Writing Across the Disciplines

RESEARCH INTO PRACTICE

Writing Across the Disciplines

RESEARCH INTO PRACTICE

Edited by

Art Young

Michigan Technological University

and

Toby Fulwiler

University of Vermont

BOYNTON/COOK PUBLISHERS, INC.
UPPER MONTCLAIR, NEW JERSEY 07043

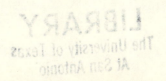

Library of Congress Cataloging-in-Publication Data

Main entry under title:

Writing across the disciplines.

Bibliography: p.
1. English language—Rhetoric—Study and teaching—
Addresses, essays, lectures.   2. Interdisciplinary approach
in education—Addresses, essays, lectures.
I. Young, Art, 1943–   II. Fulwiler, Toby, 1942–
PE1404.W693   1986   808'.042   85-24329
ISBN 0-86709-131-2

For information address Boynton/Cook Publishers, Inc., 52 Upper
Montclair Plaza, P.O. Box 860, Upper Montclair, NJ 07043.

Printed in the United States of America.
86   87   88   89   10   9   8   7   6   5   4   3   2   1

Permissions

Certain selections in this book appeared elsewhere. For permission to use these selections, the editors are grateful to the following publishers:

The Modern Language Association of America, for "Rebuilding Community in the English Department" by Art Young from the *ADE Bulletin* 77 (1984), 13-21. Reprinted by permission of the Modern Language Association of America.

The National Council of Teachers of English, for "Composing Responses to Literary Texts: A Process Approach" by Elizabeth A. Flynn from *College Composition and Communication* (October, 1983), 342-348. For "How Well Does Writing Across the Curriculum Work" by Toby Fulwiler from *College English* (February, 1984), 113-125. For portions of "Showing, Not Telling, (1981), 55-63, which appear in *Chapter 2* of this book. For the "Writing Apprehension Test" by John Daly and M. D. Miller in *Research in the Teaching of English* 9 (Fall, 1975), 246, which appears as an appendix to *Chapter 8* of this book. For "Criteria for Holistic Scoring" by Paul Diederich in *Measuring Growth in English* (1974), 53-58, which appears as an appendix to *Chapter 9*. All are reprinted with permission of the National Council of Teachers of English.

The American Society for Engineering Education, for "Writing to Learn: Engineering Student Journals" by Cynthia L. Selfe and Freydoon Arbabi from *Engineering Education,* vol. 74, no. 2 (November, 1983) 86-90. Reprinted with permission of the American Society for Engineering Education.

College English Association Publications, for portions of "Interdisciplinary Writing Workshops" by Toby Fulwiler from *CEA Critic* (January, 1981), 27-32, which appear in *Chapter 2* of this book. Reprinted with permission of CEA Publications.

Jossey-Bass Inc., Publishers, for portions of "Writing: An Act of Cognition" by Toby Fulwiler from *New Directions in Teaching and Learning: Teaching Writing in All Disciplines,* ed. C. W. Griffin, (San Francisco: Jossey-Bass, Inc. Publishers, 1982), 15–26, which appear in *Chapter 2* of this book. Reprinted with permission of Jossey-Bass Inc., Publishers.

Acknowledgments

We would like to thank all those who have supported our teaching and research efforts in the writing-across-the-curriculum program at Michigan Technological University. We appreciate the strong endorsement provided by the MTU administration, especially President Dale F. Stein, Vice President E. H. Timothy Whitten, and Dean William Powers. We are grateful to the General Motors Foundation for a series of gifts to the University which supported the program for the first five years, 1977-82, and grateful for GM's continuing financial support in 1983-84 which sponsored, in part, the writing of this book. We will always have special memories for the departmental Research and Evaluation Committee, chaired by Mike Gorman, which met every . . . well, almost every Friday morning at eight over coffee and doughnuts. This committee developed most of the research and evaluation projects described in the book, and it spent most of the summer of 1983 in cubicles in the wrestling room of old Sherman gymnasium, writing up the results which became many of the chapters in this book. In addition to Mike Gorman and the editors, committee members were Margaret Gorman, Jim Kalmbach, George Mc Culley, and Cindy Selfe. Special thanks to Pam Kuivanen and Lynn Foss, who did most of the secretarial work connected with this project with accuracy, promptness, and good sense. Finally, thanks to Laura, Ann, Megan, Molly, Anna, Sarah, and Kelsey for their good humor and patience.

Art Young
Toby Fulwiler

Foreword

At a national conference on writing, one of the principal speakers made this observation: *"Writing across the curriculum?* That's nothing new. We've had it for quite some time. It used to be called *liberal education."* The remark was, as someone noted later, "a good line"; it merited the round of laughter that greeted it. And the comment is worth our consideration now, for it invites questions with which one should approach any discussion of writing across the curriculum: What is the status of the writing-across-the-curriculum movement? Does it deserve to be called a movement? Does it represent a significant change in theory or pedagogy? Is it a proper subject for rigorous scholarly inquiry?

In some respects, even the most avid proponent of writing across the curriculum would have to agree with the speaker's comments. It has always been true that the attempt to formulate and express one's ideas through writing can be closely and complexly related to the process of learning. Furthermore, liberal education at its best has always acknowledged the significance of writing; students have been asked to do a great deal of written work, and that work has often been subjected to careful analysis.

However, even granted this point, we can question the claim that writing across the curriculum is nothing new. In a number of previous publications, contributors to this volume have described teaching practices that, for a great many faculty, in English as well as in other disciplines, represent substantial changes in the ways faculty conduct their courses and the way scholars conceive of knowledge.

Furthermore, the present volume demonstrates that there are at least two profound reasons for engaging in a careful study of writing across the curriculum. The first is made explicit in the first and last chapters and is implicit throughout the rest of the book: the attempt to carry out and assess a writing-across-the-curriculum project invites—indeed, requires—an extraordinary level of collegiality. Faculty from various disciplines must collaborate in ways that they ordinarily do not. They must learn to share teaching procedures and to synthesize diverse scholarly methodologies in an attempt to assess the program. Perhaps even more important, they must experience the hard work, occasional disagreement, and, eventually, trust that will allow them to function as a true community.

Another reason for studying writing across the curriculum is that every time we look closely at a school's program, we discover compelling questions for which we have, at best, only partial or unsatisfactory answers. Some of these questions lead us to reconsider our basic assumptions about the meaning of the phrase *good writing* and about the scholarly conventions of various disciplines. For example, from reading the essays in this volume, it's clear that we need to answer such questions as these: Are there characteristics of "good" writing that pervade most academic contexts? Are there specific conventions of style and editing that change from discipline to discipline? Do the rules of evidence for an essay in, say, Cellular Biology differ from the rules of evidence for essays in history or mathematics? What types of organizational structures are most appropriate for different writing tasks in different disciplines? Do students need different inquiry strategies for different disciplines?

Another more pragmatic set of questions arises from the fact that writing-across-the-curriculum programs are expensive and time-consuming and that, consequently, proponents of these programs will need to demonstrate that the programs are having some positive effect on teachers and students. This need leads to such questions as these: If the program is accompanied, as it should be, by workshops for participating faculty, are those workshops changing faculty attitudes and practices? Are faculty actually using pedagogical procedures—e.g., journals, peer review of essays—introduced in the workshops? Have they come to a more sophisticated understanding of ways that writing can be integrated into their courses? If faculty attitudes and practices have been changed, are those changes beneficial? Is student writing improving? Are students beginning to change their attitudes toward writing and their perceptions of what writing entails? Are they able to use writing as a means of learning the subject matter of their various courses?

These are the kinds of questions addressed throughout this volume. Sometimes investigation of these questions produces clearcut results, sometimes not. Occasionally results are equivocal or are different from what one might hope. Moreover, one could argue that even the most positive, clear-cut results may be peculiar to one institution, that results of some of these studies may not be generalizable. But to do so would be to miss the real value of investigations reported in this volume, for these studies are remarkably successful and valuable in several ways:

- they identify and exemplify principles that can help other researchers;
- they suggest that we may have to look for new types of data and we may have to invent new ways of analyzing this data;
- they help other researchers understand the complexity and difficulty of research in this area; they warn us against research methodology that is uncritically or inappropriately borrowed from other disciplines, and consequently,

essays in this volume reassure us that our difficulties reflect the complexity of our enterprise, and not just our own limitations as researchers.

And always, contributors to this volume force us to continue to ask new questions. For every conclusion they draw, they raise any number of new problems. Using their own experience, contributors to this volume keep pushing us, challenging us, expanding our sense of what's worth knowing. Liberal education—and professional education and technical education—can only benefit from their effort.

Lee Odell
Troy, New York

Contents

Introduction

Writing Across the Disciplines describes the impact of a writing-across-the-curriculum program on the professional life of a single university department and on the pedagogical life of an entire campus community. The idea that writing is the business of the whole school community has been long supported by major scholars in composition, including James Moffett, James Britton, James Kinneavy, Mina Shaughnessy, and Janet Emig. Collectively, they have argued that student writing will not improve substantially until students see writing at the center of their academic curriculum; that is, until they learn to value writing, and to practice it in the daily business of learning in all disciplines.

In an attempt to put this central idea into practice, writing-across-the-curriculum programs have emerged at dozens of colleges and universities during the past decade. Such comprehensive writing programs currently exist at small liberal arts colleges such as Beaver and Grinnell, major state universities such as Michigan and Maryland, as well as Ivy League schools such as Harvard and Yale (*Forum for Liberal Education:* April, 1981). These programs vary widely in scope and method, but most attempt to accomplish essentially the same thing: to improve student learning and writing by encouraging faculty in all disciplines to use writing more often and more thoughtfully in their classrooms. While some schools have developed placement instruments or initiated junior-year competency examinations, other schools have required the cooperation or direct action of large numbers of university professors in areas such as history, business, biology and engineering—teachers who have never been trained formally to teach writing and who don't, in many cases, know where to start or what to do. Ours has been such a program.

A comprehensive writing-across-the-curriculum program asks students to work on their writing in all disciplines and at all grade levels, placing some responsibility for assigning and evaluating writing with every teacher. In this way, language

1

instruction becomes the business of all teachers who use language. As a consequence, students can't view English teachers alone as concerned about good writing. Nor does it matter at what age students begin to take writing more seriously
or which academic major they select: at every turn of the university curriculum
someone is paying the serious attention to writing that any fundamental learning
skill requires.

During the last several years, many colleges have supported interdisciplinary
writing workshops to introduce colleagues across the curriculum to the *why's* and
how's of teaching writing. Such workshops typically last from a few days to a few
weeks and involve twenty to thirty faculty at a time. Those of us who conduct
these workshops have developed a variety of strategies, exercises, and presentations
to give our colleagues a better handle on how to use writing more often in their
classes. Teachers commonly learn how to assign different kinds of writing to serve
different purposes to a variety of audiences. A few teachers even alter their basic
approach toward teaching as a result of the workshop pedagogy.

From 1977 to 1984 workshop leaders from our Humanities Department
conducted fourteen writing workshops for approximately two hundred and fifty
Michigan Tech faculty from virtually every discipline on campus. We aimed consistently at giving teachers more than one or two "best practices" to try out on
Monday morning in their classes. Instead, we designed the workshops to introduce
faculty to a comprehensive, process-oriented view of writing in the hopes that such
a general attitude conversion would produce, in turn, a classroom conversion.
From the start we believed that inductive, experiential activities would make a
stronger impact on participants than didactic, passive lectures. Consequently we
worked with a small number of ideas, but investigated them more thoroughly:
teachers would try something out, then examine collectively what they tried, then
consider implications for their own individual classrooms.

Three ideas we worked with can be stated succinctly: 1) language is a tool
for learning; 2) writing must be viewed as a process as well as a product; 3) students have difficulty writing for a variety of reasons, which we can often identify
and then address. If teachers at a writing workshop explored these few pedagogical
principles, we expected their attitudes toward using writing in their classrooms
would change—and in turn that their classroom pedagogy would change and so,
eventually, would student writing proficiency. Though we gave few answers at
these workshops, we did provide an arena for interchange and discussion, from
which many practical ideas emerged.

And so the genesis of this book. Did the experience of these workshops
change faculty attitudes and the ways faculty assigned and evaluated student writing? If so, how and in what ways? Have changes instituted by teachers changed
student attitudes or performance? Have workshops and all the follow-up activity
associated with them created a more literate environment, a community which
values written language, at Michigan Tech?

As we discussed purposes and methodologies, designed and redesigned
experiments, interpreted and sometimes misinterpreted results, we realized that

we were learning as much about the process of research as we were about writing across the curriculum. Whether we were attempting to measure growth in learning by students who kept journals in a mathematics class, figuring out what, if anything, the assessment of a one-shot fifty-minute writing sample has to do with measuring the success of a program that emphasized revision, or debating the differences in results we could expect if we trained readers of biology laboratory reports by holistic or primary-trait guidelines, we knew that all our results would be tentative.

We valued the way Donald H. Graves reports on his research with young children: "Why not tell a story as it unfolds, and tell it from the inside? In this way, readers will be acquainted with study problems and decisions as well as specific changes in children (1979, p. 77). And as he added later on: "We wanted to tell the story of children, teachers and researchers (warts and all) from the beginning" (1983, p. 841). We, too, will tell of decisions made and unmade, problems and possibilities, mistakes and success, warts and all.

The essays in the first section explain writing across the curriculum and provide a context for collective writing research. This section demonstrates the process by which an organized effort in writing-across-the-curriculum research can occur, and suggests that such an effort can have benefits beyond the immediate research goals.

The second section focuses on evaluation, describing, as concretely as possible, what happened on one campus as a result of six years of a writing-across-the-curriculum program. Each chapter looks at a different area of impact, discusses how we went about making our investigations, and states our findings. By using a variety of methodologies accessible to teachers trained in the humanities, we attempt to describe the impact of the program on the entire campus.

The third section examines individual classrooms where instructors initiated writing-to-learn assignments promoted by the workshops. In particular, the authors describe what occurred when three functions of writing, the expressive, the transactional, and the poetic, were assigned to promote learning in such diverse areas as psychology, biology, civil engineering, mathematics, and literature. Thus the second section focuses on global change on the campus as a whole, and the third section evaluates specific techniques (e.g., journals, peer groups, poetry writing) in individual classes.

The final section contains essays on the possibilities and the problems that come with the territory of a writing-across-the-curriculum program—academic and political as well as theoretical and practical.

Art Young and *Toby Fulwiler*
March, 1985

I.
Writing Across the Disciplines
Community and Purpose

The essays in the first section introduce basic issues about writing across the curriculum which the Michigan Tech program addressed. Collectively, they describe the development of an educational community which values written language, as well as the process by which that community continues to nurture both instruction and research in writing across disciplines.

The first chapter, "Rebuilding Community in the English Department," by Art Young, examines the academic and social context of a writing-across-the-curriculum program. Young suggests that the introduction of a single, powerful program influenced the research and pedagogy of both the Humanities Department and whole university community.

The following essay, "The Argument for Writing Across the Curriculum," by Toby Fulwiler, provides the theoretical basis for the program at Michigan Tech and delineates the history and the nature of the faculty writing workshops on which the program is built. Fulwiler argues for the introduction of "writing to learn" as a powerful function of written language in all courses, at all levels, and he describes how the Tech workshop model accomplishes these purposes.

In "Developing Our Research Model," Michael E. Gorman recounts the problem-solving activity of seven teachers who took for themselves the task of evaluating this many-faceted program. Gorman's essay not only describes the process by which the research model came into being, but also illuminates the glories and the hazards of collaboration.

The final essay in the first section, "Research in Writing Across the Curriculum," by George A. Mc Culley, explains why a research component is central to a comprehensive new program such as the one described here. Mc Culley describes how research questions grow naturally out of teaching and program development, and argues that teachers from different disciplines, working together, will provide the best answers to some of these questions.

5

Chapter 1
Rebuilding Community
in the English Department

ART YOUNG

English departments can be tense and divisive places these days. We hear frequently of splits between literature and composition faculties and sometimes of the formal dividing of English departments in two. Our profession continues its pursuit of increased specialization in literary study and the separation of extraneous activities into separate departments and eventually separate professions. Theory and practice in reading and in speech are not integral to the formal study of English, and neither are the theory and practice of writing. Reading and speech are housed in separate departments in buildings across the campus from English, have their own professional organizations and meetings in faraway cities, and set their own standards for promotion and recognition within their departments and their professions. If the study of writing is to develop similarly, must it too separate itself from a department and a profession primarily concerned with the study of literature?

Most English departments have individual faculty members who value the teaching of writing, but most departments, either as administrative units or as collections of English teachers and scholars, don't value it. They view writing as a service course to be taught by the least experienced teachers to the most troublesome groups of students—freshmen and nonmajors.

The main reasons given for keeping literature and writing together are usually economic and political; English departments can't afford to give writing away. Nationally, the teaching of writing makes up more than sixty percent of the instructional load of English departments, it finances graduate students, it provides jobs, and it supports the study and teaching of literature. Writing and literature might share the same profession by historical accident and might continue to do so for some brief period because of such practical considerations. In the long term, however, we can become one profession only if we dissolve the tensions between writing and literature conceptually and emotionally. Our coming together must seem logical and feel right.

We need to begin by realizing that we give away more than economic and political power when we regard the teaching of writing as an auxiliary or expendable enterprise. We also give away the opportunity to establish the college or university as a community of scholars. The study and teaching of writing can make an English department a community, and the study of all discourse, not just literary discourse, can make an English department the center of the entire campus community—for language study is the integrative activity of all disciplines. It works as a spider spins a web, using language as filament.

Paul Goodman (1962), working from historical antecedents in the Middle Ages, viewed the "community of scholars" as a place where teachers and students (both are scholars) develop personal relationships for the pursuit of knowledge free of the economic, political, and social demands of the larger society. He insisted on giving new life to the community-of-scholars ideal as a defense against the increasing bureaucratic dehumanization and conformism of contemporary institutional education—a bureaucratization that undervalues liberal learning in favor of the impersonal and the servile. "The *ultima ratio* of administration is that a school is a teaching machine, to train the young by predigested programs in order to get pre-ordained marketable skills" (p. 172).

Of course skillful writing can be used in support of either liberal or servile education, as Richard Ohmann has reminded us. And when English faculties view it as a service industry, they treat it as a value-neutral activity of primary importance to the postindustrial state and of only secondary importance to the individual's search for knowledge and identity. When writing becomes a service industry, then the study, teaching, and learning of it become fractured, isolated, and servile within the English department and throughout the campus. When writing becomes a cornerstone of a liberal education, a humanistic activity for discovery and commitment, embraced as central to the English department's life and mission, then it nurtures and is nurtured by a community of scholars.

This essay is about one department's attempt to create a working community of scholars. We began by taking the study and teaching of writing as the central concept that informed our academic responsibilities and that spun out connections to the study and teaching not only of reading, literature, language, women's studies, and speech but of engineering, psychology, computer science, biology, business, and the rest of the disciplines on our campus. After making writing central, we made additional decisions regarding departmental policy and practice, many of which we had not foreseen and which, when implemented, changed individual faculty responsibilities and relationships within the department. The changing of individual responsibilities brought further change to departmental policies, and the symbiotic relationships among the members of the community emerged.

This retrospective look at a decade's change in the role of "English" at one midwestern university makes change appear orderly and preordained. But such an exercise offers one perspective from which to enter the dialogue about the definition of English studies and the role of the English department in a technological society. And it may generate responses from others whose departments are struggling with self-definition because of the current tension between writing and literature, changing instructional needs, increasingly demanding publish-or-perish policies, new student populations, and a confusing array of campus and societal demands and expectations.

Historical Background

In the early 1970s our department was fairly typical of those in middle-sized state-supported institutions.[1] We had a small undergraduate program for majors but no graduate program. Each faculty member taught twelve hours per term, or four three-credit courses. Of the four courses, two or three were composition classes. A year of freshman English was required of all students and, of course, we had no graduate assistants to ease the load. By mandate, all faculty members taught writing courses. Teaching responsibilities and committee service consumed the time of most of them; very little research, publication, or other professional activity took place. Such activities were not part of who we were and what we did. The teaching loads were prohibitive, the library inadequate, travel funds scarce, and so on. When scholarship occurred, it was by accident and in isolation, not because of department vision, environment, or encouragement.

We used to recruit new teachers by literary period or specialty: we might need a twentieth-century Americanist but not another Renaissance person. We recruited this way knowing that our medievalist would teach one course in Chaucer every other year, that our library holdings in medieval literature and Chaucer were pitiful, that we had few majors, and that nonmajors were increasingly shying away from specialized literature courses. Our medievalist would teach six to nine writing courses annually, for which he had absolutely no formal training. We saw nothing amiss. Our department was following a well-established model for English departments, the model we had observed in graduate school and the model that may work well for Ph.D.-granting institutions. Private liberal arts colleges and large research universities have traditionally had a well-defined sense of their role and purpose. Middle-sized M.A.-B.A. institutions have not, especially since the vanishing dominance of teacher education. We have gone in search of glory and imitated that from which we came. Badly.

We didn't realize at the time that writing was at the center of our enterprise. It was the mission most identified with the department and statistically the course each individual taught most. It wasn't necessarily what we taught best. And, happy for brief reprieves, we certainly didn't teach writing in our literature courses. Rhetoric may once have been the center of an advanced education, but that was long ago and far away. We had become specialists in keeping with our time and place. Yet we were called on to teach students, many of them first-generation college goers, who didn't want to specialize in our specialties but who did want other things they assumed we had to offer—the proficiency with language that mediates experience for educated persons, the proficiency with language that generates economic and social opportunities.

Writing Workshops

In 1976 we moved writing to the center. We began to hire writing teachers with experience in the theories and pedagogies of writing that emerged during the 1970s. In the next year we initiated a writing-across-the-curriculum program. My colleague Toby Fulwiler developed a model of intensive writing workshops for faculty members in all disciplines. These workshops were hands-on-pen experiences that lasted two to four consecutive days and nights, and participants themselves spent much of the time writing in a variety of contexts, for a variety of purposes, and for a variety of audiences. Individual workshops were structured in such a way that teacher-writers experienced firsthand the pedagogical theories of James Britton, Peter Elbow, Janet Emig, Ken Macrorie, James Moffett, and others who advised teachers to consider the writing process in instruction and to emphasize writing as a learning activity as well as a means of communication. Thus far, over two hundred teachers on our campus have attended at least one such workshop, including ninety percent of the English teachers, many of whom have become leaders of the workshop process.

Teachers who participated in the workshops experienced, in one way or another, collaborative writing exercises, small-group dynamics, oral and written peer feedback between successive drafts, writing anxiety, writer's block, writing for themselves, writing for others, writing for discovery, writing to communicate, and feeling good about writing. Most of us experienced anew the power of writing and the importance of a supportive environment in which to write. We took back to our classrooms new and renewed strategies for teaching writing: conferences, peer groups, journal writing, prewriting, revision exercises, sharing our own writing with students. But perhaps more important for our departmental and professional lives, we began to duplicate within the department itself the supportive environment we strove for in our individual classrooms.

During the four-day faculty writing workshop we experienced intellectually and emotionally the power and the possibilities of a community of scholars searching for knowledge through writing and the sharing of writing. We attempted to re-create certain aspects of the workshops in our classrooms and in our department, and what emerged blurred the traditional distributions between classrooms and departments. For one thing, students and teachers began writing to each other.

Most of us who teach college English today inherited a rather distorted view of the community-of-scholars legacy in academia. Whatever its illustrious origins in the Middle Ages, when scholars wrote and spoke about uncommon things to one another as part of their common search for Truth, most of us were trained in universities where physicists didn't write and speak to literary historians, or engineers to psychologists, or philosophers to economists. Indeed, the Lydgate scholar in the English department didn't share professional ideas with the Camus scholar in the French department or, as likely as not, with anyone at his university. Departmental colleagues read his work only at tenure time. Very rarely did he circulate early drafts of essays to several departmental colleagues for suggestions and guidance, nor did he encourage graduate students in his seminars to share emerging ideas, outlines, and first drafts. Indeed, one medieval legacy remained, that of the monk slaving away in his solitary cell. Writing is a lonely business, and writing about Lydgate is more lonely than most. And in an age of tenure quotas it can be a competitive activity as well.

Certainly much good writing is produced by monks in cells as well as by Lydgate scholars in library carrels. But the problem remains, as noted by Richard Ohmann: "It is shocking how little use we make of our colleagues as colleagues, beyond the routines of committee work" (1976, p. 19). We have begun to understand that good writing is also produced when we leave the carrel with half-baked ideas or rough drafts to share with supportive colleagues or when we enlist a co-author to generate more knowledge about a difficult topic or to help manage an unwieldy subject. Often such cooperative strategies provide the nourishment necessary for more productivity and for better writing. And when practiced widely by numerous faculty in an English department, they can help create a community of scholars interacting with one another's professional work at every stage of the process that creates it.

Process Writing

I use the phrase "process writing" to refer to writing generated in expectation of an immediate response. Although the ultimate goal of the finished piece of writing might be publication in a periodical, with a three-month period before a response from the editor and a two-year gap before responses from the periodical's readers, process writing is unfinished work submitted to trusted readers for quick feedback. Indeed, some published pieces of writing by members of our department began as "freewrites." An idea occurs to a faculty member that *might* make a good article, and she quickly writes her thoughts on what such an article might be and do. She duplicates her notes and shares them with two or three colleagues from whom she expects early replies. Their comments may range from suggestions for further reading to develop her ideas, thoughts on other directions in which the proposed article might move, requests for further information where her thoughts aren't clear, notations of similar work that has been done elsewhere. If the topic is appropriate, she might also share her freewrite with her class, and by listening to her students' comments and reading their responses, she may further refine her ideas and her writing. In this way, she demonstrates that she values the process she teaches and respects her students' abilities to generate insight. The decision on whether to continue with the piece of writing, of course, will be hers. If she should decide to write further, she will seek responses from these or other colleagues after each draft or part of a draft. She may ask for a specific kind of reading—say, to judge the organization—or a more general one. She may ask a colleague or two to assist her throughout the process of successive drafts and request others to help her only with specific areas—like the early brainstorming or the final editing. She always expects a quick response—which usually takes from a day to a week, depending on the length of the draft. She must get on with the planning, thinking, writing; and her readers know this. They write, too.

Another aspect of process writing within the department is that the supportive readers themselves practice writing to learn. The environment of trust developed by these colleagues encourages taking risks with words. Such colleagues understand that some attempts at writing well are pretty awful and that some attempts at thinking clearly are pretty fuzzy, but they also understand that, through process writing, language can be shaped and thought clarified, sometimes to the point that the writing may eventually interest a larger group of readers. But they also know that some writing will only interest a few, or only the writer, or will be thrown away. To discard writing is in the very nature of being a writer and learner, and no stigma is attached to a colleague when individual pieces fail and ideas are stillborn. There may be other ways to get the job done.

Writers and readers together need to understand the difference between writing to learn and writing to communicate. When an individual writer explores a subject through writing to learn what she thinks about it, or to explore alternative ways of organizing information, then the reader's response must be cued to the writer's purpose. It should be encouraging, collaborative, helpful, and personal. If the writer wants the writing to be as clear and effective as possible, to have the style and tone appropriate for a particular audience, to have the best supporting evidence and organizational delivery, then the reader's response should change accordingly. While remaining supportive, the reader should adopt the critical stance of the intended audience, clearly delineate the strengths and shortcomings of the writing, and provide suggestions for improvement. When the same readers have assisted a writer through the entire process, from the first writing-to-learn exercises through successive drafts to a finished essay, they share a pride in their colleague's publication that in itself renews the entire process.

All writers have different work habits, and not all create finished essays in the same way. Indeed, the same writer will tackle different tasks in different ways. There are people who, if they do freewrites at all, would never share them with others. But one aspect of the process does appear universal: anyone who does share a piece of writing hopes for a quick response. Important ingredients in this process are colleagues who are knowledgeable, supportive, and responsible readers —readers who understand process writing, who do it themselves. When such writing activities are going on widely among faculty members, benefits accrue to the department in intangible ways, in all departmental activities that are enhanced by cooperation and trust, including teaching. Those who share essays with one another also share syllabi and handouts—before handing them out. Such a departmental environment enables writing teachers to write even though teaching loads remain heavy. They are supported in their realization that their own writing, when shared with colleagues and students, is as important to their teaching as is grading student essays. It is a part of who they are as writing teachers.

Collaboration

Unlike the arts, the sciences have long encouraged collaboration. Most scientific papers have coauthors. We need only read autobiographies of scientists, such as James Watson's *Double Helix* or Freeman Dyson's *Discovering the Universe,* to glimpse some of the excitement and involvement that are generated when two or more colleagues tackle a project together. It's an excitement that many scholars in English, and many humanists generally, seldom experience. Perhaps because our work traditionally has emphasized the historical and the theoretical and because our primary resource has been the library not the laboratory, our avoidance is understandable. But when the study of writing becomes integral to English studies, important changes occur. Scholars become interested in current problems of practicing writers, in state legislatures' demands for standardized tests, in the classroom as laboratory. These new interests frequently demand collaboration in much the same way that science does. And if the profession of English, as opposed to the profession of writing, is going to respond to these new interests, then it must learn to value and nurture collaboration. For one thing, such activities must become a familiar and respected part of graduate education.

In our experience, it frequently happens that colleagues who read one another's first drafts become interested in one another's projects. In the academic games associated with publish or perish, this development could be a distinct danger. Because ideas can be stolen, many prefer to work in isolation, remaining competitive and watchful. But for colleagues willing to risk basing relationships on trust, the rewards, both emotional and intellectual, can be substantial. Ego is present in all of us, but if the discovery of knowledge is preferable to self-aggrandizement, then the collaborative sharing of ideas is generally preferable to going it alone. When two colleagues discover they are working on the same thing, it needn't be an occasion for panic and writer's cramp. It can be a unique opportunity in writing and learning.

When writers and readers share their ideas, they find opportunities for collaboration, and the collaborative experience is essential in creating and nurturing community. When someone learns about a colleague's current research and becomes interested in it, he sometimes perceives areas where their current research is complementary, or where a colleague's teaching strategy might work in his own classes, or where he has substantial information that might be useful to a colleague's work but where mastery would be tedious and difficult without collaboration. From such situations and numerous others, collaboration will emerge in an environment that encourages it.

Not all projects want collaboration, and not all people work well in collaboration. But writing can be and often is a collaborative activity, and the study and teaching of writing can be an important avenue for encouraging collaborative activity. In addition to increasing productivity in scholarly activities, widely practiced collaboration within a department brings many tangential benefits: 1) it informs other departmental activities, such as teaching, committee work, and grant writing; 2) it nurtures scholarly creativity despite heavy teaching loads; 3) collaborative efforts to study writing lead to collaboration to study literature, language, literary theory, and other areas of traditional English; and 4) collaboration within the department leads to collaborative projects with colleagues across disciplines. The collaborative process is fundamentally dialectic and consensual; it seeks to know. When collaborative projects operate across disciplines to study language and learning, then English moves to the center of the community of scholars.

Teaching at the Center

Teaching, as we conceive of it, is the central activity of a community of scholars. It is the most important scholarly activity, not just a routine task. To realize this importance is often difficult when scholars are torn in many directions, some of which appear to operate against teaching and against community. Although teaching often shares with writing a misbegotten image as an isolated and individualistic activity it too can flourish as an integrated and communal endeavor. Our experience in writing has taught us much about teaching. We have learned what Paul Goodman already knew: "Merely to expound a subject matter is not teaching" (p. 177).

We conceived writing across the curriculum as a teacher-centered program. Our program recognizes, computers and competencies notwithstanding, that teachers are still the center of the educational experience. We used strategies learned from the NEH Institute on Writing in the Humanities (1977) and the National Writing Project to help teachers develop the ability and the confidence to use writing in teaching their disciplines. We chose to focus on teaching, rather than on curricular change or extensive testing of student performance, because curriculum and testing derive meaning only from knowledgeable and committed teachers. Some educational and political bureaucrats use curricular change and testing programs as measures to force teachers to change; we hope to empower teachers to transform routine teaching and testing by developing pedagogies that thwart conformism and successfully encourage critical thinking. But to effect change, teachers must understand that the study and teaching of language, especially writing, have the potential to empower that change.

Many writing activities—process writing, collaboration, participation in reading groups—that we have put to use in research and publication can play an identical role in the development of teaching philosophies and strategies. When colleagues teach different sections of the same course, they can collaborate in the teaching of those sections. Faculty members who seek peer feedback in preparing assignments, handouts, and classroom units, as well as in writing an article, not only bring a communal knowledge and support system to those activities but participate in giving the departmental teaching mission an increased sense of purpose and importance. Innovation and renewal in the classroom can occur more frequently and easily to teachers working in such an environment.

For teaching to be recognized as the central activity of English scholars, faculty members must see it as worthy of scholarly inquiry in itself. The artificial dichotomy we inherited from graduate school says that teaching goes on in the classroom and scholarship goes on in the library. How students learn to write and to improve their confidence in writing, how they learn to read and to relate literature to their lives, and how the expression of knowledge contributes to that learning are all questions of interest to the scholar. And if the English scholar teaches undergraduate writing and literature courses, these questions are central to that activity. Theory and practice in the teaching of writing, reading, and literature are one area that all scholars in an English department have in common; what we need to do is change this shared responsibility from being the lowest common denominator to being the highest. All teachers should be studying pedagogy every time they teach. And because pedagogy is intimately related to how people develop knowledge, every class presents an opportunity to develop fresh insight or new knowledge about the act of writing or about a literary text, knowledge that may be of interest beyond the individual classroom to the profession at large. We need to encourage and reward knowledge developed in this way, when the teacher and the scholar are one.

Writing, reading, and teaching are all individualistic as well as communal activities. Each of us has teaching strategies that work for us and others that don't. This truism can be the untested hypothesis that, on investigation, leads to personal understanding. Scholarship in English consists in personal understandings shared in community. Dixie Goswami, of the Bread Loaf School of English, has a phrase for the teacher who unifies the dual activities of discovering and transmitting knowledge: "teacher as researcher." Because the scholars in their libraries and the educationists in their laboratories have not generated a particular kind of knowledge useful to teachers, teachers must accept the responsibility for generating it *in their own classrooms.* This knowledge is related to how individual students (the ones in the class at that time) learn the skills, content, and values of "English" and how the individual teacher (you) can best teach these students. In one sense, with new students introduced each term, generating this knowledge is a scholarly project without end—a metaphor, when applied to learning, that we like to share with our students. Students become collaborators with their teacher-researcher in this project, developing new knowledge as well as learning the wisdom of the past. The teacher relearns the content to be mastered, the rigor of interpretation, the environment for discovery. The collaboration with students must be supported by collaboration with other teachers who pose similar questions for themselves, thus enlarging the supportive community that encourages learning.

When teaching becomes the center of a community of scholars our view of students changes. We disregard the we-they mentality, the metaphor of the givers and the receivers of knowledge, and we accept a collaborative model for teaching and learning. In such a model some people know more about some things than others do, and they teach even as they learn. It is more important to teach and to learn than to be taught. Central to the collaborative model, no matter what the discipline, is language. Writing, reading, talking, and listening are means to the discovery of knowledge, self, and power.

English Studies

J. N. Hook has argued that while there have been departments of English literature since about 1880 (of English and American literature since 1930), "what have not existed, as strong, unified wholes, are departments of English which include everything that belongs in the domain" (1978, p. 269). He issued the now familiar warning that writing teachers might secede from English literature departments, as speech, journalism, and logic teachers had before them. But he also fantasized that a baby would be born, "a real department of English, with literature in an honored but not dominant role" (p. 270). Real departments of English would deal equally with composition, language, literature, and reading.

Hook's fantasy is appealing. When our department began to shape a role for itself based on the centrality of the study and teaching of writing, we didn't want to repeat the mistakes of the past by separating writing and literature in the department and simply reversing the power structure in favor of writing. We put writing at the center because it was what we taught the most and what gave us the greatest influence on the greatest numbers. (At MTU, courses in writing are required, but literature is an elective.) Taking "language and learning" as a theme for our departmental mission, we meant to include writing, reading, literature, rhetoric, linguistics, and selected interdisciplinary areas as equally important within our mission. But more than that, we tried to see these separate academic areas as integral and whole, as an area of learning and teaching called English studies.

Some of our goals for English studies were to affirm the centrality of teaching, to respect research and scholarship on pedagogy, to emphasize the connections between reading and writing, and to recognize our special interest in teaching and studying the reading and interpreting of literature. We envisioned English studies as related to the missions of other departments on campus and as central to the education of all students. We agreed with Paul Goodman that liberal arts is the core of a college education because the liberal arts faculty "teaches the language of intellectual discourse and the nature (and limits) of the different kinds of evidence used by the other studies" (p. 185). We thus agreed that all faculty would teach both writing and literature courses; we wouldn't have writing specialists who taught only writing courses and literature specialists who taught only literature courses. Faculty members, consequently, now strive to have the teaching of one course inform the teaching of another. We attempt to have students do as we do: write for readers, read as learners, reason carefully, and talk together to understand.

In the world of college academics the study of reading is separated from the study of literature, an even more ironic situation than the separation of reading from writing. Most of us trained in traditional English departments never had a course in the reading process or in psycholinguistic reading theory. English departments need to give the reading process the same attention and stature that the composing process is now coming to have. All English professors should have some understanding of the reading process and the writing process, the interrelations between the two, and the ways in which both can inform the study and teaching of literature. The person who clearly showed several of us in our department the relations among reading theory, literature, and teaching was Alan Hollingsworth, former chair of the English department and now dean of arts and letters at Michigan State University. He introduced us and the profession generally to the value of psycholinguistic reading theories, both as an antidote to bankrupt behavioral theories of reading and as a stimulant for understanding how people read literature and make meaning from it. The work of Frank Smith and Ken and Yetta Goodman in psycholinguistic reading theory took on special meaning for us as we sought to unify the teaching of writing, reading, and literature. Hollingsworth also introduced us to a new group of literary theorists, reader-response critics and scholars who were interested in the reader as well as in the text: David Bleich, Norman Holland, Stanley Fish, and others. And he introduced us to Louise Rosenblatt, who characterizes the reading of a poem as an event, a transaction between reader and text (see Hollingsworth's review). Rosenblatt's transactional theory of reading, that readers and texts are equally significant in the reading experience, and her treatment of reading in literary and nonliterary discourse provided us not only with a base for teaching both readers and texts—that is, both the students and the literature—but with a base for making connections to the teaching of both writers and texts—that is, both our students and their personal and public discourse.

Just as many of us during the past decade have developed new ways of teaching and studying writing, we have developed new ways of teaching and studying literature. We have changed partly because the new critical method of reading and teaching presumed a preprofessional disposition on the part of students, now inappropriate when literature contributes to the general education and liberal learning of students interested in other professions. This method also separated the experience of the reader from the text and left reading knowledge almost exclusively in the hands of the master interpreter, the teacher. The Rosenblatt theory made sense to us and provided us with a rationale for action as we sought to integrate the teaching of writing, reading, and literature,[2] to move teaching to the center, to create a community of scholars for students and teachers alike.

Experiencing Rosenblatt's work on reading led us back to the teaching of writing. It afforded us a better understanding of writing as a humanistic activity, not just a survival skill similar to balancing a checkbook. We relearned that writing has its personal and public domain; that it can be creative and informative, that it can serve, and be served by, the writer; and that all its functions occur simultaneously on a continuum. We make meaning from writing as we do from reading, and the meaning we make shapes our values and our lives.

Thus we make meaning of the term "English studies": a community of scholars teaching and studying writing, reading, and literature as one subject. No more the schizophrenia of having to teach three sections of composition while publishing on Lydgate or perishing. If reading Lydgate and reading and writing about Lydgate are to be made activities of value to the community of scholars, then the Lydgate scholar must integrate his work into the lives of his students and colleagues. Not to do so is to work without the nurturing and the support the department offers and to run the risk of contributing to the fracturing of community.

Departmental Environment

A departmental environment is created by the values, goals, and practices of the individual faculty members. When most members reach consensus about what a department should be and do, then the prerequisite exists for an interactive relationship between individuals and the department in the shaping of shared values, the generation of knowledge, and the nurturing of community. These shared values and the environment that nurtures them will not and should not be the same in all departments of English. Each department must discover its own role, based on the students it serves, its institution's role, and the faculty's interpretation of how English studies can best contribute to education locally and to the profession at large. Religious institutions will differ from technical institutes, small liberal arts colleges from research-oriented doctoral institutions. But the faculty members of each department should strive to establish its definition by consensus in order to give identity to the work they do. The department's identity shapes the work the department does, and the work it does shapes its identity. When this occurs, individual members talk about "our" work rather than "my" work, as we have learned to talk and think about "our" writing-across-the-curriculum work at Michigan Tech. The departmental environment must support this work. Resources must be marshalled and allocated in support of the shared values and purposes of the community; departmental policies and practices must be constituted to enable the community of scholars to do its work.

For example, our departmental self-definition has led to a change in our hiring practices. Instead of recruiting teachers to fill gaps in a particular literary period or genre, we have adopted a policy we call "redundant hiring." This entails recruiting people who already know a great deal of what we know, who are committed to the concept of English studies, and who have the knowledge, aptitude, and inclination to work collaboratively on existing and new projects within the department. Certainly we ask that they be able to contribute something new, perhaps sociolinguistics or classical rhetoric or contemporary literary theory, but we also expect them by training or self-education to have a generalist background in the primary interest of the department—the integrated study and teaching of writing, reading, and literature. Thus we don't hire composition specialists or literature specialists; rather, we hire people from all areas of English studies who will strengthen our community of scholars. We look not for ideological conformity but for an ideological commitment to our department's work. How best to accomplish that work is always an open matter of discussion, as is the changing nature of the work. Nor do we recruit people with the same narrow background disguised as generalists; on the contrary, we have hired psychologists, philosophers, and historians committed to the department's work but offering different perspectives. Toby Fulwiler provided us with another phrase for what we do—"healthy irreverence." The irreverence is directed at the traditional ways of doing things and at our own experimental ways. Such phrases as "redundant hiring" and "healthy irreverence," and the practices that create them, indicate growth in community spirit.

Beyond recruiting and hiring faculty members, the department must nurture them on a continual basis for the duration of their careers. Obviously reward systems, such as promotion, tenure, perks, and merit raises, must be consistent with departmental work. A department can't encourage pedagogical research or collaborative projects and then have their value discounted at tenure time, from either within or without. On the contrary, a department must affirm its values whenever possible, by supporting such efforts through grant monies, released time, and when the quality of work warrants, tenure and promotion. It's normal for teachers to want to change their scholarly interests at various times in their careers, and such changes are possible under the broad rubric of English studies. A faculty member who moves from technical writing to literature and then to women's studies can be accommodated as long as such moves are in the framework of wider departmental goals regarding the integration of English studies, teachers as scholars, and the collaborative community.

The collaborative community demands participation and responsibility from faculty members in all areas of departmental life. It means the risk of establishing personal relationships based on trust and respect in committees, on special projects, in proposal writing, in teaching and research, and in policy-making. It means delegating authority and accepting rule by consensus. It means allocating resources in such a way that collaborative projects central to the department's interest receive priority over individual projects of specialized interest. It means all faculty taking responsibility for providing emotional and intellectual support for others, not to mention searching and lobbying for the financial support needed by all: for word processors, copiers, secretaries, released time—all the goodies that we have discovered we need to increase exponentially as the sense of community grows. In return for the risk and the participation, faculty members empower themselves to make a difference in students' education and in their own professional lives.

In making language and learning our department's special mission and writing across the curriculum the vehicle for its implementation, we influenced and shaped numerous programs throughout the department. From the beginning we saw writing across the curriculum as integrated and central. For many of us it assumes the place that rhetoric once had at the center of education. This positioning has helped mold and define our freshman English program, our language skills laboratory, our programs for majors, and our future planning. Because writing across the curriculum means that faculty members in other disciplines use writing to teach their disciplines, freshman English doesn't include teaching technical writing or the writing required in the various disciplines. Freshman English for us is fundamentally a humanities course concerned with the teaching and learning of writing, reading, and literature. It is a general education course, not a preprofessional course. Students may later take business writing or technical writing as part of a professional curriculum, and teachers in all disciplines can integrate reading and writing into their courses using the student's freshman English experience as a base. Teachers of composition and teachers in other disciplines share many assumptions about language and learning, thanks to a high rate of participation by both groups in the writing-across-the-curriculum workshops and program. Having developed a comprehensive writing program, we have been able to answer those who ask why we don't make freshman English a grammar and report-writing course and teach "the things our students really need to know." Freshman English is only one part, a very important part, of our students' language education in their four years of schooling.

Likewise, our language skills laboratory is set up to assist students on a tutorial basis in reading or writing or both. But the lab does not serve just remedial students, or just freshman English students; it serves students at all levels of skill development in all courses throughout the university. Its role developed out of our program's premise that all people can benefit from collaborative writing experiences, personal feedback from readers, and a supportive environment that encourages learning. The lab is important to the success of our comprehensive writing program, playing a clearly defined role that has served it well in an age of budget reductions.

One final example of how the acting out of departmental philosophy has changed departmental programs. In 1976, when we took language and learning as our departmental mission and launched our writing-across-the-curriculum program, we had ten English majors. We still have ten English majors. But we also have over a hundred majors in a new degree program entitled Scientific and Technical Communications. This program was created and developed to accord with the broader interest of the department—reading and writing across disciplines. Students in the program take substantial courses in other disciplines, usually engineering or science; courses in communications theory and practice; and courses in the traditional liberal arts. All students must complete senior projects in which they attempt to generate knowledge about communication in the disciplines, either in collaboration with faculty members or with faculty members as supportive readers offering critical feedback. We are just now beginning to realize the potential of this program, as well as of our more traditional programs, in creating the community of scholars. In stepping outside the field of English, we got the perspective we needed to identify for ourselves the field of English studies. We thus have been able to develop a perspective on both the literary and the nonliterary and recognize our need to study and teach both with equal commitment and equal rewards and as one community of scholars in English studies.

Coda

There is much to be done and much we don't know—about scientific discourse, about reading literature, about language development, about conformism in education, and about teaching Lydgate. But we have discovered a concept, as ancient as word processors are modern, for getting on with the work: the English department as a community of scholars. It thinks and feels right.

Notes

1. Although Michigan Tech has a humanities department comprising several disciplines, including English, for the purposes of this discussion I use "department" to stand for the English department—the various programs and the thirty faculty members within the discipline of English at MTU.

2. Some of our published attempts at integration are Fulwiler and Young, co-authored by fifteen colleagues at MTU; Petersen; Freisinger; and the journal *Reader: Essays in Reader-Oriented Theory, Criticism, and Pedagogy,* begun in 1983 under the editorship of Elizabeth Flynn.

Chapter 2
The Argument for Writing Across the Curriculum

TOBY FULWILER

In order to make the abstract concept of "writing across the curriculum" more concrete, the Humanities Department of Michigan Tech planned, organized, and conducted a series of off-campus writing workshops to which teachers from all disciplines were invited. These workshops introduced participants to three premises which we believed crucial to developing a truly interdisciplinary writing program. We wanted teachers to understand (1) that the act of composing a piece of writing is a complex intellectual process; (2) that writing is a mode of learning as well as communicating; and (3) that people have trouble writing for a variety of reasons; no quick fixes will "solve" everybody's writing problem. In the next few pages I'd like to explain these assumptions, as they are the core ideas around which all of our workshop activities are designed.

Composing

Many teachers—and whole school systems—have identified writing as a basic communication skill which is often taught as spelling, punctuation and penman-ship in the early grades. In the later grades it is still taught as a technical skill, nec-essary for the clear transmission of knowledge. This limited understanding of writ-ing takes no account of the process we call "composing," the mental activity which may be said to characterize our very species, and which Professor Ann Berthoff de-scribes as the essense of thinking: "The work of the active mind is seeing relation-ships, finding forms, making meanings: when we write, we are doing in a particular way what we are already doing when we make sense of the world. We are com-posers by virtue of being human" (1978, p. 12).

Janet Emig of Rutgers has made an international reputation studying the composing processes of student writers (1971). She believes that writing "repre-sents a unique mode of learning—not merely valuable, not merely special, but unique" (1977, p. 122). The act of writing, according to Emig, allows us to ma-nipulate thought in unique ways because writing makes our thoughts visible and concrete and allows us to interact with and modify them. Writing one word, one sentence, one paragraph suggests still other words, sentences and paragraphs. She points out that writing progresses as an act of discovery—and furthermore, that no other thinking process helps us develop a given train of thought as thoroughly. Scientists, artists, mathematicians, lawyers, engineers—all "think" with pen to paper, chalk to blackboard, hands on terminal keys. Emig argues that developed thinking is not really possible, for most of us, any other way. She also points out that we can hold only so many discreet ideas in our heads at one time; when we talk out loud and have dialogues with friends—or with ourselves in the garage or bathtub—we lose much of what we say because it isn't written down. More importantly, we can't extend or expand our ideas fully because we cannot *see* them. Sartre quit writing when he lost his sight because he couldn't see words, the symbols of this thought; he needed to visualize his thought in order to compose, manipulate and develop it (Emig, 1977).

When we speak we compose. When we write we compose even better—usually—because as Emig posits we can manipulate our compositions on paper in addition to holding them in our heads. We can re-view them, re-vise them and re-write them because they are now visible and concrete. Both activities, speaking and writing, are important because they generate understanding and communication. Only in particular circumstances, however, such as English and speech classrooms, is the precision, shape and correctness of the speech or writing *act* itself viewed as more important than the *thought* engendered in the act. In other words, we usually speak or write to understand or communicate—not to evaluate our language medium. Some of us do communicate well because our pronunciation and articulation are careful, or because our spelling, punctuation and penmanship are fine, but most often the power of our language depends on profound "skills," much harder to identify and teach than the mere mechanical ones. Sometimes these composing skills are called "logical" or "rhetorical"; always they involve complex activities which we don't fully understand—and which are harder to teach.

Good teachers don't worry about how mysterious or difficult the composing process is to teach. For example, Peter Elbow tells students that "meaning is not what you start with, but what you end up with" (1973, p. 15). Writing is an act of making meaning—making thought—and not the other way around. James Moffett describes this same process as "hauling in a long line from the depths to find out what things are strung on it" (1982, p. 234). It's not important that writers know exactly where they are going when they start; it's important they trust the process of composing to take them somewhere. James McCrimmon calls writing an act of continual choice making: "Often the writer does not know at the beginning what choices he will make, or even what his choices are; but each fresh choice tends to dictate those that follow, and gradually a pattern begins to emerge and the constellating fragments fall into place . . ." (1970, p. 4).

This happens in my own writing all the time, even as I write and shape these words. I begin writing with a more or less clear direction in mind—in my head—and *always* discover that the act of writing takes me places I never imagined. I continually make the choices McCrimmon talks about, and each one takes me someplace I hadn't fully anticipated going. I've learned to trust this process; like Elbow and Moffett, I can *predict* that writing for a certain period of time will usually create meaning. It is this trust, especially, that we need to teach our students.

This assumption, the notion that writing is a process, "something which shows continuous change in time like growth in organic nature," is at once familiar and foreign to teachers in disciplines other than English. Familiar, because, as writers of articles, proposals and books, college teachers struggle with "process" each time they do a piece of writing; foreign, because these same teachers often require single-draft writing in the form of term papers and essay tests from their own students.

At the writing workshop teachers are asked to engage in exercises which reacquaint them with the frustrations (and joys) of the composing process: participants do various prewriting activities such as journal writing, freewriting, and brainstorming in order to select and focus on a writing topic. Later they develop one idea into a draft based on colleague response. Finally, they revise this piece and publish it for all in the workshop to read.

After sweating through this condensed composing process most teachers admit to having more empathy with student writers. Few teachers who had simplistic notions about "the writing product" when they began the workshop still retain that attitude. Prewriting, writing, responding and revising, brought to consciousness through group discussion, emphasize clearly the process involved in generating a serious piece of public prose.

Writing and Learning

A research team headed by James Britton investigated the relationship between writing and learning in a study published in 1975. Britton's team collected 2,000 pieces of writing from British school children aged 11-18 and classified each according to the function it served: transactional, poetic or expressive. They defined transactional as writing "to perform a transaction which seeks outcomes in the real world" (1975, p. 160). Transactional writing aims to inform, persuade or instruct an audience in clear, conventional, concise prose. Most school writing is transactional: term papers, laboratory reports, essay examinations, book reviews and the like; it accounted for 63% of the total sample collected.

Poetic writing, Britton's second category, is akin to what we call "creative writing" in this country; language which functions as art, shaped as "an independent verbal construct" (1975, p. 161). Readers don't expect poetic writing to be true in the same sense as transactional writing; fiction, poetry, drama and song are works of the imagination, which of course, deal with "larger" not "literal" kinds of truth. Nor is poetic writing governed by any stringent rules or formulas, as the work of Joyce, Faulkner, e. e. cummings and many others will attest. Poetic writing accounted for 18% of the total sample collected, with little evidence of its use outside of English classes.

Britton calls his third category of writing "expressive," after Sapir's term "expressive speech" (1961). Expressive writing is "self-expressive," or "close to the self"; that is, it "reveals the speaker, verbalizing his consciousness" (1975, p. 90). This form of writing is essentially written *to* oneself, as in diaries, journals and first-draft papers—or to trusted people very close to the writer, as in personal letters. Since it isn't intended for external audiences, it has few conventional constraints of form, usage or style. Expressive writing often looks like speech written down and is usually characterized by first-person pronouns, informal style, and colloquial diction. It accounted for 5.5% of the total sample collected, with no evidence of its use outside of English classes.

The complete neglect of expressive writing across the curriculum is a clue to the value of writing in schools. According to Britton's classification, expressive is the most personal writing, the closest to "inner speech" and the thinking process itself. The absence of expressive writing in school curricula suggests a limited understanding of the way language works. As co-researcher Nancy Martin explains: "The expressive is basic. Expressive speech is how we communicate with each other most of the time and expressive writing, being the form of writing nearest speech, is crucial for trying out and coming to terms with new ideas" (1976, p. 26). According to the research team, personal or expressive writing is the matrix from which both transactional and poetic writing evolve. This chapter is concerned primarily with the expressive-transactional continuum; there is some evidence, however, that poetic writing, also neglected across the curriculum, promotes significant learning (Young, 1982). Serious writers who undertake writing tasks almost naturally put their writing through "expressive" stages as they go about finding out what they believe and what they want to write. Pulitzer Prize-winning author Donald Murray, talking about both his poetic and transactional work explains: "I believe increasingly that the process of discovery, of using language to find out what you are going to say, is a key part of the writing process" (1978, p. 91).

Teachers need to understand how writing promotes thought. If school writing showed no evidence of exploratory written language being encouraged by teachers, students were not being taught to use all the learning tools at their disposal. The Britton research team concluded: "The small amount of speculative writing certainly suggests that, for whatever reason, curricular aims did not include the fostering of writing that reflects independent thinking; rather, attention was directed towards classificatory writing which reflects information in the form in which both teacher and textbook traditionally present it" (1975, p. 197). My colleague, Randall Freisinger, insists that: "Excessive reliance on the transactional function of language may be substantially responsible for our students' inability to think critically and independently. . . . Product oriented, transactional language promotes closure" (1982, p. 9).

Reading-thinking, listening-thinking, speaking-thinking, writing-thinking: these processes are the essential activities of civilized, educated people. In this context, Brazilian educator Paulo Friere contends that "liberating education" occurs only when people develop their critical thinking skills, including self-knowledge and self-awareness; the ability to think critically separates the autonomous, independent people, capable of making free choices, from mere passive receivers of information. Friere describes liberating education as "acts of cognition, not transferrals of information" (1970, p. 67). I believe that writing is the specific activity which most promotes independent thought. Both the decision to write and the process of writing are actions; one cannot be passive and at the same time generate words, sentences and paragraphs—thoughts.

However, as we have seen, some writing activities clearly promote independent thought more than others—expressive of "self-sponsored" writing, for example, seems more likely to advance thought than note copying. Writing to people who care about us—or what we have to say—engages us as writers more than writing to people who read our work in order to grade us. As we come to understand the role of writing in generating and formulating ideas, we must also examine the traditional role writing is assigned in schools. If writing promotes independent thought, to what extent can teachers across the curriculum take advantage of this unique capacity?

For the duration of a writing workshop we ask teachers to keep a journal—an organized place for day-to-day expressive writing—and we ask them to write in a variety of ways to themselves about the content and process of the workshop. At times we ask them to brainstorm in the journal, other times to summarize what they've learned, and still other times to reflect about how they *feel* about the work of the workshop. Through this assignment we hope to show participants firsthand the value of keeping a running personal—expressive—written commentary on one's own learning process. If the journal works for them at the workshops, maybe it will work for students in their classes.

Writing Problems

Many participants initially sign up for the workshop with a stereotyped idea of what constitutes "student writing problems." From the first session to the last, whether at a one-day or a five-day workshop, we attempt to expand our colleague's notion of the range, variety and complexity of "writing problems," One method that works well is to ask people at the opening session to each suggest one writing problem. We then list these on the board. A typical list looks something like this:

1. attitude
2. having something to say
3. faulty reasoning
4. having a thesis
5. understanding what the reader doesn't understand
6. value of writing
7. rules of writing (spelling, punctuation, etc.)
8. context of writing
9. organization
10. revising

11. developing ideas logically
12. writing like they talk
13. coherence (in a whole essay)
14. being concise
15. self-confidence
16. ignorance of conventions
17. sentence errors
18. including irrelevant and digressive information
19. using correct references and sources
20. writing introductions

From this point on, it becomes clear that we aren't talking about one solution for all problems; the solution must suit the particular problem. For example, the idea that spelling or grammar drills will cure all (or most) writing problems disappears fast. The "solution" to a "motivation" problem is far different from (though perhaps related to) an "editing" problem. Student "skill" problems (spelling, punctuation) require teacher responses different from student "developmental" problems (cognitive maturity, reading background); teacher-centered problems (poor assignments, vague feedback) differ from institutional problems (credit hours, course loads, grades). The whole concept of "writing problems" expands and teachers begin to understand both its complexity and diversity. It is then possible to conduct individual workshop sessions which address themselves to one problem or another in meaningful ways.

To conclude this introductory session on writing problems, I ask the teachers to condense the long list of problems they have generated into fewer, more general categories. We try to combine, for example, "spelling," "punctuating" and "staying on the line" into one category which we agree to call "mechanics," and so on. The following list reproduced from a recent college workshop is typical of the kind developed by most groups:

1. Attitude (motivation, interest)
2. Mechanical skills (spelling, punctuation)
3. Organizational skills (how to piece it together)
4. Style (conventions appropriate to task and audience)
5. Reasoning ability (thinking, logic)
6. Knowledge (something to write about)

This briefer list, while it doesn't cover every single item on the longer lists, organizes areas of concern so workshop participants can better understand them and, at the same time, gives us a common vocabulary to speak from. Looking at such a list highlights the problem categories and makes them easier to discuss and perhaps solve. Actual solution, of course, will be the business of later workshops. The dialogue has begun.

Classroom Practices

Once teachers understand and accept the major premises which inform our writing workshops, we believe they will make their own best translations of those premises into classroom practices suitable for their own disciplines and teaching situation. However, nearly all teachers seem to be interested in two general pedagogical problems associated with teaching writing: making assignments which generate good writing, and evaluating or responding to the writing once written.

Assignments

Let me outline a few of the most practical and useful suggestions that emerge from workshops about creating good out-of-class writing assignments:

1. Prepare a context for each assignment. When students are asked to write about something related to the subject in your class, it's often possible to plant fertile ideas in advance that will help generate more comprehensive writing. For example, ask students to do a series of journal writes or freewrites on a related subject a week or two prior to a major assignment, and use those writings to stimulate class talk, again about the coming assignment (Macrorie, 1970; Elbow, 1973). Informal writing can prime the pump, pave the way for a steady flow of ideas which is the necessary complement to all good writing.

2. Allow time for the composing process to work. In addition to informal writing to start the process, make room for students to write several drafts before the final paper is due. Ask students to share some of these drafts with each other—to give both readers and writers a sense of each other's ideas and capabilities. And try to have a short conference with each writer about a draft stage of his or her paper so your critical response can be addressed *before* the paper is completed. A process approach simply gives an assignment room to grow.

3. Ask students to write about what *they* know, not what you already know. Where possible, make your assignments approximate real communications situations, where the writer/speaker communicates something to a reader/listener who wants to learn more about it. This is the reverse of a "test" situation where an examiner already knows the answers and simply wants to make sure that you do too. In out-of-class paper assignments (as opposed to essay tests) students should be encouraged to use all the resources and wits at their disposal to teach you, the instructor, something new.

4. Use peer groups to motivate and educate each other (Bruffee, 1973). If you can find time in your classroom schedule to divide students into small groups of three or five each, you can ask them to read their writing out loud to each other and share oral responses. This peer-review process, carefully used, adds to student comprehension of course material as well as helps them with their writing. Small groups of students, with clear tasks to accomplish, take responsibility for their thinking and writing and thus add a dimension of active self-sponsored learning to whatever subject they are investigating. The more times they do this, across the curriculum,

the better at it they become; however, in a given class they may be a bit quiet and altogether too uncritical of each other's work. With each subsequent meeting, the groups may trust each other more and become more critically articulate about each other's work. Peer review is an easy and natural part of the composing process.

5. Show models of student writing to students. An excellent way to set up your students for a given assignment is to project on an overhead screen samples of student papers from a similar assignment last year. Show both well and poorly-done work and ask students to judge why which is which. Such an exercise draws students into the learning process by making student texts part of the course and by trusting student judgment to make critical distinctions about quality. Students who see other good student work recognize that successful completion of the assignment is also within their grasp.

6. Assign students to write to a variety of different audiences. Ask students to write to each other sometimes, and depend on such peer feedback for further revision. Ask students to write to professionals in their field by sending letters or reports out for comment (Faigley, 1981; Goswami, 1981). Ask students to write for publication, if possible, helping them do an appropriate analysis of the publication for which they are writing. And pose for your students as many challenging hypothetical audiences as you can, asking them to role play and stretch their usual school voice as far as possible (Field and Weiss, 1979). Play with audiences in your assignments and you'll be teaching writing lessons most suitable to the outside world for which they are preparing.

7. Require a series of short papers rather than one long one. The advantage of seeing several shorter pieces of student work are several: you can find out almost as much about writing skills in a page or two as you can in ten; you can also request careful, thoughtful and efficient treatment of some idea in five pages and make that as demanding a task as a more loosely-written ten- or twenty-page assignment. It's also a lot easier on you—and more enjoyable—when you come to read the papers. But the real value may be in teaching students progressively, through your comments on each successive paper, to think and write even more sharply each successive time. At the end of the term you can ask to see these several papers and assess the progress from assignment to assignment.

8. Put directions clearly and comprehensively in writing. This may sound like common sense, but it's surprising how often poor writing results from an inadequate student understanding of what is expected—and often this problem is as much the teacher's fault as the students'. Include in your instructions: (a) a clear articulation of the problem or question to be addressed; (b) your expectations regarding paper scope, depth, format, length and so forth; (c) what resources you expect to be used; and (d) the evaluation procedures and standards you will apply to the paper. Composing a set of lucid assignment directions for your students is a demanding exercise in technical writing for yourself.

9. Write some of your own assignments; watch how you do it; show students the results. This is hard to do often, but doing it once a year in even one course can be a humbling experience. It *will* be easier for you to do than for your students, of

course, but in actually thinking through the assignment, with the intention of sharing it with the class, you'll have to be quite concerned with audience and economy yourself. When you pass it out or project a transparency of it on a screen, you may wish to explain why you did what you did. At the same time, be prepared for some tough questions about this assertion or that sentence construction. Best of all, share a rough draft with your class and let them see your fuzzy thinking in the raw.

10. Integrate writing into the daily activity of your classroom. Effecting this generalized advice can actually have a profound effect on all the formal writing you require of your students. Once they understand that writing is a way of learning more about every subject and is something that you, a professional and a professor, do yourself, the routine bitching that so often accompanies writing assignments will probably dissipate. The majority of students are in school because they really do want to learn—and learn how to learn.

Evaluation

The other end of making assignments is responding to or evaluating them. Many teachers have signed up for the writing workshop in the first place because they hoped we'd have some magical suggestions for grading student papers. As they often find out from sharing ideas with each other, how teachers go about grading papers may depend a lot on how they have assigned them and on what else happened in between—revision, editing, peer reading, teacher conference or whatever. But eventually, in most academic situations, teachers must respond to and grade student writing in some fashion or other. The following ideas were generated by various teachers over the course of several workshops; they are general guidelines and not meant to be prescriptive in any way; however, teachers who follow these suggestions when commenting on out-of-class writing will help their students considerably with both their writing and thinking.

1. Respond to the content first, not the mechanics, of each paper you read. Too often we become a bit jaded or tired as readers of student writing and spend more time looking for errors than ideas. In the process we can become absolutely fixated on sentence- or word-level problems and never read the paper for its larger intention. While I'm not counseling that we ignore sentence inconsistencies, I am reminding us to let the writer know that we have considered—for good or ill—the integrity of that intention. Otherwise we treat this act of communication as a mechanical exercise—and surely, if we have made a careful, thoughtful assignment we don't want to do that.

2. Respond positively and personally where possible. Again, no absolutes here, but I believe that writers begin to care about their writing when they see that we care about it. Caring is the necessary first step to actually writing better. A corollary of that is that it's difficult to work on a piece—revising and editing it—when nothing encouraging has been said about it. Most acts of student writing are mixtures of more and less good work; be sure to comment as much on the "more" as you do

the "less." I address my comment to students by name, as I would in a letter, and I sign my comments with my name—a dimension of personal interaction that improves our communication with each other.

3. Revise early drafts; edit later drafts; grade final drafts. When you put a grade on a piece of writing you have treated it as a finished product, as if the learning is already and altogether over (Martin, 1976). If you are asking students to put their writing through several draft stages, keep in mind that the motive to revise a *D*-paper is rather low. Better, I think, to point out where the paper is strong as well as weak, conceptually, and ask for a rewrite, grade aside. Once a draft is conceptually together, with good internal logic and evidence, then we can turn attention to matters of voice, tone and style, which are really acts of editing on the sentence level. When you and the student pronounce this act of writing/learning finished, that's the time to grade it.

4. Comment critically on one item at a time. It's easy to overwhelm students who have written a weak or uncertain paper with all sorts of negative comments and a plethora of suggestions for what to do next. While the intention behind such active criticism is well-intentioned—certainly better than giving the paper a rote *F*—such teacher commentary may not accomplish its purpose. Once you see that a paper has multiple problems, it may be a good idea to single out one or two conceptual or organizational problems for comment, suggesting that other problems will be dealt with on subsequent drafts. This way the student has a clearer idea of what to do next; it may also surprise you both how many smaller problems will be cleared up in that initial act of revision, so that you may never need to spend time on this at all. And use pencil—it's more forgiving on both of you.

5. Be specific when you comment on problems. I remember being coached by a fine writing teacher to avoid all those funny symbols inside the front covers of handbooks (*frag., comma splice,* etc.); he argued that students were only more confused by them and that not all teachers used the same symbols anyhow. He suggested instead just using one comment, "Awk," for everything. But his solution, while it worked for him because he had frequent personal conferences, can be equally confusing advice for novice writers who don't yet trust their own ears. Point out exactly what you object to, but without necessarily correcting it yourself: that way the writer has something concrete to go on when he or she turns attention to revision.

6. Edit a page or two, not the whole paper. Too often colleagues report going over an entire error-filled student paper with their best critical eye, suggesting changes in language everywhere, but in the process doing most of the work which should be done by the writer. And too often at the end of a term we've all seen piles of papers meticulously edited by the teachers and never even picked up by the students. What a waste of professional time and energy! To solve both problems at once, show the student what constructions or stylistic problems bother you on the first page or two and how to fix these, then ask the student to edit by example the rest of his or her work. That saves all of us time and places the editing responsibility where it rightfully belongs.

7. Learning to critique is part of learning to write; include peer evaluation where you can in your class. In addition to receiving help with one's own paper in a writing group, one learns what to look for and how to respond in order to help others with their papers (Hawkins, 1976). Learning how to be critical is part of learning how to write yourself. We all know how much easier it is to see problems in someone else's writing; what that suggests, of course, is that we have a critical distance here that we don't have from our own work. But the process needs to start somewhere. When I first introduce peer criticism into a class, I do it with students, myself, and sometimes provide directions for what to look for. As I said before, the first time they do it will not usually be successful—but the subsequent meetings will get better quickly.

8. Discuss samples of good and bad writing with your class. I use the same technique here as for making assignments. I project anonymous papers that are well-written as well as those with problems and talk them over with my class. They see, often as quickly as I, what works and what doesn't, but especially they see by example what they have done well or poorly on their own work. Here again, you're bringing the students into the evaluation process, trusting them to have responsible voices and make reasonable judgments. Another good idea, suggested to me first by a history teacher: before handing papers back—and I always do this now—read out loud from several papers you consider good and explain *why* you liked them. Students seem to find this both unusual and highly enjoyable: taking time to introduce the students' expression of a relevant idea to the class.

9. *What* is said includes *how* it is said: Don't split grades. I never find agreement at a workshop on this one, but I believe it's important to quit separating ideas from the language in which they're expressed. For one thing, when something is known or understood well the chances are that a writer will express it well; conversely, a lot of poor writing (wordy, rambling, evasive, digressive, disorganized, over-generalized) results from inadequate knowledge and understanding. For another thing, such grade splitting reinforces the notion that English teachers are rightfully concerned with "mere expression" and the other folks with "true content." Politically, across the university, that's a troublesome belief; conceptually, for me, it's unacceptable. One grade: how good a job is it?

10. Understand that good writing depends on audience and purpose. At writing workshops we all spend some time exploring what kind of language may be appropriate for a given situation or audience. The academy seems to sanction a distanced, objective, neutral voice as that which best conveys fact and truth; however, most human beings enjoy reading more lively, personal writing that shows a clear authorial voice—which voice is fully capable of conveying some pretty hefty ideas. The consensus which emerges from most workshop groups is that style is a matter of what is appropriate rather than what is correct. So we need to show students that different voices work well for different purposes, that memos demand one style and letters another, depending upon for whom they've written; that the same goes for book reviews, term papers and professional reports. The trick is, of course, to be good in all modes to all audiences.

Getting Down to Earth

This essay could go on at some length with further suggestions for including more writing across the college curriculum. However, similar information has been presented in a variety of places before, as the reader will discover from browsing through the list of references at the end of this book. Suffice it to say that, after conducting more than fifty workshops in a variety of school settings, I believe that the ideas presented here can work in all sorts of different disciplines and instructional situations. Of that I am convinced. The writing workshop is based on simple, sound premises which teachers explore through the very best modes of learning—reading, writing, talking, listening.

As far as we can tell it doesn't make all that much difference what precise format the workshop takes or even for how many days it is offered. An ideal workshop is a week long at an off-campus setting where participants interact socially as well as intellectually and get paid for attending. A less intense but still fairly effective workshop can be offered for two six-hour days, on campus, with no evening sessions. In this shorter format participants need to pledge not to cut out to meet students and check mail, for this in-and-out business has a strong negative effect on workshop morale. But the point is that a good two-day workshop can accomplish much in the way of attitude change—while obviously less in terms of the variety of particular ideas or time to test those ideas on each other.

The primary ingredients for a strong workshop-based writing-across-the-curriculum program seem to be a combination of (1) knowledgeable, flexible writing teachers, (2) a core of concerned, flexible teachers from other disciplines, (3) administrative sanction, (4) belief in a process-oriented pedagogy and (5) plans for activities and communication once the workshop ends. Of course I write all this, as I have often in the last six years, knowing that once a commitment is made to develop a cross-disciplinary writing program, no quick fixes will result and no magical cures for poor literacy skills will be discovered. What we have learned, however, is that such comprehensive writing programs, fraught with administrative difficulties as they are, will also pay good dividends, because writing is one of the elemental, cross-disciplinary, comprehensive subjects around which to unite a faculty.

But I get ahead of myself here. This chapter has outlined why the workshops were conceived, how they operate, and what they teach. The rest of the book is concerned with three further questions: Did the time, energy and resources spent on this program really make a difference? If so, how? And how do we know?

Chapter 3
Developing Our Research Model

MICHAEL E. GORMAN

"I'm forming a committee to evaluate our writing-across-the-curriculum program. Would you mind chairing it?" Art spoke casually, as though this were a matter of little importance. I said, "Sure," wondering what I was getting into.

Only a few months ago, I had made the same response when Art Young offered me a job at MTU. Sure I'd teach writing, psychology, and education courses. What the hell, that's only three disciplines to stretch across. I'd always considered myself a generalist.

And now I was in a department where people assumed I had heard of Britton and Kinneavy and asked me whether I was going to go to 4Cs—whatever that was. The only name I could drop was Don Murray. I had taken Advanced Non-Fiction Writing from him at the University of New Hampshire, where he untaught me most of what I knew about writing. But my Ph.D. was in psychology, not rhetoric and composition, or even literature, or English education. Because there was only one other overworked psychologist on campus, Art had hired me to help the Humanities Department with their research. I didn't want to prove him wrong.

Soon after arriving in Houghton, I realized that my reserved, professional, gentlemanly department head was a riverboat gambler at heart. Not content with just hiring a psychologist, Art was going to triple the stakes by asking a first-year faculty member with little experience in composition research to evaluate a quarter-million dollar-project.

Not only that, he assigned two other first-year faculty to the Evaluation Committee: George Mc Culley (Utah State) and Cindy Selfe (University of Texas). Fortunately, both were trained in English composition. The fourth committee member, second-year man Jim Kalmbach (Michigan State) was trained in reading and linguistics. Fortunately, Art and Toby Fulwiler, who co-designed the writing-across-the-curriculum program in 1977, sat in on the committee's debates. For once I was relieved to have somebody looking over my shoulder.

At the first meeting, Art gave us a sense of what he was trying to do. The General Motors grant that funded Tech's writing program called for a modest, small-scale evaluation. However, he wanted to make this evaluation into a major research project with implications that stretched far beyond Michigan Tech.

Art and Toby had already collected some data, asking faculty to rate their attitudes about teaching writing before and after each workshop, but they needed someone to analyze these surveys. Plans were also underway to compare holistic paper scores in 1979, '81 and '83. But Art made it clear that he welcomed ideas for other projects.

After Art finished, I got my first sense of the other committee members. George began asking questions, Cindy started outlining proposals, and Jim said very little—but when he spoke, he was careful and thoughtful.

By the next meeting, Cindy already had plans for two pieces of research: Project Recruiter, in which she would find out what kinds of skills corporate recruiters looked for in MTU graduates, and Project Predictor, in which she would find out how well G.P.A. in Humanities courses—particularly freshman composition—predicted success at MTU. I realized that I was going to have to sprint to keep this colleague in sight.

I decided to start by helping Toby make sense of his Faculty Attitude Survey, which already had been administered before and after several workshops. I took a quick look at the raw survey data and concluded that this analysis would be easy. I knew the statistical test I wanted to use; it was simple, and there were statistical packages to run it on the computer. I remember Toby's looking at me and saying, "Can you really do all this?"

I said yes—and promised something I couldn't deliver. When I looked more closely at the data from the survey, I knew I was in trouble. There were several different versions, with questions worded differently and reordered. A scale that went one way on one version often went the other way on another version, then reversed again on a third. It would take hours just to get the questions and reversals straightened out.

In short, I had a big mess on my hands. Fortunately, a saviour came: my wife Margaret, who had spent two years analyzing experimental data at the National Institutes of Mental Health. She joined the evaluation team and spent over a year helping me analyze those questionnaires. Initially, she worked as a volunteer, but it quickly became apparent that she was indispensable. Art found money for her as soon as he could; she became our number cruncher and organizer, making sense out of masses of data.

But even with Margaret's help, the survey still took forever to analyze. Toby reminded me several times of my promise to complete this analysis rapidly. Meanwhile, Cindy was racing along on her projects, George was asking questions at an even more furious rate and Jim was proceeding quietly but surely in his own direction.

Writing samples and Writing Apprehension Tests had been collected from MTU freshmen in 1979. The idea was to collect writing samples again in 1983 and have the students fill out the Writing Apprehension Tests for a second time. If we were going to do this, we had to move *fast,* so I decided to make my mark on this data set. I'd show them what a psychologist could do. I whipped off a dazzling, three-page memo that described how we could do a repeated-measures analysis, comparing the writing-sample score of each senior to his or her score as a freshman. We could determine, via a questionnaire, how many writing-across-the-curriculum-intensive courses each senior had been exposed to and use that variable to predict the amount of improvement in each student's writing. I called a meeting to discuss this plan. George asked, "Did we really expect our writing-across-the-curriculum program to affect the way students performed on a 50-minute writing sample?" We all answered "No." In 50 minutes, students would have too little time to brainstorm, freewrite, revise. The topics would be selected for them, not generated by the students themselves. In short, the 50-minute writing sample ran contrary to all the things the workshops had emphasized. One good question had blown my plan apart.

My design was excellent, but my goals were weak. I felt embarrassed but grateful to George. If I had been working alone, I would have spent a year on the repeated-measures study, only to find nothing. I began to realize that I didn't have to whip off dazzling designs on my own—that I could rely on the team to make up for my deficiencies.

That discussion had been so valuable that I decided to keep a record of future ones. I decided to propose less and listen more and so started taking notes on the group meetings. These notes started out short, but kept getting longer and longer as we debated George's question. We realized we had been trying to design an evaluation without being clear what the focus of the writing-across-the-curriculum program was. As a writer, I had learned that one of the best ways to start a piece was to dive right in, knowing that sooner or later, I'd have to step back and develop a plan. Similarly, we had thrown ourselves into the evaluation without having a clear idea of where we were headed. That was good for starters; now we needed a plan.

We asked Toby to describe the goals of the GM-funded program. We met every week for two hours to debate and refine his initial description—"The Evaluation Ball Park." (See p. 36.) Getting to first base was changing faculty attitudes, the explicit goal of the workshops. Getting to second meant changes in classroom teaching, which in turn should lead to third base—changing students attitudes toward writing—and home, improving how they wrote. Individual projects were aimed at seeing to what extent we had reached each of the bases. Most of us liked the model, but several questioned what happened to runners left on base and, worse, how could some runners skip bases? For example, we might give students a more positive attitude toward writing without improving their ability to write.

Reacting to this debate, Toby wondered if the GM Grant wasn't schizophrenic, in that it tried to change student writing by changing teachers' attitudes. Eventually, he came up with a less flamboyant, but more accurate flow-chart model. (See p. 37.)

The Evaluation Ball Park

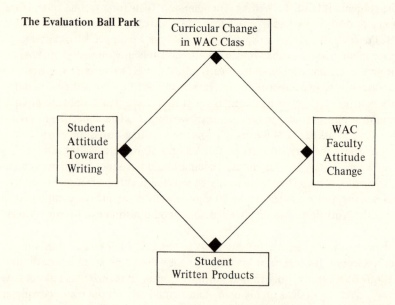

The problem of how the workshops should affect student writing was answered in the central line of the flow-chart: changes in faculty attitudes trickle down through faculty teaching and changes in student attitudes to student writing. But, unlike in the baseball diamond, indirect lines of influence are now possible: for example, classroom pedagogy can affect student writing independently of changes in student attitudes.

Designing this model had given our evaluation a focus. The really important projects would be the ones that related directly to the central line of the evaluation. Most of our existing projects lined up right on the central line: e.g., the attitude survey given out before and after the workshops was our main measure of changes in faculty attitudes. Other projects that related to side-lines would play a smaller role in the evaluation: e.g., Cindy's Project Recruiter which related to successful job performance. But this model also raised new questions: How were we going to measure "student ability to solve writing problems" and relate that to changes in student attitudes and classroom pedagogy?

Methodology Depends on Goals

Composition researchers are beginning to do what psychologists have been doing for years: argue about methods. Some people love ethnography and case studies and advocate their widespread use (e.g., Don Graves, Dixie Goswami); others (e.g., John Daley) prefer quantitative methods: experiments, surveys, etc. At its worst, this argument boils down to a "who is doing the right catechism" debate. Because each of us on the committee had been trained in a different catechism, we had numerous debates about methods. The clashes over methods showed us the strengths and weaknesses of each approach so that we all became advocates

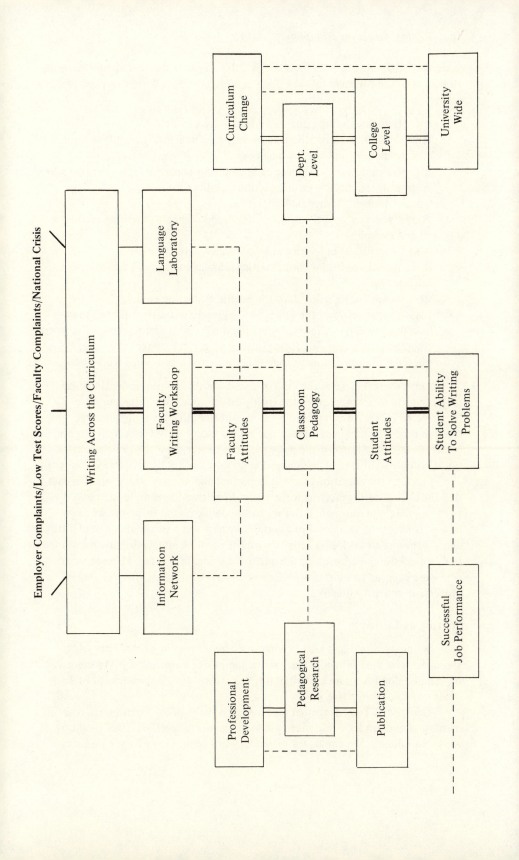

Employer Complaints/Low Test Scores/Faculty Complaints/National Crisis

Writing Across the Curriculum

Language Laboratory

Faculty Writing Workshop

Information Network

Faculty Attitudes

Professional Development

Pedagogical Research

Publication

Classroom Pedagogy

Student Attitudes

Student Ability To Solve Writing Problems

Successful Job Performance

Curriculum Change

Dept. Level

College Level

University Wide

of using what Jim called a "conspiracy of different methods." Eventually, even the 50-minute writing samples found a place in our conspiracy. Witness the following debate:

JIM: How does writing quality fit into Toby's model?

TOBY: The workshops discuss how writing can be used to improve both content mastery and writing quality.

JIM: We could use the College of Engineering assessment (involving 50-minute writing samples) to measure writing quality.

MIKE: I thought George sank that idea.

TOBY: Learning to write multiple drafts should improve writing even on a 50-minute sample.

MIKE: I feel like I'm looking at a resurrected corpse!

JIM: We have to deal with the writing samples conducted by the College of Englneering.

MIKE: Okay, so let's fit it into the general evaluation model.

JIM: The objective of the College of Engineering study would be to assess how WAC techniques have affected the quality of student writing. The more complementary views of writing quality we get, the better off we are. Besides, the College of Engineering study isn't much additional work for us.

This debate illustrates the kind of discussion that helped us decide which projects made sense, in terms of the trickle-down model. My initial horror at the "resurrected corpse" was replaced by an insight that, like the writing process, the research process is non-linear. Ideas that are cut out of early drafts may reappear in later ones, as the focus of the piece becomes clearer. Similarly, a new role for the 50-minute writing samples emerged as we developed a clearer sense of our goals.

Practical considerations are also important and interact with goals. The fact that the College of Engineering was already doing a writing sample encouraged us to fit this data into our model. But we had to define how it fit before we knew how to conduct the samples. For example, we gave out a survey that assessed students' exposure to workshop activities *after* the writing sample because we wanted to relate classroom pedagogy to the quality of students' writing. Those students who were exposed to a lot of workshop activities should show the greatest improvement in writing quality.

Writing as Learning

We now had a rough idea of what to do about writing *quality*. But what about the workshop principle that "writing improves learning"? Fifty-minute writing samples don't measure growth in learning through writing; we had to find another way of assessing this.

George and Toby suggested that we assess the impact of writing activities on mastery of content by doing a series of experiments in specific classes taught by workshop alumni. We could, for example, work with an instructor on using journals in one section of her class and compare the results with those from other, comparable sections.

I played devil's advocate, arguing that working with a workshop alumnus didn't measure the impact of the workshops: it showed what happened when you manipulated someone's class. Furious debate ensued. To resolve it, we had to hold a day-long meeting before we went our separate ways for the summer of 1982. We decided that working with worshop alumni would help us assess whether the workshop *premises* were sound. If we helped an instructor develop a set of journal entries especially designed to promote learning, that would assess the impact of journals *under ideal circumstances,* answering the question, does this sort of writing really promote learning? Then we could use the Curricular Practices Survey to help us find out what techniques facluty were actually using. If workshop alumni used journals heavily in classes, and we knew from an experiment that journals promoted learning, then we could *infer* that student learning was being improved on campus.

Yelling and Screaming

Cindy Selfe planned an experiment to measure the effect of journal writing on learning in a mathematics class taught by C. L. Nahrgang. At our first meeting in the fall, Cindy brought in some journal assignments that she felt would improve students' learning in the mathematics class. The following debate ensued:

TOBY: These assigned journal entries are fun and cute, but they're not really expressive writing. They're just problem-solving assignments phrased in a cuter way.

GEORGE: Expressive writing involves values, emotions.

CINDY: Remember, we're using an objective test to assess students' learning. The students have to master content, not just express their emotions.

TOBY: When people see Nahrgang's journal entries, will they think this is what the Humanities research team stands for? I'm willing to stand behind a lot of our crazy ideas, but this assignment may be going too far. An example of a good journal assignment from a Chemical Engineering class: "Explain the mole concept to a class of freshmen." This kind of entry forces them to speculate.

GEORGE: An entry like that really forces you to know your stuff.

CINDY: So help me figure out what to tell Nahrgang.

MIKE: Use several different kinds of entries. Each of us should come up with several examples for Cindy.

ART: Keep the ones Nahrgang has got—and add five carefully-crafted speculative ones.

TOBY: But I'd predict that only four or five journal entries wouldn't make any difference on a final exam.

GEORGE: We could do a kind of experiment within an experiment: Do speculative journal assignments produce more learning than Nahrgang's "cute" assignments?

We ended up following George's final suggestion, but the credit belongs to the whole group: we avoided what Irving Janis calls "groupthink"—the tendency for some groups to reach a consensus too quickly and make serious errors. As an example of the right group atmosphere, Janis discusses the Policy Planning Group, headed by George Kennan, that developed the Marshall Plan.

> As leader of the group, Kennan seems to have made it quite clear to the members that open-minded, freewheeling, unconstrained debating was precisely what they should be doing. Everyone was urged to express any idea that might embody a useful proposal and to help spell out all the drawbacks as well as the good consequences. One of the main group norms was to subject everyone's ideas to thorough criticism. The members applied this norm to Kennan's own seemingly brilliant proposals, some of which he had painstakingly developed during the months preceding the group's deliberations: "[They] put me personally over the bumps, to drive whole series of cliches and oversimplifications out of my head, to spare me no complications." (p. 175)

Like Kennan, I learned to trust the group process: to avoid playing leader and encourage the kind of atmosphere in which "yelling and screaming" flourished and my ideas, like everyone else's, were put over the bumps.

But the "yelling and screaming" could not get personal. During the planning period, we met two hours every Friday morning—intense sessions which left us all so exhausted we knew we'd need a weekend to recover. To keep the debate from getting bitter, we used coffeecake and humor. Each of us took turns bringing in goodies. It's hard to get angry while you're stuffing your face. When things got really tough, Toby brought in a concoction that tasted suspiciously like Bloody Marys. "Spicy tomato juice," he said with a smile.

> "A poem is never finished, it is just abandoned."
> *Verlaine*

Recently, we were debating the results from our analysis of changes in student writing apprehensions across four years at MTU. You may recognize in this project a vestige of my old design to note changes in student writing across four years. I told the committee that there was no clear pattern of correlations between the Writing Apprehension Test and the exposure questionnaire. George didn't think it was worth debating what to do next. Cindy wanted to correlate clusters with WAT scores. Jim wanted to look at what happened to the "high-exposure" students only. Toby shook his head slowly and Art smiled. By now, I was no longer the nervous rookie who had tried to lead the committee. I trusted the process. It seemed like we were getting nowhere, but I knew a consensus would emerge. If the consensus was, "Do more analyses," I'd make the time to do them—because by then, we'd know why more analyses were essential.

Finally, Toby came up with an analogy to the Viet Nam War: should we "escalate," or had time come to consolidate resources and withdraw gracefully?

We realized that like the American military in Viet Nam we had no clear idea what sending in more troops would accomplish. We had learned that analyses, like methods, depend on goals.

But we all knew that this decision was tentative and flexible—at a future meeting, the whole debate could be resurrected and a rationale for further analyses discovered. Fortunately, the book deadline intervened and solved the problem for us. Art's gamble paid off—the green kids out of grad school managed to shape a reasonable evaluation of the writing-across-the-curriculum program at MTU. But, just as I always see the flaws in what I have written, when I look over our evaluation I see all the holes—the lack of open-ended questions on the Faculty Attitude Survey, the clumsy surveys to assess student exposure to workshop techniques and attitude change, the sixteen experiments we didn't have time to do. The results of each evaluation study tell us how we could have done that study better; each piece of research raises more questions than it answers. This is the joy of research—like writing, it leads to constant discoveries.

But research is too often portrayed as a totally logical enterprise. Researchers are always supposed to be testing precise hypotheses, formulated in advance—just as we once imagined that writers were supposed to know exactly what they were going to say before they said it. Nonsense. As the prominent evaluation researcher Lee Cronbach (1982, p. x) said:

> "Those who become investigators quickly learn that the formal, preplanned design is no more than a framework within which imaginative, catch-as-catch-can improvisation does the productive work. Even in basic research, nature does not stick to the script. Planned treatments go awry, and surprises lead the investigator down new paths. Questions posed to get the inquiry under way prove to be far less interesting than the questions that emerge as observations are made and puzzled over. Not infrequently, questions arising out of the observations prove to be more important in the long run that the facts that the study was designed to pin down."

As we began our research, we also began to articulate our goals, but the two went hand-in-hand. Now, finally, as we sit down to write the report, we are beginning to understand fully what we have and haven't accomplished. This understanding is the beginning of our next research project.

Chapter 4

Research in Writing Across the Curriculum

Beginnings

GEORGE A. MC CULLEY

Three Scenarios:

Partially hidden behind a stack of student papers that are waiting to be read, the phone rings. "Hi. This is Martie. I want to ask you a couple of questions. I assigned a term paper in my cellular biology course this quarter—no specific topic, just about something related to cellular biology. I tried peer critiques in the same course last year, but they didn't work out so well. Some students complained because they thought the students who critiqued their papers were dull—didn't know enough about the subject to offer helpful comments. I'd like to use peer critiques again, but I think I need some help. What do you think?

"Well . . ." long pause.

Since Martie had attended one of our writing-across-the-curriculum workshops and had participated in peer critiques, she didn't want to know how peer critiques could be used; she *knew* the process. She knew what she expected in these papers, based on her experience and training in biology, but she wasn't quite sure how to articulate her expectations into specific criteria that students could use to evaluate each other's papers during the critique sessions.

What criteria should be used to judge papers in Cellular Biology? What do English teachers know about writing in biology? Do we know, for instance, if the rules of evidence are different in biology than in composition? In mathematics? In history? That is, in composition and literature we regularly accept (in fact, demand) authoritative opinion as sufficient evidence to support a point: "Which critics assert that Chaucer's *Troilus and Creseyde* had its roots in Boccaccio's *Decameron*?" But is authoritative opinion ever appropriate evidence in biology? If so, under what conditions? If not, what is appropriate evidence? Is writing in biology always grounded in the scientific method, from theory building to hypothesis testing? Or are there cases when the logic of narrative or some other type of reasoning is appropriate? If so, what are they? Do they also hold for physics?

42

Elsewhere? All of these questions concerning writing in disciplines outside of English are important, yet remain largely unanswered.

*   *   *

Outside the third-story windows autumn sweeps through the campus, day-glo red and gold. Inside the faculty lounge there is a din of lunch conversation:

"May I join you, George? I've been meaning to call you for a while."

"Sure! Sit down, Jon. What's up?"

"Well, as I'm sure you're aware, the College of Engineering has approved the development of 'writing-intensive' courses—you know, putting in as much writing as possible in some of our upper-division courses to improve content knowledge as well as writing ability. I think my 406 course would be a natural choice—course concepts highly interrelated, requiring the kind of synthesis that writing seems to develop so well. But I'm not quite sure how writing can be best integrated in the course."

Eagerly, "What's 406, Jon?"

"Microwave Devices."

"Oh . . ."

"Resonant cavities," "slow-wave structures," "two-cavity klystrons" and much more make up the content of a "Microwave Devices" course in electrical engineering. Can writing effectively be used to teach at least part of this? If so, which part? How "rectangular, cylindrical, and re-entrant cavities" physically differ and how these differences "influence fields"? How "phase and group velocities" and "cutoff frequencies" are interrelated? How "slow-wave structures" get their name? Assuming that writing can help students learn about slow-wave structures and the rest, what types of writing assignments work best? Journal entries? Term papers? Essay examinations? Moreover, what works best within an hour-and-a-half, twice-weekly Microwave Devices course? Several short papers? One long paper?

Finally, even if answers to questions about effective writing assignments, related to course content and physical constraints, are known, what are the answers to these questions in other electrical engineering courses? In mathematics courses? History courses? All courses across the curriculum?

*   *   *

The civil engineering professor steps in front of his Professional Practices class, cradling a small stack of one-page handouts in his left arm that he begins to distribute as he tells the students:

"Today, we're going to work on developing a clear, technical style—something that's very important in the career of a professional civil engineer. We're going to use something called the 'Paramedic Technique' (Lanham, 1981), accurately named as I believe it helps breathe life back into moribund writing."

After his discussion of the "Paramedic Technique," the students dive in, reading something about the problems with the public address system and the ceiling in the Michigan Tech ice arena:

> The Michigan Tech Ice Arena has a serious voice reproduction problem during hockey games. In much of the seating area, the announcer is impossible to understand, due to the constant echo in near-capacity situations. Indirectly related is a ceiling paint problem—the paint is flaking off and landing on the ice, tripping up several hockey players. The suggestion to solve this problem and to also improve acoustical characteristics of the arena is to suspend a thin tarp of material just below the rafters. This material supposedly has some acoustical effectiveness. This suggestion must be analyzed for acoustical effectiveness, and possible alternative solutions must be explored. Changes in speaker tuning and positioning will also be considered.

The students begin by circling *is's, are's,* and every word resembling a preposition. They ask "Who's kicking who" in each sentence, find it very awkward to put "real" subjects and "active" verbs into some sentences, such as "Changes in speaker tuning and positioning will also be considered," but keep trying.

During the next class and throughout the rest of the quarter, the professor encourages students to use the "Paramedic Technique" when editing their writing. But he realizes that the students soon internalize the circling of *to be* and prepositions—indeed, find these steps in the method tedious and abandon them—so he deletes these steps in next quarter's course, only mentioning the evils of *to be* verbs and prepositional strings in his opening discussion of the technique. He wonders if he should go through the whole process next term—or could he skip some of the prescribed steps?

These are real questions: Are there hallmarks of "good" writing that pervade most writing contexts, such as Lanham (1981), Williams (1981), Reddish (1983), and others suggest? Many authorities agree on the horrors of overly nominalized prose and convoluted syntax. But when does nominalization become extreme and syntax convoluted? Obviously the answer depends on the context. But what do we know of the rhetorical contexts in each discipline?

If there are truisms of good style that span most disciplines and contexts, do the specific stylistic and editorial conventions change from discipline to discipline, from context to context? What do experienced readers in each discipline expect? In what situations? Fundamentally, what emphasis should be put on teaching specific stylistic and editorial conventions, particularly when many students will change careers several times during their lives? Odell, Goswami, and Quick (1983) believe that we should turn our attention from style and focus on invention, echoing the concern for process-oriented instruction that has permeated all levels of composition theory and practice in recent years. If Odell and his colleagues' reasoning is sound, and common sense suggests that it is, what invention strategies should be employed in each context? What are the questions about audience(s) and purpose(s) a civil engineer should answer before drafting an environmental impact statement? An accountant writing a letter to the file? And so forth . . .

Quite clearly, we don't yet know what the specific stylistic considerations across the curriculum are nor how important they may be. Nor do we know how invention can best be managed from biology to history, from philosophy to applied statistics.

Writing to Communicate

Kinneavy (1971) argues that we don't know much about the principles of logic, organization, and style in informative and exploratory discourses—the two primary aims of most lab reports in biology courses and many writing tasks in other disciplines. Other researchers who have carefully examined writing outside of the composition classroom echo Kinneavy's conclusions (e.g., see Odell and Goswami, 1982).

Writing texts in courses from law to engineering do exist. But most authorities, including some authors, admit that the general prescriptions for quality in too many texts are static, immune to the constantly changing contexts for writing, and largely ignorant of the specific logical, organizational, and stylistic requirements for separate writing tasks. Houp and Pearsall (1984), the authors of a widely used technical writing text, make this clear in their first chapter:

> Because the qualities of good reports vary from report to report, depending upon audience and objective, we cannot offer . . . a list [the criteria for quality] that applies equally to all reports (pp. 8–9).

Of course, we can't determine the specific requisites of quality for every writing task. Nevertheless, if we are to make writing a viable concept in biology, physics, electrical engineering classes, and all across the curriculum, we must begin filling in the gaps in our knowledge of how writing is best used within the specific discourse aims across the curriculum. To do this, we must carefully investigate writing and the writing process in a myriad of contexts—that is, we must conduct research.

Writing to Learn

Beyond the general speculations of Berthoff (1983), Britton (1970), Emig (1983), and Moffett (1981) and the seminal research of Applebee (1983), Britton, Burgess, Martin, McLeod, and Rosen (1975), we know little about the specifics of writing to learn. We don't know what content can be taught using writing, especially in the more scientific and technical areas. We also don't know if writing is a more effective means of teaching content than other more "traditional" methods. (Intuitively, most of us will agree that writing is not the most efficient pedagogical technique for teaching multiplication tables or other rote learning tasks.) Worse yet, we haven't done much to match types of writing (exposition, for instance) and their inherent logical and organizational structures with specific learning tasks. In general, Kinneavy (1971) suggests that if students are just acquainting themselves with the subject matter (such as "slow-wave structures" and "resonant cavities"), then the logic and organization of classification and narration would be most applicable, usually calling for an essay. But we aren't sure if this holds true for all new content in all areas. Following the same reasoning, it would appear that when students are asked to design, construct and test microwave devices, necessitating the use of "slow-wave structures" and "resonant cavities," then inductive and deductive logic and organization become necessary characteristics of reports and proposals. But again we aren't sure. Further, if students must understand the limitations of these concepts in the theory of microwave devices, where and why they don't work (applied research), or are asked to extend them, how they might be improved (basic research), then the logic and organization of evaluation and exploration (if any exists) become necessary and would require argumentative papers and theoretical treatises. We aren't certain, however.

Even if we did know what type of writing is best suited for what type of learning, we would still have to guess which physical constraints (class size, term length, credit hours) limit the usefulness of writing as a pedagogical technique. Since our hunches are often misleading, only research can answer our questions and guide us as to where (in electrical engineering and elsewhere) and how writing can be best used for teaching and learning.

Rhetorical Considerations

In the last few years "packaged" editing schemes, like Lanham's "Paramedic Technique" (1981), have exploded into the literature and texts on writing. Yet, just a decade before, some authorities, like Kinneavy (1971), were asking which stylistic and editorial conventions were appropriate to each discipline. Have we now discovered that there are no unique conventions, that they are the same everywhere?

Reddish (1983), writing about bureaucratic language, distinguishes three styles of writing: simple ("Dick-and-Jane" style), complex (mature but graceful style), and "complexified" (a highly legalistic, convoluted style which largely ignores the rhetorical context within which the writing is placed). For Reddish and many others, then, "good" style largely depends on the rhetorical context—who is writing, for what purposes, and for whom. In this sense, good style is like good manners—what may be appropriate behavior at a white-tie dinner may not be necessary at McDonalds. although there are probably threads common to both situations. What we don't fully know is what readers need to make meaning out of written texts as the contexts for writing change and what, if any, are the universals of good style within all contexts.

This relativistic notion of good style is also much closer to the position of others, like Odell and his colleagues (1983), who call for more specific knowledge about invention in varying contexts. If the elements of good style are dependent upon changing conditions, then logically the most effective invention strategies should also vary. Selzer's (1983) investigation of the composing processes of a practicing engineer, considered a successful writer, depicts that this engineer spends most of his composing time planning. But is this engineer unique? Are the invention strategies he employs in planning common to other successful engineers? For most writing tasks? What about other professionals and nonprofessionals who must write to succeed on the job? And what is the interrelation between invention and style across disciplines, among writing tasks? Without at least partial answers to these questions, our efforts to foster and improve writing across the curriculum will be greatly handicapped.

Why Research and Evaluation in Writing Across the Curriculum Programs?

For Martie, the clear articulation of criteria for Cellular Biology papers was essential to her efforts to instill writing in biology. For Jon, the knowledge of which type of writing could be best used to teach and extend which course concept made writing a fixture in his Microwave Devices course. For the civil engineering professor, the discovery of how style could be best taught in his Professional Practices course cemented his attention to style and opened his eyes to other rhetorical concerns in his civil engineering report writing courses.

Although these three scenarios, all brief and insular but typical, represent glances of the writing-across-the-curriculum program at Michigan Tech, they point out three strong reasons for conducting writing research across the curriculum:

1. to discover the uses and roles of writing to communicate across the curriculum;
2. to determine how writing can best be used to structure and improve learning across the curriculum;
3. to identify and develop the appropriate rhetorical concerns across the curriculum.

Individually, each of these three reasons represents strong motivation for conducting research in writing-across-the-curriculum programs, and together they comprise a compelling argument for making research central to such programs. But there are still other reasons.

Writing-across-the-curriculum programs require time and money. To gain these resources, program developers need to demonstrate that their programs work and that classrooms are improving—the evaluation function of research. Evaluations, if properly designed, can tell us not only if our programs are working, but *why* they are working. Such evaluations add to program growth by providing diagnostic and prescriptive information as well as evaluative data; they do not just statistically assume that the program is as good as it is ever going to get. In evaluation jargon, these dynamic evaluations are known as formative evaluations; static assessments as summative evaluations. Obviously, if writing-across-the-curriculum programs are to succeed, satisfying the needs of administrators and/or funding agencies, and to improve, satisfying the need of students and teachers, our evaluations of them must be both formative and summative—that is, they must include research in its fullest sense.

With increasing frequency, faculty members outside of the English area at our institution seek us out and ask questions like: "What do you think is the best way to incorporate writing into my CAD/CAM (computer-assisted design/computer-assisted manufacturing) course?" The gravity of such a question is hard to appreciate unless you have worked in an institution like Michigan Tech where engineering and the sciences are the popular concerns. All too often a well-intentioned faculty member, seated at a crowded luncheon table, prefaces a comment with: "You people in the humanities won't appreciate this, but . . ." Our best explanation of these surprising questions, which occur just about anywhere and anytime, even between periods at Tech hockey games, is that we are now seen as authorities in an area where a wide range of faculty have an interest. These "shared interests," more than anything else, have led to the collaborative research which has benefited us all, as Art Young accurately pointed out in the first chapter of this book.

Even at a technological university like Michigan Tech, the curriculum is extensive, from Outdoor Recreation Development in the School of Technology to Drill and Ceremonies in Army ROTC. Within this varied curriculum, the diversity of classrooms and instructors is large, and writing is beginning to pervade this spectrum of different courses and teachers. Students write "letters to the file" in their Accounting I and II courses, documenting their procedures. Students in an intermediate algebra course must summarize basic concepts in a journal. Students in many engineering courses write lab reports, field reports, proposals, feasibility studies and more, and it is the same in the life and physical sciences. Because we believe that writing should be at the center of the curriculum, we see the whole curriculum as a laboratory, full of opportunities. The questions within our own curriculum provide the motivation for research in writing across the curriculum.

II.
Evaluation
Assumptions and Discoveries

The Michigan Tech writing-across-the-curriculum program was founded on the premise that teachers are the most permanently influential members of the university community; if teachers would incorporate more writing in their classes, they, in turn, would influence the students. However, this presented a problem. If our original goal was to have an impact on *student* writing and learning ability, we had certainly taken the long way around. If we actually diagrammed the flow of influence, it might look like this:

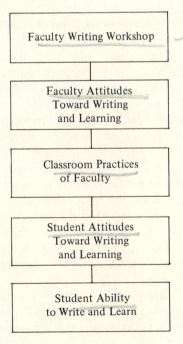

The faculty writing workshops should change how participating teachers view writing in the curriculum. This attitude change should lead, in turn, to changes in how teachers assign and respond to student writing. These changes in classroom practice should produce changes in how students view writing, which, finally, should influence, in a positive way, their writing and learning abilities. This model relies heavily on a trickle-down theory of behavior—"supply-side pedagogy," as one colleague called it.

But this flow chart, which so neatly outlines on paper what our workshops were meant to accomplish in practice, is deceptively simple. A necessary distortion occurs any time one attempts to make a linear graph of anything as complex as "attitude" and "behavior." For instance, we know already, from talking to colleagues, that some teachers incorporate workshop ideas into their classes without ever changing their basic attitude toward the role of writing in the curriculum. At the same time, we know other faculty who actually changed their attitude about writing only *after* trying something out in their class. One must start somewhere, however, and this schematic flow of influence gave us just that.

This flow chart is deceptive in still another way: logical though it looks, the process by which it was arrived at was, if anything, highly emotional. When we formed our seven-member evaluation team in 1981, we knew dimly that we wanted to measure the change in student writing ability because we had promised our grant source we would produce such a measurement. (Sound familiar?) We didn't know what, precisely, about writing ability to evaluate, nor the means by which to do it. Lee Odell counseled us to use multiple measures for a program as ambitious and amorphous as ours—a recommendation similar to that of Davis, Gross, Scriven, and Thomas in *The Evaluation of Composition Instruction* (1981), a highly useful book which we discovered only after our own evaluation project was underway.

With only this general principle in mind, our evaluation team began a series of two-hour meetings at 8:00 on Friday mornings, complete with muffins and coffee, to see what sort of diagrammatic sense we could make from a program already four years old. The more we attempted to sketch the lines of influence leading toward demonstrable improvement in student writing ability, the more we began to doubt we would find it. It now seems surprising how slowly it dawned on us that if we wanted to measure any effect produced directly by the program we should measure the effect closest to the actual treatment itself and not some effect several removes later. In other words, we should measure the impact on the faculty first and only later try to measure the impact on students. In addition, we recognized that even if we could show that Michigan Tech students did write better somewhere down the line, it would be hard to prove "beyond a shadow of a doubt" that our program was responsible for the improvement; there were simply too many variables to control. But we get ahead of ourselves here—that is the very story this section is meant to tell.

But all was not lost simply because it was difficult to measure what we had promised to measure. There were observations to make, data to collect, and new instruments to design. The act of retrospectively constructing this model showed us what, where, and when to measure. With this larger perspective, borne of our paper diagram, we found a place to start: faculty attitudes—how could we measure them? Since we were already collecting qualitative workshop evaluation, could we add something more quantitatively measurable? And, after that, could we collect information about classroom practices. And how should we do that?

This section, then, attempts to answer some of those questions as well as show you the process of questing for answers. The following five chapters measure the program at points where it is measurable. As you read through these particular pieces, keep in mind the flow chart depicting the workshop influence: these reports were designed to find out what was happening to (1) faculty attitudes, (2) faculty practices, (3) student attitudes, and (4) student writing and learning ability. As you will see, some of the findings are surprising, others predictable, still others disappointing. However, each study attempts to convey process and method as well as result and conclusion.

In "Changing Faculty Attitudes Toward Writing," Fulwiler, Gorman and Gorman describe the attempt to measure the impact of the workshops on faculty beliefs about writing and teaching writing. In the process they developed a "Faculty Attitude Survey" which may be useful to others interested in finding similar information.

In "How Teachers Teach Writing: A Survey of Classroom Practices," Kalmbach and Gorman report the results of a survey conducted in the fall of 1982 to assess which ideas about teaching writing had actually found their way into the pedagogy of participating teachers. Here again, the researchers developed a survey instrument, the "Student Attitude Survey," to accomplish this task.

In "Student Exposure to Writing Across the Curriculum," Selfe and Mc Culley designed a survey to monitor the effect of the faculty workshops on students enrolled in the classes taught by participating faculty. In most respects, this student-generated information compares favorably to the faculty-generated information in another study, yet the researchers also found some surprising differences.

In "Watching Our Garden Grow," Selfe, Gorman, and Gorman attempt to measure (1) whether students between 1979 and 1983 had changed their attitude about writing and (2) if so, whether such a change could be attributed to the writing-across-the-curriculum program. In this piece it is interesting to watch the researchers struggle to make sense of especially difficult data.

In the final piece in this section, "Assessing the Writing Skills of Engineering Students: 1978–1983," Mc Culley and Soper report the results of a study to measure gross improvements in writing skills of college seniors during the most active years of the project. This study, more than any other, illustrates the difficult terrain over which our evaluation project has traveled. In 1978, we promised our grant source, General Motors, that we would evaluate the project according to gross changes in student writing ability over four years. At the time, however, we had a rather simplistic notion of what such an evaluation might look like: a holistic scoring of senior student writing in successive years. However, soon after we actually began to collect such samples, with the help of the College of Engineering, we began to have questions about the wisdom of this particular design as an accurate reflection of the program we were conducting.

For one thing, our writing-across-the-curriculum program was aimed directly at faculty and only indirectly at students; if one class of seniors did in fact show improvement over another class it would be very difficult to demonstrate that our project, alone, made the difference. But we had an even more serious theoretical problem with administering a one-shot, fifty-minute writing sample on an arbitrary topic as a test of our program: from the beginning we had argued that students would write better only if they came to value their writing and put in the necessary time in revision activities to make it better.

So, while we felt obligated to conduct this gross assessment of student writing ability on the one hand, on the other, most of us on the evaluation team now doubted that it would provide useful information. However, we continued with this project for two good reasons: first, our multiple-measures strategy encouraged us to collect all the data possible because it would simply give us more information on which to base our overall assessment. Second, George Mc Culley wanted to find out if switching from holistic to primary-trait scoring would produce more meaningful results. This chapter provides an inside look at some of the best laid plans . . .

Chapter 5
Changing Faculty Attitudes Toward Writing

TOBY FULWILER, MICHAEL E. GORMAN
and MARGARET E. GORMAN

We didn't start our writing-across-the-curriculum program with the intention of developing a replicable model for other institutions. However, as we learned how to help Michigan Tech faculty change the nature and quality of their writing instruction, we realized that our workshop model functioned in a variety of settings with equally beneficial results. We designed a survey to provide some measure of quantitative evidence that we were correct—that the workshops worked—though we who conducted such workshops knew or *felt* that workshop participants were having a highly beneficial experience.

In order to find out whether or not we were successful in creating significant attitude changes among the interdisciplinary faculty who attended the workshops, we developed a twenty-five statement survey to tell us specifically with what attitudes teachers came to the writing workshops and with what attitudes they left. We believed this would be a valid approach because we don't teach "right answers" at the workshops, but instead encourage exploration through questions and exercises. We will explain more about this directly.

The Writing Attitude Survey (WAS)—Pre-Test (see pp. 66–67.) is filled out by participants during the first ten minutes of a writing workshop, before the business of the workshop is introduced or explained. The WAS—Post-Test (the same survey) is filled out sometime during the final session of a multi-day workshop, after participants have explored a variety of composition activities. We use this survey only for workshops of two days or more.

There were several versions of the survey from 1979 to 1982. With the help of several colleagues, including James Kalmbach and George Mc Culley, we changed or replaced some original statements because their wording was vague or ambiguous. Therefore, later versions of the survey differ somewhat from earlier ones. Approximately one-third of the statements remained the same from the earliest draft of the survey to the latest. 221 participants from MTU and several other institutions responded to these eight unchanged statements, whose results we will report in detail. We will also report briefly the results for ten other statements that appeared in the most recent version of the survey. Seventy-one workshop participants responded to these statements.

In analyzing the survey, we grouped the statements under the three premises on which our program was based: (1) that writing is a learning activity; (2) that writing is a complex process; and (3) that students write poorly for a variety of reasons. Following is a discussion of the survey statements which support each premise.

Premise I. *Writing is a Learning Activity.*   We believe this premise is best explained by James Britton (1975) through his discussion of the function categories of writing. Essentially, Britton argues that expressive or personal writing is the matrix from which the other more audience-oriented writing functions evolve. As Britton defines it, expressive writing is close to informal speech or thought; it is fragmented, exploratory, speculative writing which one does for oneself, to try out new ideas and see what's on one's mind. First drafts, diaries, journals and letters to very close friends are places where such writing can be found. Britton's other two function categories of writing are already familiar to academic audiences: "transactional" writing, where one uses writing to inform, instruct or persuade an audience and "poetic" or "creative" writing, which is language used aesthetically to create certain effects, as in poetry, fiction or drama. Britton argues, essentially, that students who learn to "express" their thoughts to themselves first will then produce better, because more thoughtful, transactional papers later. Prior to attending a writing workshop, most participants will not have considered expressive writing as in any way relevant to their classroom teaching, but we try to change that by asking faculty to (1) keep journals for the duration of the workshop, (2) share their entries periodically with each other, (3) explore, through practice, the value of "freewriting," "mapping" and "brainstorming" and, finally, (4) read and think about some of the ideas of Britton, Flower, and Emig which present writing as a learning activity.

To find out whether participants accepted this premise by the end of the workshop, we constructed statements which we hoped would allow faculty members to find uses for writing which they neither graded nor necessarily collected. An analysis of each statement follows.

Statement 2. Faculty members should grade rigorously every writing assignment done by their students.

This statement appeared on every version of the survey, so 221 participants responded to it before and after their workshops. We hoped that participants would leave the workshop disagreeing with it: grading measures how much people know and does not, as a policy, encourage exploration or risk-taking.

In the table on the next page, we have noted the number of people who agreed with this statement (i.e., marked it a one or a two), the number who disagreed (i.e., marked it a four or a five), and the number who were neutral (i.e., marked it a three).

	Before the Workshop	*After* the Workshop
Agreed	127	36
Disagreed	77	179
Neutral	16	5

The table shows that far more people disagreed with this statement at the end of the workshop than at the beginning. In fact, of the 143 participants who initially agreed with or were neutral towards this statement (marked it a 1, 2 or 3), 112 changed to disagree with it (marked it a 4 or 5). This is exactly the kind of attitude change we were hoping we would get.

In contrast, only ten people who began the workshop disagreeing with this statement ended up agreeing with it. It's obvious that the change in the expected direction greatly exceeded the change in the opposite direction. On other statements, however, this difference between the attitude change we hoped for and attitude change in the opposite direction was not as marked. So we computed a statistical test to make sure that the change in one direction significantly exceeded the change in the other. The Wilcoxson Signed-Rank Test (Ferguson, 1976) permits us to compute the probability that the observed pattern of attitude changes occurred by chance. On statement two, the probability that 112 people could have shifted their attitudes in one direction and only ten in the other is less than one in a hundred thousand (which is abbreviated as $P < .00001$). So we conclude that this pattern of results didn't arise by chance alone; it was the workshops that made the difference. (In fact, the Wilcoxson test also takes into account the *magnitude* of the change; for example, whether a person changed from a 5 to a 1 or only from a 4 to a 2. So the Wilcoxson compares both the number of people who changed in each direction and the amount each person changed.) We will refer to this test again as we describe the results from the other statements.

Statement 10. Writing can play an important role in classes that enroll over 100 students.

We hoped that workshop participants would realize that teachers can assign all sorts of informal, non-graded writing to promote learning regardless of class size.

	Before the Workshop	*After* the Workshop
Agreed	120	169
Disagreed	58	35
Neutral	43	16

Sixty-three of the participants who initially disagreed with or were neutral towards this statement had changed to agree by the end of the workshop. On the other hand, eleven moved from agreeing to disagreeing, and another three moved from agree to neutral. Finally, eleven people who initially agreed didn't change.

So the attitudes of twenty-five participants either changed or remained in the wrong direction on this question. The overall pattern of change in the desired direction is also highly significant as measured by the Wilcoxson (P < .00001).

This result illustrates both the strength and the weakness of this kind of quantitative measure. When we showed these numbers to one workshop leader, he objected: "But I'm sure everyone changed in the right direction!" If we relied solely on subjective judgments such as this one, we would consistently overstate our case. Of course, what the numbers can't tell us is why the fourteen people changed in the wrong direction. Were they alienated by something in their particular workshop? Did some simply misread the statement and mark a wrong number? We don't know.

On the whole, we were pleased with the attitude change on the statements under this premise. Table 1 puts the figures for these two statements in context with those that appeared only on the most recent form of the survey. What we have done in this table is to note the percentage of those participants who were initially neutral towards, or opposed to, the attitudes promoted by the workshop who changed to an attitude consonant with that promoted by the workshop. Figures for those who changed in the opposite direction are not reported, but are factored into the Wilcoxson, which checks to make sure the desired change significantly exceeds any undesired change. Hence the inclusion of asterisks to denote the probability values for the Wilcoxson. Each asterisk denotes an additional factor of ten in the probability, starting with a single asterisk to denote a probability of less than one in a hundred. Where no asterisks are printed, the results are not significant. This means the change in the opposite direction was equal to, or exceeded, change in the desired direction.

Table 1. Attitude Change for All Questions Supporting Premise I

Statement #	Total # initially opposed	Total # change to support	Percentage	
2	143	112	78	****
10	100	63	63	***
(18)	43	20	47	***
(19)	28	16	57	**
(24)	70	18	26	**

(Numbers in parentheses denote statements that appeared on the latest form of the survey only, so just 71 participants responded to them. After each statement, we have noted, in parentheses, whether we hoped participants would agree or disagree with this statement.)

18. Writers should always make an outline before beginning to write. *(Disagree)*
19. Before beginning to write, writers should know precisely what they want to say. *(Disagree)*
24. Student journals should be evaluated according to the quantity of writing rather than the quality of ideas. *(Agree)*

Overall, the new statements show less change than the older ones, but the recent numbers are small so that it's hard to be conclusive. On statement 18 it's possible that a specific technique like outlining has long proved valuable to certain participants who therefore adhere to it as a fundamental skill. Still others may elevate it to a "rule" since it is one strategy which specifically teaches students to organize—one of the most discussed student deficiencies at a workshop. On statement 19 most of the participants agreed with us initially, anyway—anyone who has written extensively knows that there are times when the writing goes in unexpected directions. On statement 24 we hoped participants would see the value of leaving journals ungraded, but the statement doesn't necessarily reflect that emphasis. Many instructors do feel that the quality of the journal should play some role in the evaluation of the journal, that fifteen pages of mindless scribble isn't better than five thoughtful pages. We intend to revise this statement to fit more closely with the idea of "writing-as-learning."

Subjectively, we feel that the writing-as-learning concept created the most frequent "Ah ha!" experiences of the workshop. A colleague in philosophy wrote that the most important thing the workshop taught was that "writing is an integral part of cognitive growth. I grasped that intuitively years ago—I used to see essay tests as a learning experience—but I really did not put the concept to work very much." An historian wrote the following about the workshop itself: "I am most pleased to see perceptual wheels turning, and I sincerely hope we are truly listening to one another as well as discovering, or rediscovering the basic common sense behind the personal, active experience of learning and helping others to learn."

Premise II. *Writing Is a Complex Process.*   The second assumption is that writing is an important and complex *process* and that faculty in all disciplines need to know and understand this in order to assign and evaluate student writing. At a writing workshop teachers develop some of their journal writing, freewriting and brainstorming into more focused transactional prose through a series of process steps. They compose a draft to share with colleagues and, still later, revise and edit that draft based on colleague response. We believed that inventing, composing, responding and revising, brought to consciousness through personal writing and group discussion, will alter significantly how teachers view both their own and student writing.

For our survey, we included a number of statements meant to reveal whether or not participants actually understood the value of teaching writing through a process approach: only statements four and thirteen under this premise were used on all forms of the survey.

Statement 4. Conscientious teachers who want to improve student writing will point out all errors on each student paper they read.

We hoped that those who initially agreed with or were neutral towards this statement would disagree by the end of the workshop: pointing out too many errors all at once actually discourages writers from doing further revisions.

	Before the Workshop	*After* the Workshop
Agreed	114	49
Disagreed	100	162
Neutral	7	10

Seventy-five participants changed from agreeing with or being neutral toward this statement to disagreeing with it. Only thirteen participants who initially disagreed changed to agree. Overall, the workshops were successful at promoting attitude change on this statement (P. $<$ .0001). But by the end, there are still 49 participants spread over 12 workshops who agree. Perhaps teachers have paid attention to error for so long that this attitude may be very hard to change altogether, especially in writers who make few errors themselves. After a two-day workwhop, one colleague in the business school, quite active in the workshop, still pointed proudly to places on his course syllabi where he took off points for spelling errors. This remained his way of emphasizing the importance of writing.

Statement 13. Asking students to rewrite assignments does not help most students to improve their writing.

We hoped that participants would leave the workshops disagreeing with this statement: rewriting is, quite simply, the most powerful means of improving writing that we know of.

	Before the Workshop	*After* the Workshop
Agreed	26	15
Disagreed	181	203
Neutral	14	3

We were pleased to discover that most participants already disagreed with this statement; there were only forty people who initially agreed with or were neutral towards it, and of those, all but six changed to disagree (P $<$ .0001). Unfortunately, nine people who initially disagreed changed to agree. Without being able to interview the individuals involved, it's hard to explain these changes that ran counter to predictions. It's hard for us to imagine anyone leaving a writing-across-the-curriculum workshop convinced that rewriting isn't useful.

Table 2 on the next page puts the results from these two statements in context with the statements under this premise that were used on the most recent version of the survey only.

Space does not permit a discussion of all the statements here. Again, because of the small numbers involved, it's difficult to speculate about changes. In numbers eight and twenty-five, for example, we are talking about what happened to ten people or fewer; the rest of the participants already agreed with us. But let's talk about two statements, one in which there was strong change in the expected direction and another in which the change in the expected direction wasn't significant.

Table 2. Attitude Change for All Questions Supporting Premise II

Of those who were initially neutral or opposed to the attitudes promoted by the workshops on Premise 2, how many changed to an attitude consonant with that promoted by the workshops?

Statement #	Total # initially opposed	Total # change to support	Percentage	
4	121	75	62	***
13	40	34	85	***
(3)	24	13	54	
(5)	23	19	83	***
(8)	6	3	50	
(11)	31	15	48	
(15)	26	18	69	**
(20)	35	20	57	
(22)	44	25	57	**
(25)	10	4	40	

3. To encourage students to revise their writing, teachers should withhold letter grades from early drafts. *(Agree)*
5. Students should read and critique each other's writing to improve their own writing. *(Agree)*
8. If teachers want to help their students learn to write better they should require several short papers spaced throughout the term rather than one long paper at the end of the term. *(Agree)*
11. Teachers in disciplines other than English should give one grade for content and a separate grade for the quality of the writing. *(Disagree)*
15. Teachers should not show their own writing to students unless it has been carefully revised, edited and proofread. *(Disagree)*
20. There are fixed rules which govern all good writing. *(Disagree)*
22. Writers should make sure they have their thesis clearly stated in the first paragraph before they write anything else. *(Disagree)*
25. Students learn bad writing habits when they read and criticize each other's writing. *(Disagree)*

Regarding number five, we hoped that participants would agree: any activity which increases students' critical awareness about style, structure, content, etc., will give them more tools with which to evaluate their own writing. Student peer-group critiques were specifically mentioned as a promising technique in most workshops. So the fact that almost all participants finished the workshop agreeing with this statement isn't surprising.

On statement eleven, we hoped that participants would realize that content and quality are inseparable in writing. Fewer than half the participants who initially agreed moved to disagree. Why? It might be that so many teachers in other disciplines have separate grading scales for content and quality already set up that it's difficult to change them. This issue was also less central to this premise than rewriting, peer-group critiques and other issues.

In a written evaluation of the workshop itself, a professor in political science summed up his attitude about process this way: "The idea that had the greatest impact on me was that of considering writing as a process—that transactional writing *can* flow out of expressive writing." Another professor in the humanities added: "What I have liked most about this workshop, I suppose, has been the opportunity to participate in a writing process of the very type that I might use with my students. One learns best, I think, by doing."

Premise III. *Students Write Poorly for a Variety of Reasons.*   The third workshop assumption stems from our belief that students write poorly for a variety of reasons, some complex and others rather simple. We discovered that many participants initially signed up for the workshop with a stereotyped idea of what constitutes "student writing problems"; for example, some teachers are convinced that poor spelling is the crux of the problem. From the first session to the last, whether at a one-day or a five-day workshop, we attempt to expand our colleagues' notions of the nature and variety of writing problems by asking them to explore these problems and share possible solutions among themselves. One teacher defers grading until a lab report is properly complete, a second teaches outlining, while a third simply hands out written copies of all assignments to eliminate confusion.

The primary purpose of the first session at a writing workshop is to initiate a dialogue among participants in which they share ideas and find points of agreement and disagreement about the role of writing in college teaching. We believe that opportunities for such focused common sharing occur rarely in the everyday lives of teachers; the workshop helps teachers simply by providing time to explore the several reasons—motivational, conceptual, rhetorical—why students write poor papers.

For our survey we used five statements meant to reveal how participants viewed writing problems differently after the workshop.

Statement 1. Rigorous spelling and grammar instruction in writing classes will solve most student writing problems.

We hoped that participants would disagree with this statement: the most serious problems listed by teachers at every workshop have to do with logic, organization and thinking rather than spelling and grammar.

	Before the Workshop	*After* the Workshop
Agreed	80	45
Disagreed	133	168
Neutral	7	7

Fifty-seven of the participants who initially agreed or were neutral towards this statement shifted to disagree as a result of the workshop. However, 20 participants who initially disagreed shifted to agree and two more shifted to a neutral position. While the overall change in the desired direction is significantly greater than change in the opposite direction ($P < .0001$), 45 participants left the workshop believing that spelling and grammar are the keys to improving student writing.

The workshops do seem to encourage participants to be more rigorous about writing in general—perhaps that emphasis on rigor causes some participants to agree with any statement that calls for rigor. Or perhaps some participants react so negatively to the workshops' emphasis on process that they register a protest on this question by calling for humanities people to "attend to the basics." Without interviewing those 45 participants who agreed with this statement, it's hard to say.

Even though there are some puzzling attitude changes on this statement, the overall pattern is still positive: most people enter the workshop disagreeing with it and significantly more disagree by the end.

Statement 6. Poor assignments from teachers often cause poor writing from students.

We hoped that participants would agree with this statement: we are convinced that poorly constructed, poorly worded and hastily graded assignments have a lot to do with poor student writing.

	Before the Workshop	*After* the Workshop
Agreed	121	213
Disagreed	72	6
Neutral	27	1

The workshops were most successful at making teachers aware of the role their own assignments play in students' writing problems than they were on any other issue investigated on the survey. Although almost a hundred people entered the workshop disagreeing with this statement or feeling neutral towards it, only seven people left the workshop still not in agreement. As one colleague in Civil Engineering commented a year later: "I worry less about the students' preparation and concentrate harder on my own performance. I try to teach by example, by giving organized lectures, by concentrating on clear expression of ideas, and by clearly telling the students what I expect of them." This engineer has realized that one of the best ways to improve student writing is to concentrate on his own performance. Good assignments are a necessary, but not sufficient, condition to insure good student writing.

Statement 7. A major cause of poor college writing is immaturity on the part of the writer.

We hoped participants would agree with this statement: the work of William Perry, Jean Piaget and others suggests the importance of knowing what developmental stage a student is at. Some students simply don't have the intellectual and emotional maturity to write as their professors expect.

	Before the Workshop	*After* the Workshop
Agreed	68	129
Disagreed	124	69
Neutral	29	23

Eighty-three participants changed to agree with this statement over the course of the workshop. Twenty-two shifted in the opposite direction, seven of them to a neutral position and the other fifteen to disagree. Again, the shift in the expected direction significantly exceeds the opposite shift (P. < .0001), but a surprisingly large minority changed their attitudes in the opposite direction.

Actually, this finding isn't a total surprise. The "student immaturity" issue isn't formally introduced in the workshop—as opposed to other issues like teacher assignments. In fact, one of the messages the workshop gives faculty is to be more demanding when it comes to student writing—to see their students as capable of being good writers. It's easy for us to imagine participants being torn on this issue, thought most finish the workshop believing the developmental level of the student is a factor in his or her writing.

Statement 16. Many students write poorly because teachers have made them afraid to write.

We hoped participants would agree with this statement: some students view writing solely as a means of measuring them and come to view all writing as judgmental—hence their anxiety about writing.

	Before the Workshop	*After* the Workshop
Agreed	109	152
Disagreed	70	42
Neutral	42	27

Sixty-one participants shifted to agree with this statement; eighteen shifted from agree to disagree or neutral. Again, the shift in the expected direction is significant (P < .0001), but reduced by movement in the opposite direction. About three-quarters of the participants finish the workshop agreeing with this statement, but there are still 69 who don't. We think that people who may not have experienced anxiety or fear connected with their own writing don't readily understand this emotion in others. Fortunately, most participants readily admitted their own anxieties about writing and discussed them with colleagues in the workshop. We see evidence in responses to statements like this one that this process helped faculty understand students' writing problems, too.

Table 3 on the next page puts the four statements we have already discussed in context with the one other question that was added to this premise on the most recent version of the survey:

Table 3 . Attitude Change for All Questions Supporting Premise III

This table, like the others before it, shows the percentage of those who changed their attitudes to a position consonant with those promoted by the workshops.

Statement #	Total # initially opposed	Total # change to support	Percentage	
1	87	57	66	***
6	99	94	95	****
7	153	83	54	***
16	100	61	61	***
(14)	19	14	74	***

14. Poor spelling and punctuation are the most serious writing problems of college students.

We hoped participants would come to disagree with this statement. The table above shows that fifty-two of the seventy-one participants who responded to this statement did disagree with it, initially, and of the rest, all but five shifted. In the workshop, faculty are asked to come up with their own list of writing problems and spelling and punctuation are typically very low on the list.

Teachers generally discovered new reasons for the student writing problems they had encountered in the past. A colleague in the math department wrote the following: "I gained insights into both the problems of the various departments in having to 'deal with' poor writing—and came away with a new (to me) explanation of the hostile attitudes of the Tech student toward writing and some aids to try and break down this hostility." An especially large number of insights came in regard to the problem of "motivation" or "attitude" on the students' part. For example, a sociologist wrote: "The major idea is that writing must be empahsized as important by literally every person teaching in every discipline. If the students can be cajoled or convinced that writing is important for their personal and professional success, then and then only will they care about their writing."

Comments on the Survey

When our colleague, Art Young, asked participants at a recent workshop to comment "expressively" about the Writing Attitude Survey—how they felt taking it, what changes they could have predicted and what it measured and didn't, he found some interesting observations. Most common were those who said something like "I have no doubt that my responses in the survey have drastically changed reflecting less concern for grammar as a separate part of writing." We believed we could change attitudes in a general way so that faculty would see writing more holistically—less atomistically—and so we were pleased by this comment. Many respondents noted that they would "concentrate on giving more positive feedback" and that their answers on the post survey would show their new conviction about "the value of revision" or "how writing can be used as a 'learning tool.'"

A number of people, responding immediately after the post survey, were sure they had developed much stronger convictions during the course of the workshop: "I found my second 'go' at the survey an instructive contrast with the [first-day] experience. My initial responses to the survey questions were, for the most part, qualified responses. Today, I found myself using '1's' or '5's.'" Another respondent wrote: "Key words in the questionnaire stand out and make sense. Sunday [the first day] I didn't even see key words. Obviously my attitudes changed over the past couple of days. I found that on the 'second' survey I recorded 1's and 5's frequently and definitely. I don't recall using either number more than once the first time." Still another recorded a similar observation about moving toward much firmer convictions by the end of the workshop: "I really enjoyed (I'm sure a strange term here) the pre/post attitude survey . . . In the initial survey I'm not sure what I put down, but in the post survey I felt urged to be either a '1' or a '5.' This surprised me because I try not to be an extremist."

Some participants reported that they didn't change their attitudes much as a result of the workshop—largely because they already believed in the premises the workshop was based on. One teacher wrote: "I'm not sure that my responses on the questionnaire were significantly different between the pre and post tests. My attitudes toward student writing were and are generally consonant with those of the project." This person wrote further, however, that he had gained concrete ideas for "incorporating the writing process into classes." Another colleague wrote: "I already came in with a pretty good set on the value of writing but I was weak on the mechanics of how to get students to do good writing." While yet a third wrote: "I think the survey will show that even before this retreat, I had a flexible attitude about writing" but went on to conclude "still, this workshop has helped me . . . I renewed my own excitement about writing."

Some faculty members had problems with the survey itself, and articulated their concerns lucidly: "I don't think my attitudes shifted much. Probably there are some numerical shifts, but I don't think they are reliable, because I couldn't get very excited about the difference between 'strongly' and 'somewhat.' I find the objective questions more maddening than usual because of all the damned 'alls' and 'always' used in the statements. A person has to be something of a fool to think that 'all writing' should be anything 'always.'" Another respondent wrote the following: "The questionnaire was transparent enough that I'm not sure the pre-test reflected all of my biases as I began the workshop. I had an idea from my pre-conceived notions and talking to those who had attended the earlier workshop what the 'right' answers were." She also went on to say "However, even though I can't remember all of my responses to the pre-test, on some items I could see the change." And several faculty pointed out the limitation of knowing how attitudes changed in the short term only: "It might be useful to measure not only that, but after a year or so to measure the amount of change that actually occurred." We agree with this and are in the process of collecting attitudes from participants a year and two years after the workshops are over.

Finally it is worth noting those items which the participants perceived as not measured by the survey. One participant simply wrote that the survey won't show "fun in writing" or "insights into one's self" or "grasping difficult concepts" through writing. Another pointed out that "The form can't, of course, measure increased cohesiveness of many participants; it doesn't make any serious attempt to measure—though it possibly could—a new or reaffirmed belief in the usefulness of the writing process in generating ideas." To encourage these kinds of comments, we are going to add an open-ended question to our survey that asks participants to reflect on their attitude change.

We understand many of the limitations of our survey instrument. We have felt, from the start, that numerical measures which report mass collective movement from one number to another pale beside the genuine transformation of one individual who significantly alters the way he or she teaches writing because of the workshop. Nevertheless, we find the survey useful for giving us a gross indication, at least, of change and, perhaps just as significant, for helping bring to consciousness the fact that one's attitude toward language use in general, and writing in particular, may have far-reaching consequences on student attitudes and abilities. While the survey attempts to "measure" on the one hand, it "reinforces" on the other, as participants are asked to consciously monitor their own attitudes through the taking of the survey. In other words the survey is an important extension of the workshop itself as much as it is an external instrument to "objectively" measure the effectiveness of the workshop in a designated area.

We continue to believe that faculty are the dominant influence on the mode and quality of education at a university and that, consequently, their attitudes and practices have direct bearing on student writing and thinking. This brief survey demonstrates that the workshops create changes in short-term attitudes—the necessary precondition to changes in teaching pedagogy, course curricula and student writing abilities. Subsequent chapters in this section follow this line of influence from workshop to classroom to student belief and ability.

Writing Across the Curriculum
Pre- and Post-Workshop Attitude Survey

ID Code: _____
Your Sex: M   F
Your Discipline: _____
Your Faculty Rank (if applicable): _____

Please complete this attitude survey using the following scale:

1 — Strongly Agree
2 — Agree with Qualification
3 — No opinion
4 — Mildly Disagree
5 — Strongly Disagree

_____ 1.   Rigorous spelling and grammar instruction in writing classes will solve most student writing problems.

_____ 2.   Faculty members should grade rigorously every writing assignment done by their students.

_____ 3.   To encourage students to revise their writing, teachers should withhold letter grades from early drafts.

_____ 4.   Conscientious teachers who want to improve student writing will point out all errors on each student paper they read.

_____ 5.   Students should read and critique each other's writing to improve their own writing.

_____ 6.   Poor assignments from teachers often cause poor writing from students.

_____ 7.   A major cause of poor college writing is immaturity on the part of the writer.

_____ 8.   If teachers want to help their students learn to write better they should require several short papers spaced throughout the term rather than one long paper at the end of the term.

_____ 9.   Writing tasks actually required in business and industry provide good models for student writing assignments in college.

_____10.   Writing can play an important role in classes that enroll over 100 students.

_____11.   Teachers in disciplines other than English should give one grade for content and a separate grade for the quality of the writing.

_____12.   Poor readers are likely to be poor writers.

_____ 13. Asking students to rewrite assignments does not help most students to improve their writing.

_____ 14. Poor spelling and punctuation are the most serious writing problems of college students.

_____ 15. Teachers should not show their own writing to students unless it has been carefully revised, edited and proofread.

_____ 16. Many students write poorly because teachers have made them afraid to write.

_____ 17. Many teachers are afraid to write because their writing has been severely criticized in the past.

_____ 18. Writers should always make an outline before beginning to write.

_____ 19. Before beginning to write, writers should know precisely what they want to say.

_____ 20. There are fixed rules which govern all good writing.

_____ 21. College students will improve their writing only when they are required to pass a writing proficiency examination in order to graduate.

_____ 22. Writers should make sure they have their thesis clearly stated in the first paragraph before they write anything else.

_____ 23. College students should always be required to write to a single audience—their teacher.

_____ 24. Student journals should be evaluated according to the quantity of writing rather than the quality of ideas.

_____ 25. Students learn bad writing habits when they read and criticize each other's writing.

Chapter 6

Surveying Classroom Practices

How Teachers Teach Writing

JAMES R. KALMBACH and *MICHAEL E. GORMAN*

We knew right from the beginning that our writing workshops were changing faculty attitudes. We could tell from lunchroom conversation and participants' voluntary responses. But there was no guarantee that attitude change would trickle down to the next level in our model: the classroom. The workshops were aimed more at introducing faculty to a comprehensive, process-oriented view of writing than at giving them one or two best practices to try out in their classes on Monday morning. We hoped that faculty would use their greater understanding of the writing process to design writing assignments and activities appropriate to their own individual classes, but we couldn't be sure.

To assess the impact of the workshops on teaching, we considered several alternatives: (1) survey asking workshop participants specific questions about the effect of the workshops on their assignments and teaching; (2) interviewing participants, either face-to-face or by telephone, about the impact of the workshops; or (3) observing classes taught by participants and recording what they were doing.

Eventually, we combined all three of these components into one comprehensive plan: we would send a survey to all workshop participants; based on survey responses, we would select a smaller number of faculty to interview; from the interviews, we would determine an even smaller number of faculty whose classes we would visit and observe, studying their writing assignments. In addition, we would conduct experiments in a small number of classes, comparing the effects of using specific workshop techniques to control classes.

In the fall quarter 1982, as we began to design the survey, we debated the relative merits of objective vs. open-ended questions. On the one hand, objective questions such as checklists or rating scales are quantifiable, specific, and quick and would increase the liklihood of a response to each item. If, for example, we wished to learn which of a series of specific activities faculty used such as journals, freewrites, multiple drafts, etc., an objective checklist of some sort would be the best approach. However, objective measures, no matter how well researched, still represented what the researchers—not the respondents—saw as important. As such, they might miss other activities which respondents found valuable. On the other hand, open-ended questions such as "What writing activities do you use?" would give us a more accurate and honest assessment of what faculty actually did, but the results would be difficult to analyze and might have a number of accidental omissions. Respondents could forget an activity or simply leave it off, believing it to be unimportant. Open-ended questions would also take longer to fill out and thus might lower the response rate.

We argued at length about whether the advantages of open-ended questions would offset their effect on our return rate. Eventually, the members of our research team favoring a quantitative approach won out, and we developed a purely quantitative version of the survey. It included a checklist of specific writing techniques which faculty may have used in *any* of their courses followed by a series of questions and rating scales faculty were supposed to apply to *a single course,* and a request that faculty give us copies of all of their writing assignments.

When we piloted this version of the questionnaire, one participant substituted a freewrite for her response to the request for assignments. She talked about how she has initially been an "enthusiastic applier" of writing-across-the-curriculum techniques but now wanted to devote more time to her own writing. As we read her freewrite, it became apparent to all members of the committee that responses of this sort had to be solicited, regardless of the return rate, so we added two open-ended questions in an effort to encourage participants to reflect on their workshop experience. (See pp. 83–85 for the final version of the questionnaire.) The pilot questionnaire also showed us that asking participants to comment in detail on a single course missed the fact that participants tended to use different techniques in different courses. In the final version of the questionnaire, we asked participants specifically to list the courses they taught which used writing, to complete a checklist of techniques they may have picked up from the workshop and to indicate what writing assignments they now used in their classes. After the respondents had gone over all of this specific information, they would have material fresh in mind to answer the first open-ended question, "How has the writing-across-the-curriculum workshop changed your teaching or use of writing in your classes?" After answering, participants, we felt, would be better prepared to answer the second question, "In retrospect, how do you feel about the writing-across-the-curriculum workshop experience?"

We piloted this new version of the questionnaire on another small group of workshop alumni and were pleased with the responses. Only one of the teachers failed to fill out both of the open-ended questions. He didn't answer the last one about the workshop experience. When we asked him why, he said that he thought it was a good question; he just hadn't taken the time to fill it out. Everyone else seemed to find the questionnaire clear and worthwhile.

By this time, we had spent several months designing the questionnaire. After analyzing responses, there would be little time to do the other steps in our original design, i.e., interview faculty, go into their classes, etc. We hoped, though, that the questionnaire would provide a base for further research by defining trends in writing practices and by identifying potential faculty for further collaborative efforts.

Who Responded?

In December, 1982, we sent the questionnaire to all of the faculty who had attended one or more of the workshops and who were still at MTU. The initial response rate was over 60%. We sent out two follow-up letters and achieved a final return rate of 82%. We saw this high rate of response to a difficult and time-consuming survey as another indication of the strong impact the workshop had on participants.

Of the 104 faculty who responded to the questionnaire, 14 had to be removed from the data base for various reasons: several sent letters instead of questionnaires, others didn't teach, and still others in the Humanities Department had been so intimately involved in the design and evaluation of the program that we felt their responses would skew the results.

For the purposes of analyzing our data, we placed respondents into four disciplinary groups: (1) engineering, (2) other disciplines, (3) humanities and social sciences, and (4) composition and literature. We placed faculty in the departments of Humanities and Social Sciences together because, during our preliminary data analysis, we found that their responses were remarkably similar and quite distinct from the other disciplines. As we analyzed the data more closely, however, we discovered that some of the differences were due to the responses of the composition and literature teachers, and we concluded that these responses should be analyzed separately. Because composition faculty have had many more opportunities to teach writing and to try out different workshop activities, their responses tended to be quite different from faculty in other content areas. We grouped the different engineering departments together because they are all part of the College of Engineering where two-thirds of our students matriculate. We placed the remaining departments—Biology, Business, Forestry, School of Forestry, ROTC, School of Technology, Education and Public Services, Math and Computer Sciences—together because, though all play an important role in the University, they don't play a role in the general education of Michigan Tech students or their courses traditionally require little or no writing. Table 1 presents the number of faculty who responded in each disciplinary group.

Table 1. Faculty by Discipline Who Responded to the Questionnaire.

Engineering	
Chemical Engineering	7
Civil Engineering	7
Electrical Engineering	4
Geological Engineering	1
Mechanical Engineering	5
Metallurgical Engineering	3
	27

Other disciplines

Biology	3
Business	8
Forestry School	1
Forestry Department	4
ROTC	1
School of Technology	5
Education and Public Services	1
Math and Computer Sciences	3
	26

Humanities and Social Sciences

Fine Arts	5
Foreign Language	2
Philosophy	2
Social Sciences	1
Anthropology	2
Geography	2
Political Science	2
Sociology	1
History	2
	19

Composition and Literature	18

What We Found, and How We Found It

We spent most of July 1983 analyzing the questionnaires, locked in an old wrestling room (*Mat burns build character*) while Portage Lake shimmered through the trees. As we coded and counted the open-ended questions, we saw the strong overall impact of the workshop; but as we assembled table after table from the computer printout of the quantitative questions, we saw that the *specific impact* of the workshop was more selective. As we expected, composition faculty had been most strongly affected, then humanities and social science faculty, then faculty from other disciplines, and engineering faculty least of all. Our open-ended, qualitative questions and our quantitative questions appeared to give us different insights into the program.

The Impact of the Workshops: Qualitative Assessment

When we asked faculty, "How has the writing-across-the-curriculum workshop changed your teaching or use of writing in your classes?" and "In retrospect, what do you think about the writing-across-the-curriculum workshop experience?" we got an overall sense of the effect of the workshop on faculty. We asked two questions, hoping to reach as many faculty as possible. Most, we knew, would respond to both questions, but some would respond only to one or the other. Often faculty members had only one thing they wanted to say about the workshop, and we wanted to offer them two different opportunities to say it. We also felt that the two questions complemented one another. Some faculty may have made few or no changes in their use of writing. Perhaps they hadn't taught since the workshop, perhaps they already used writing extensively in their courses, or perhaps they simply hadn't decided yet what changes to make. These faculty may still have had a very positive and useful experience at a workshop. Conversely, other faculty could have used ideas from the workshop to profitably change their teaching, but at the same time have had a negative experience at the workshop, perhaps because of the way the ideas were presented.

All of the responses were coded by two separate readers who then met and resolved any disagreements they had. We discovered, in coding, that a seemingly innocent question such as "How has the writing-across-the-curriculum workshop changed your teaching or use of writing in your classes?" actually asked two separate questions: (1) In what specific ways has your teaching of writing changed? and (2) What has been the significance of those changes? Some faculty responded only to the former question, some only to the latter and some to both—which made coding difficult. In general, however, faculty were quite clear on whether or not their teaching *had* changed. Faculty who felt their teaching hadn't changed said so explicitly with comments such as "It really has not changed," "no change," "very little," etc. Some faculty, especially in composition, said that their teaching hadn't changed because they already used workshop activities, and that the effect of the workshop was to reinforce what they were doing:

> Because I was aware of the writing process and had been teaching writing for several years, the workshop did not change teaching techniques. It did, however, reinforce those techniques such as journal writing and peer critiquing that I had been using.

Faculty who felt their teaching of writing had changed described that change clearly—although the nature of the change varied enormously from one faculty member who said he now stresses mechanics more to other faculty who reported that incorporating writing had changed their entire mode of teaching. One math teacher, for example, who began using journals, commented that:

> Previously I had only taught the mechanics of mathematics. Since initiating writing assignments, both journals and term papers, I have begun teaching a basic understanding of the concepts of mathematics.

No one reported that they felt their teaching had changed for the worse. Where change was reported, it was always positive.

In all, 82% (65) of the faculty who responded said that their teaching of writing had improved since the workshop. In the specific disciplines, 64% of the engineering faculty, 91% of the rest of the faculty, 94% of the humanities/social sciences and 82% of the composition faculty all said their teaching had changed.

In addition to noting whether or not teaching had changed, we also coded any comments or complaints about teaching that faculty had made. These comments were spread evenly across the disciplines, and two groups of comments in particular stood out. Ten faculty felt that they could not adapt writing to their particular discipline; either the content was inappropriate or the courses were too large. Another group of faculty complained about the lack of institutional support for incorporating writing in their courses: three faculty said they were using less writing now than before because of other demands on their time, another seven faculty members commented that they simply didn't have the time to make the changes they would like to make:

> I have a better understanding of writing; a better understanding of the areas of writing in teaching; and the desire to incorporate more writing into my course work. However, it is difficult to find the time to develop meaningful assignments (in a special area), incorporate them into the course content, and develop the grading methodology, etc.

While the number of responses isn't large, that these faculty volunteered this information is particularly significant. It suggests what workshop leaders have long argued, that faculty members need both the opportunity to learn how to incorporate more writing in their classes and support for their efforts to make changes.

Next we asked faculty "How, in retrospect, do you feel about the workshop experience?" We grouped responses into four categories:

Positive - reports that he/she feels very good about experience
Mixed - reports good features of workshops, and includes at least one criticism of workshop
Negative - reports only criticisms of workshop
Neutral - doesn't say how he/she feels—often goes off on an unrelated tangent

Positive, negative, and mixed responses were all easy to sort. Only the small neutral category was ambiguous. Occasionally faculty would respond to the question with a comment unrelated to the workshop. We coded these as neutral because we couldn't infer anything from them. Faculty responses in these four categories are summarized in Table 2. In all, 78% of the faculty were positive about the experience, while 7% were negative.

Table 2. Faculty Perceptions of the Workshop Experience.

	Engineering $N = 20$	Other Disciplines $N = 23$	Social Sciences Humanities $N = 18$	Composition $N = 13$	Avg. $N = 74$
Positive experience	80%	65%	75%	92%	78%
Mixed experience	5%	22%	19%	8%	13%
Negative	10%	9%	6%	0	7%
Neutral	5%	4%	0	0	2%

Overall comments about the workshop ranged from positive: "Excellent— very worthwhile," "Great," "It re-awakened all my lofty ideals about teaching," to negative: "A waste of time." The five completely negative comments generally focused on the inability of the workshop to address the needs of specific disciplines while the fifty-eight positive comments focused on what was learned about the writing process, the pedagogical activities which the participants took away and the opportunity to meet with colleagues from other disciplines. Nearly a third of the faculty (22) mentioned that they found the interaction with colleagues valuable. As one faculty member in forestry put it: "Last, but not least, I thoroughly enjoyed the opportunity to get to know other faculty members." Even faculty who were otherwise critical of the program found the interaction with faculty valuable:

> As an instructional experience, my net gain was two or three items. The time productivity, four days for three ideas, seems very low. The most productive portion of the workshop was the interchange with the other participants.

Table 2, however, is somewhat misleading. A question such as "In retrospect, how do you feel about the writing-across-the-curriculum workshop experience?" doesn't measure the strengths or weaknesses of the program; rather it measures the impression the workshop left in participants' minds; the climate the workshop created. The trickle-down model assumes that the workshops will, first of all, leave faculty with positive attitudes toward writing and teaching writing. If faculty are not positive about the experience, chances are they won't go back and, on their own, make changes in their classes. The fact that 78% of the faculty were positive— while another 13% were both positive and negative—and that only 7% were negative suggests that the program has succeeded in creating a climate where change is possible.

The Impact of the Workshops: Quantitative Assessment

Most teachers came away from the workshops ready to try out some ideas. A climate for change existed, but did any change take place? To find out, we asked faculty to list the courses they taught which used writing, along with the number of times the course was taught each year, the approximate enrollment, and whether they felt the workshop improved the course, made no change or that they weren't sure. Their responses didn't, of course, represent an objective measure of improvement. Rather, they indicated the faculty's opinion, which again told us something about the climate for writing across the curriculum. If a critical mass of faculty felt that the inclusion of writing was improving their courses, then their success and enthusiasm would help sustain the program. Our analysis of the question is summarized in Table 3.

The degree to which the interdisciplinary writing workshops affected teaching varies by discipline: composition shows the most impact and engineering the least, with the other disciplines falling in between. It is tempting to attribute these

Table 3 .   Overall Impact of Writing-Across-the-Curriculum Workshops on Courses That Use Writing.

	Engineering N = 78	Other Disciplines N = 89	Social Sciences Humanities N = 63	Composition N = 86	Total N = 316
Improve	53%	59%	63%	71%	61%
No Change	34%	26%	17%	28%	27%
Not sure	13%	15%	20%	0	12%
Made Worse	0	0	0	1%	.3%

differences to differences in the content and methodology of the various disciplines. We quickly discovered, however, that these gross differences were the result of more subtle patterns. We found, for example, that the workshops had an equally strong effect across disciplines for courses of twenty or fewer students. In engineering, humanities and social sciences and composition, 67% of the courses were improved, while in the other disciplines, 61% were improved. Similarly, the impact was constant in courses taught once a year. About 57% of those courses were improved, regardless of discipline. Thus, for small courses *and* for courses taught once a year, the writing-across-the-curriculum workshops have had a uniform effect.

In courses with thirty-six or more students, taught two or three times a year, a different pattern emerges: only 45% of the engineering courses were improved, whereas 58% of the other disciplines' courses were improved, as were about two-thirds of humanities and social sciences courses. The workshops were not as effective with large engineering courses as with the smaller ones, and the majority of engineering courses in our sample (about 63%) were taught in sections of more than 36 students.

Similarly, in courses taught twice or more a year, engineering showed the least improvement (50%), with other disciplines next (63%), social sciences next (71%), and humanities the highest (84%). In this case, the impact of the workshop on engineering is just about the same, regardless of the frequency with which the course is taught, but the impact in other disciplines increases with the frequency with which the course is taught. Without more detailed information about the specific kinds of courses in various disciplines that are taught two, three or more times a year, it's useless to speculate on the reasons for the impact of the workshops on them. We were, of course, pleased to see that those courses taught most frequently are the ones most likely to be improved by the workshops.

We also gave faculty a checklist of writing activities which they may have used in their courses. While the workshops sought to help faculty learn about the nature of the writing process and student writing problems rather than providing them with a set list of writing activities to implement in their classes, the process orientation of the workshop did cause certain writing activities to be stressed either through group discussion or because exercises were built around them and all participants tried them out. For example, everyone at a workshop kept journals and wrote in them often. Similarly all participants worked on several drafts of a paper during the workshop and read those drafts in peer-critiquing sessions. Thus while the workshops were not overly programmatic, they did introduce faculty to rather specific writing activities.

We developed the checklist to assess whether or not faculty actually used the activities presented during the workshop. Table 4 summarizes the responses of the faculty to the checklist. We have reduced the complex response matrix in the original questionnaire to before/after responses: Did faculty use these activities and assignments before attending a workshop, and did they use them after attending a workshop? Although there was a good deal of variation in the responses of faculty in various disciplines, only two activities were used by at least half of all the faculty before attending the workshop (conferencing with students, 53%; and assigning oral reports, 61%). After attending a workshop, however, eleven of the fifteen activities were used by at least half the faculty (brainstorming, 52%; assigning journals, 52%; ungraded writing, 62%; sharing student writing, 51%; sharing your writing, 55%; conferencing with students, 71%; assigning multiple drafts, 63%; assigning proposals, 52%; writing for an audience, 50%; assigning oral reports, 73%; and assigning several short papers, 62%).

That at least half the alumni of the workshops were using so many of the workshop ideas again suggests that a strong climate for change exists. After the workshops, faculty were willing to try out or continue using these various activities and assignments. Although we were pleased with the "after" figures in Table 4, we recognized that these figures did not truly measure the impact of the workshop because they combined faculty who had used these activities and assignments before attending a workshop with faculty who hadn't tried them before and thus were experimenting with workshop ideas for the first time afterwards. Even the participants themselves recognized these differences among faculty. For example, one faculty member from forestry noted that:

> I believe it [the workshop] is good for everybody even if for different reasons. I discovered that some faculty pay much less attention to writing than others. The workshop did essentially two things. It stimulated those who do not use much writing in their teaching to do more of it and it gave everyone, regardless of experience, ideas on how to improve what we are already doing.

As this teacher suggests, faculty who have used writing in their courses and those who haven't face different tasks in making sense of and using the ideas from the workshop. Teachers who have already used multiple drafts, freewrites or journals bring a context of experiences to the workshop which they can use to make sense of workshop ideas and to better integrate those ideas into their own teaching. However, teachers who are encountering these ideas for the first time must both make sense of them and find a place for them in their courses.

We hope that even faculty who had tried these activities before found ideas to improve their teaching at the workshop. But removing the people who had

Table 4. Curricular Practices Survey Data:
Faculty who used writing assignments and activities before attending a workshop and after

	Engineering N = 27		Other Disciplines N = 26		Humanities & Social Sciences N = 19		Composition N = 18		Total N = 90	
	Before	*After*	*Before*	*After*	*Before*	*After*	*Before*	*After*	*Before*	*After*
Freewriting	0	23%	4%	39%	0	42%	39%	100%	39%	48%
Brainstorming	12%	19%	12%	46%	15%	68%	66%	94%	23%	52%
Journal Writing	15%	27%	8%	35%	10%	68%	67%	100%	22%	52%
Ungraded Writing	8%	42%	12%	46%	25%	84%	56%	94%	22%	62%
Revising	8%	27%	0	31%	20%	37%	72%	94%	21%	44%
Peer Critiquing	12%	39%	8%	39%	5%	26%	50%	100%	17%	47%
Sharing Student Writing	19%	34%	4%	31%	45%	84%	50%	66%	27%	51%
Sharing Your Writing	35%	50%	35%	46%	35%	58%	50%	72%	38%	55%
Conferencing with Students	56%	73%	35%	54%	47%	63%	83%	100%	53%	71%
Assigning Multiple Drafts	31%	65%	15%	50%	10%	53%	56%	94%	27%	63%
Assigning Proposals	35%	42%	35%	39%	45%	58%	44%	83%	39%	52%
Assigning Collaborative Writing	27%	39%	27%	46%	25%	58%	28%	55%	27%	48%
Writing for an Audience	35%	46%	19%	39%	10%	26%	44%	94%	27%	50%
Assigning Oral Reports	52%	53%	62%	81%	63%	74%	72%	89%	61%	73%
Assigning Several Short Papers	31%	39%	35%	54%	30%	74%	78%	100%	41%	62%

already used various activities before the workshop left a pool of people for whom the workshop activities were either new or untried.

How well did we reach faculty who hadn't tried various techniques before the workshop? On the whole, 22% of the engineering faculty tried one or another activity for the first time, 31% of the other disciplines, 41% of social sciences and humanities and 84% of the composition faculty. This overall effect, however, proves, on closer inspection, to be made up of several different patterns of effect. First, there were three activities with no particular differences. Oral reports, student collaboration, and sharing writing were equally likely to be picked in all of the disciplines. Secondly, there is a group of activities which composition faculty adopted much more often than participants from other disciplines, and, excluding composition, the percentage of faculty who used the activities was very similar across disciplines. This second pattern is summarized in Table 5.

Table 5. Workshop Ideas Which an Equal Number of Faculty in All Disciplines Other Than Composition Picked Up.

	Engineering	Other Disciplines	Social Sciences Humanities	Composition	Total
Assigning Proposals	11% (2)	6% (1)	20% (2)	70% (7)	22%
Writing for an Audience	22% (4)	24% (5)	18% (3)	90% (9)	32%
Revising	21% (5)	31% (8)	20% (3)	100% (5)	30%
Peer Critiquing	29% (7)	33% (8)	22% (4)	89% (9)	37%
Conferencing with students	42% (5)	29% (5)	30% (3)	100% (3)	38%
Assigning Multiple Drafts	47% (9)	41% (9)	47% (8)	87% (7)	50%

Techniques such as writing proposals, revising, peer critiquing, conferencing, etc. are primarily ways that faculty can improve the quality of the written work they receive in the classes where they already *require* writing. Having students submit a written proposal before doing a paper gives the teacher control over the appropriateness and scope of the topic; having students aim their paper at audiences other than the teacher frequently results in better work because it forces the student to do a more careful analysis of his or her audience; revising, peer critiquing, conferencing and requiring multiple drafts are techniques which usually result in better writing because students spend more time on their papers and get better feedback in what they need to do to improve them. These activities were probably used in the courses with smaller enrollments, which were taught once a year where there was little reported difference in course improvement among the disciplines.

It's tempting to speculate that these courses were upper-division courses, central to students' major areas of study. Unfortunately, we can't be sure which activities were used in which courses because our checklists on course improvement and specific activities were kept completely separate in the interests of simplicity. We see more clearly now the need for combining this information on future versions of the questionnaire.

Table 6 summarizes the final pattern, a group of activities not used before the workshops which were adopted least often by engineering faculty, somewhat more often by other disciplines, more often yet by social sciences and humanities faculty, and most often by composition faculty. It is the same selective pattern that we found in course improvement for courses taught two or three times per year and courses enrolling 36 students or more: engineering faculty were the least affected, composition the most, and the other two in between.

Table 6. Workshop Ideas Which Engineering Faculty Picked Up Least Frequently and Composition Faculty Most Frequently.

	Engineering	Other Disciplines	Social Sciences Humanities	Composition	Total
Assigning Several Short Papers	11% (2)	29% (5)	62% (8)	100% (4)	36%
Sharing Student Writing	18% (4)	28% (7)	80% (8)	100% (3)	37%
Brainstorming	9% (2)	39% (9)	63% (10)	83% (5)	38%
Journal Writing	14% (3)	29% (7)	65% (11)	100% (6)	39%
Freewriting	26% (7)	36% (9)	44% (8)	100% (11)	43%
Ungraded Writing	36% (9)	39% (3)	79% (11)	87% (7)	55%

The strong effect the workshop had on composition and social sciences and humanities faculty is a strength of the program. No matter how much writing students may do across the curriculum, their general education courses will continue to be a critical component of their education in written communication. The data in Table 6 suggests that the program has had a strong effect on the general education faculty in the Departments of Humanities and Social Science who didn't already use these writing activities and assignments.

However, just as faculty in engineering and other disciplines were least likely to report improvement in the teaching of writing in large and frequently taught courses, they also appeared to be less likely to use activities such as brainstorming, freewriting and ungraded writing, activities which could most easily be adapted to such large, frequently taught courses.

In such courses, it might appear that there simply wasn't room in the course to assign journals or freewrites. That is, these activities were seen as adding new work to a course already crammed with material and thus were resisted. For example, a faculty member in engineering commented that:

> Through the workshop, I believe I have improved the way of teaching writing assignments (or reports, strictly speaking). However, I am still trying to find effective ways to implement those techniques (which I learned from the workshop) to *a large class*.

By way of contrast, several teachers in other disciplines commented about how much they felt their large lecture sections had been improved by using freewrites. For example, one colleague from business said that:

> Students get to freewrite earlier on issues, write more on "homework" and explain answers on quantitative problems. This helps even in "larger" introductory classes in quantitative subjects.

And a faculty member from the music division commented that:

> The techniques I use the most often is to have the students write their reactions to work I have just played for them; then use this writing (which is not turned in) as the basis for class discussions. This seems to force them to think about each work on their own.

The resistance which many engineers and science faculty expressed towards these activities may be a result of the way the activities were presented in the workshop. Faculty were asked to keep a journal where they wrote on why they thought writing problems existed and what could be done. They also used their journals to brainstorm for their paper topic and to freewrite a rough draft. These activities brought out the critical links between writing and thinking and writing and values, but perhaps it also made it difficult for science and engineering teachers to see how to make the leap from using journals and freewrites to improve *writing* to using them to improve *learning* and *thinking* in science. One faculty member in forestry seemed to be raising this problem when he commented that:

> I still have the feeling that the workshop was not adequately oriented to teachers who have a "certain amount of material" to cover in professionally oriented courses.

It would appear that the workshops have not been as successful as we would like in exploring the connections between writing and learning in a large course with a lot of material to cover. If this is true, it is a particularly unfortunate result of the workshops, as a number of faculty who attended workshops have used these same activities with success in their professionally-oriented classes. For example, one engineering faculty member commented:

> I have tried freewriting as a problem-solving tool and for communicating with students in large classes where personal contact is not possible. The results have been good.

Throughout the program, workshop teachers have commented about how difficult it was to get science and engineering faculty to see ways of using writing as learning in their classes. The survey confirms workshop leaders' suspicions. Faculty on the whole have done a good job of picking up ideas from the workshop to improve their teaching of traditional writing assignments. They have been inconsistent, however, in their use of other techniques such as freewriting or journals which enlarge the role writing can play in the classroom. The problem is shown dramatically by the comments of a chemical engineering professor who gave us a complete history of his attempts to incorporate more writing in his classroom:

First year after program

I did the brainstorming and freewriting in lectures for the physical chemistry lab. Students liked the possibility of having an effect on coursework through this method but were uncomfortable with having a variable curriculum (some of the brainstorming ideas were incorporated immediately). I also tried peer evaluation of each group's work. The students were extremely uncomfortable with this. They did not like making decisions that affected other grades.

Second year after program

I took one lab period and had them write rough drafts of various parts of reports, and they were graded on these parts. This was not satisfactory to me because they were not required to write complete reports.

Third year after program

Two lab periods were devoted to peer evaluation of rough drafts. I also help and answer questions. Then long reports (15–25 pages) are turned in to me for grading. Students like this and seem to do better.

This faculty member tried brainstorming and freewriting with some success and some problems. He then went to a multiple draft format for lab reports which he refined. The workshop apparently convinced him of the value of trying writing as learning, but he needed follow-up consultation to help him make the best use of techniques like brainstorming and peer evaluation. On the other hand, he was able to refine a multiple draft format for lab reports on his own and seemed pleased with the result.

To help faculty in scientific and technical disciplines make the leap from *experiencing* writing-as-learning activities such as journals, freewrites and brainstorming to *incorporating* them in their classes, the workshops will have to be better supplemented by regular consultation with faculty as they try activities out in their classes.

Conclusions

This study has two major conclusions: (1) overall the writing-across-the-curriculum program at Michigan Technological University has had a strong impact on faculty, but (2) the effect of the program on specific courses and specific activities for the teaching of writing has been selective, with composition faculty the most strongly affected and engineering faculty the least affected.

The study has also taught us the value of combining qualitative with quantitative questions. We all agree now that both are essential. Had our questionnaire been either purely quantitative or qualitative, we would have missed a major insight about the program. Writing-across-the-curriculum programs are for the most part complex efforts which succeed or fail on many different levels. If we are to assess these programs properly, we must use a variety of different instruments which examine programs in a variety of different ways.

In Chapter Five, we saw that the workshops at Michigan Tech have changed faculty attitudes towards the teaching of writing and faculty conceptions of the writing process. In this chapter we have seen that faculty then went out and made changes, that a large number of faculty felt their teaching of writing has improved, and that, after trying out workshop ideas in the classroom, they have continued to view the workshop as a significant and worthwhile experience. In short, the attitude change achieved by the workshop resulted in changes in the classroom. To the extent that activities such as assigning multiple drafts, conferencing with students, requiring oral reports, etc. will improve the quality of student communication, the program has had an important impact on the campus.

When, however, we examine more specifically the faculty's use of writing activities such as keeping journals, doing freewrites, brainstorming, etc. which in many cases involved incorporating additional writing into the curriculum, we see that the overall success of the program must be qualified. The workshops have done a good job of reaching faculty in composition and literature, the humanities, and the social sciences with these activities, but less well in reaching faculty in sciences, mathematics, and engineering.

One of the major reasons we have been so successful with composition and humanities faculty is that after the workshops these faculty are continually exposed to workshop ideas from their colleagues. To a lesser extent, this is true of some people in social sciences who maintained close contact with their humanities colleagues. Faculty in science, mathematics and engineering had fewer opportunities for this kind of contact. In the cases where there was strong follow-up, e.g., with a mathematics professor (see Chapter 14), two biologists (see Chapter 11), and an engineer (see Chapter 12); results were very good. But the lack of a *systematic* program of follow-up activities, adapted to the needs of specific disciplines and specific courses, may account in part for the selective effect of the workshops.

Currently, we are working on a systematic follow-up program. We feel this questionnaire demonstrates the success of the workshops at creating a core of faculty at MTU who share common assumptions about the writing process and are willing to experiment with ways of improving student writing at MTU. Now we need to help those faculty channel that energy in productive ways.

Curricular Practices Survey for
Writing-Across-the-Curriculum Workshop Participants

Completion Time: 20 minutes

Your Name: _____

Your Department: _____

Years at MTU: _____

Current Academic Rank: _____

1. Check the date(s) you attended a Writing Across the Curriculum Workshop:

____ October, 1977	____ May, 1980	____ February, 1982
____ March, 1978	____ August, 1980	____ May, 1982
____ October, 1978	____ May, 1981	____ August, 1982
____ August, 1979	____ August, 1981	____ Other
____ August, 1979 Humanities Faculty Workshop		

2. List below the courses you teach in which you give writing assignments. (Essay exams count as writing assignments. Journals, term papers, freewrites in class, etc., all count as writing assignments.) Include their *approximate* enrollments and a rough estimate of how often you teach them. Please also note whether the Writing Across the Curriculum Workshop you attended changed the way you use writing in these courses.

Course (just the # is OK)	approximate enrollment	number of times taught each year	Did the workshop change the way you use writing in this course?
			____ improved ____ made worse ____ no change ____ not sure
			____ improved ____ made worse ____ no change ____ not sure
			____ improved ____ made worse ____ no change ____ not sure
			____ improved ____ made worse ____ no change ____ not sure
			____ improved ____ made worse ____ no change ____ not sure
			____ improved ____ made worse ____ no change ____ not sure

3. Below is a list of activities that you might have used in your classes. Check those activities that you used before attending a Writing Across the Curriculum Workshop. Also indicate the activities you tried *after* the workshop and those you use *now* in your classes.

Used Before Workshop	Used After Workshop	Used Last Year in Classes	Never Used	Activity
				Brainstorm (freewrites, lists, diagrams)
				Assigning freewriting before, during or after lectures
				Journal, notebook or log
				Ungraded writing
				Multiple drafts of papers
				Revision and editing exercises
				Reading techniques (preview text, use Cloze procedure)
				Sentence combining exercises
				Written proposals for papers/ projects
				Writing for a variety of audiences
				Model essay analyzed in your class
				Several short assignments in place of one long one
				Peer group critique of papers
				Students collaborating on a piece of writing
				Student writing shared within class
				Student papers analyzed in class

Used Before Workshop	Used After Workshop	Used Last Year in Classes	Never Used	Activity
				Oral reports and presentations
				Conference with students about their writing
				Your writing shared with students
				Language Lab referral: Spelling and Mechanics
				Clarity of style
				Paper revision
				Organization and thinking problems

4. As part of our evaluation of the Writing Across the Curriculum program, we would like to assemble a file of course syllabi and writing assignments used by faculty after they have attended a workshop. Please attach as many of your assignments or syllabi as possible and identify any changes you've made in the syllabi or assignments since the workshop.

If you can't locate copies of assignments, please complete the questionnaire and return it without them. We would appreciate it, however, if you could describe below the writing assignments you have used since the writing-across-the-curriculum workshop.

5. How has the writing-across-the-curriculum workshop changed your teaching or use of writing in your classes? You may want to comment on areas such as design of course, nature of writing assignments, writing activities you used or evaluation of writing.

6. In retrospect, what do you think about the writing-across-the-curriculum workshop experience?

Chapter 7

Student Exposure to Writing Across the Curriculum

CYNTHIA L. SELFE and GEORGE A. MC CULLEY

By the spring of 1983 we had made considerable progress in assessing the impact of our writing-across-the-curriculum program on faculty at Michigan Technological University. Mike and Margaret Gorman and Toby Fulwiler collected evidence that told us our writing-across-the-curriculum workshops changed faculty attitudes toward writing (See Chapter 5), and soon thereafter Jim Kalmbach presented us with evidence that the workshops had prompted a number of our faculty in geography, engineering, philosophy, forestry, biology, chemistry, math, and computer science to include writing-across-the-curriculum activities in their classrooms. (See Chapter 6.)

What we were missing in our evaluation, however, was whether Tech students were feeling the impact of our writing program. We wanted to know, among other things, which specific writing-across-the-curriculum activities taught to faculty at the 12 MTU writing-across-the-curriculum workshops bewteen 1979 and 1983 trickled down to the students at our institution and how often, during the same period, did students encounter each trickled-down activity.

For our own curiosity, we also wanted to examine faculty and student perceptions of this trickle-down effect. Faculty participants in our workshops had already identified a list of those writing activities they thought that they used most commonly in their classes. We wanted to know whether the students at our institution identified these same activities as those they most often encountered in their classes. Making this connection, we reasoned, would give us one more piece of information about the process by which the workshop activities reached the average student at our university.

Designing a Survey Instrument

To gauge the extent to which our students had been exposed to particular writing activities, we had to design an instrument that would accomplish two tasks:

1. describe the specific writing-across-the-curriculum activities taught at faculty workshops so that students could understand and identify them.
2. identify the frequency with which students had been exposed to each activity.

Our initial attempts to design such a measure seemed feeble indeed. Our earliest instrument was over five pages long and would have taken students forty-five minutes to complete. A later survey draft asked students to remember the names of all the professors they had taken courses from over a period of four years, the name, number, term of the courses each professor taught, and the specific writing-across-the-curriculum techniques that were used in each class—a daunting array of tasks that we quickly discarded. In all, we wrote four different drafts of our survey in two months.

In retrospect, at least, it seems we were embarrassingly slow on the uptake. It took us several months and at least as many false starts to learn one very obvious lesson from our labors: we were asking for too much information. We didn't need to know in which classes the writing activities were being used or when during a four-year period those classes were taught, or even by whom they were taught. All we needed to know, from this survey at least, was *which* workshop activities students encountered and *how often* they encountered them.

This simple realization, which the evaluation team came to at one of our regular Friday morning meetings, was liberating. Once we understood just what we needed to know, we were able to sketch a simple solution. Our survey would list the sixteen major writing activities taught at the writing workshops, (including such items as brainstorming, keeping journals, multiple drafting, conferencing, peer critiquing) and, to the right of each item, ask students to estimate the number of classes they had taken over a four-year period which employed that technique. (See questionnaire, p. 95.) For example:

1. Brainstorming ideas before writing   0   1-2   3-5   6 or more
   (freewriting or listening).
2. Keeping journals or logs.   0   1-2   3-5   6 or more

Although this instrument required student respondents to recall far less information than our previous draft, we were still worried that memory would limit the reliability of our investigation. Could students, we asked ourselves, remember the number of classes in which they encountered each of the listed writing activities? To help answer this question, we piloted our instrument (the Student Exposure Survey) on 84 upper-level students in four of our own classes. For the pilot we added under each item on the instrument an indicator of confidence:

1. Brainstorming ideas before writing   0   1-2   3-5   6 or more
   (freewriting or listening).
   My confidence in the above answer: low   medium   high

The answers we received from this pilot added to our own confidence: The students expressed "high" confidence in 77% of their answers, "medium" confidence in 21% of their answers, and "low" confidence in less than 2% of their answers. The pilot of the survey also gave us the chance to rewrite those items that students indicated were unclear or confusing.

Selecting a Sample

After we developed the exposure survey into an instrument that would ask what we wanted to know, we had to find a way to administer it. Initially, we considered giving it to all the 1983 seniors at MTU. These 2,100 students were, after all, the only accessible population which had experienced four years of courses influenced by our program. We first thought of asking all teachers of senior-level courses in the university to administer the survey during one particular class period on a special date. Fortunately, the logistics of convincing our colleagues to interrupt over *sixty* classes in twenty-five different disciplines in two different colleges and three schools quickly convinced us that sampling a smaller number of seniors would be a more realistic goal. We did, however, want to make sure that the sample of seniors we chose was representative of the larger population of seniors from which it was selected. In other words, we wanted the sample group's responses to be generalizable to the entire population of Tech seniors.

We solved our sampling problem by giving the survey to two different groups of students: 206 engineering seniors, who were gathered to produce a writing sample for a college-wide assessment of writing abilities (See Chapter 9), and 31 randomly selected non-engineering students who were part of Project Registrar (See Chapter 8).

Because we wanted to determine how representative our combined sample was of the entire university population of seniors, we used a statistical technique generally known as the "bootstrap." The results of the "bootstrap" analysis indicated that the sample of seniors was respresentative of the entire senior class.

What We Found

The first thing we wanted to learn from the survey was how many writing activities specifically promoted by the workshops the students in our sample encountered in their classes from 1979 to 1983. So we counted the number of activities each student reported experiencing in at least one class during this four-year period.

Although the results of this first analysis, as shown in Table 1, were heartening—81.01% of our sample had encountered 10 or more of the activities in at least one of their classes—we weren't satisfied. We suspected after studying the findings that many of the students could have encountered these activities in their first-year composition courses and not in their content area classes. To determine if our suspicions were valid, we decided to count only those responses that indicated exposure to one technique in three or more classes (See Table 2), knowing that our first-year composition sequence consisted of three courses and that a response of three or more classes would suggest exposure beyond the composition courses.

Table 1. Percentage of Students Exposed to WAC Activities in One or More Classes Between 1979 and 1983

% of students exposed	# of WAC Activities					
	16–14	13–10	9–6	5–3	2–1	0
	35.49%	45.57%	13.50%	4.22%	.84%	.42%

Table 2. Percentage of Students Exposed to WAC Activities in Three or More Courses Between 1979–1983

% of students exposed	# of WAC Activities					
	16–14	13–10	9–6	5–3	2–1	0
	1.69%	10.13%	22.79%	24.05%	21.10%	20.25%

Though these figures were considerably lower, we felt that they gave us a more realistic picture. This second analysis told us that 12% of our sample had been exposed to 10 or more writing activities in three or more of their classes and that 47% of the sample had been exposed to between 3 and 9 activities at the same level.

Frequency of Student Exposure

After we found out how many of the activities used in the writing workshops had reached the students in our sample, we set out to determine which of those activities on the survey enjoyed the widest exposure. We recorded the number of times each student encountered each activity, converted these raw scores to percentages, and then ranked them as shown on Table 3.

Our first glance at this table was sobering. We found, for example, that between 3% and 32% of the students in our sample reported no exposure at all to the 10 activities most consistently stressed at our faculty workshops and that between 37% and 64% of our sample reported only "low" exposure (1–2 classes during four years) to these same activities. We were even more disheartened when we realized the "low" exposure could have occurred in the first-year composition sequence and not in content area classes. But gross numbers alone don't always provide definitive answers.

A closer look at the data yielded more encouraging findings. On the survey, 20% to 50% of our student sample registered a "moderate" level of exposure (3–5 classes during four years) to 9 of the 10 most important WAC activities. We felt better about these "moderate" figures because they indicated exposure outside of first-year composition, although we were disappointed that the one top-ten item ("writing to different audiences") had been encountered by only 17% of our sample at a "moderate level." These figures were encouraging because they revealed that our program had been successful in providing between one-fifth and one-half of the MTU seniors with what we considered a healthy dose of these 9 WAC activities, impressive when we considered that only one-third of the faculty currently at MTU had attended our workshop series.

Finally, our data told us that between 5% and 7% of our sample reported "high" exposure (6 or more classes during four years) to 5 of the 10 most consistently stressed writing activities (doing "more than one draft of a paper," writing "several short papers" in lieu of "one long one," "sharing your writing with other students," "working with other students on papers" and "brainstorming").

Summary

The information we obtained from the Student Exposure Survey allowed us to draw a reasonably accurate profile of student exposure to writing activities on our campuses. From our findings, we now believe that at least half of our students during their academic careers at MTU are required to write more than one draft of papers assigned in classes outside of the first-year composition sequence; over

Table 3. WAC Activities Rank Ordered for Exposure to Sample

			Percentage of students		
Rank	Activity	No Exposure (0 classes)	Low Exposure (1–2 classes)	Moderate Exposure (3–5 classes)	High Exposure (6 or more)
1.	Doing more than one draft of papers	3.4	38.8	51.0	6.8
2.	Writing several short papers rather than one long paper	5.9	44.7	44.3	5.0
3.	Sharing your writing with other students	13.1	46.0	35.9	5.1
4.	Working with other students on papers	21.1	37.1	36.7	5.0
5.	Brainstorming ideas before writing (freewriting or listening)	21.5	50.2	22.8	5.5
6.	*Giving oral reports	14.8	57.4	24.9	2.9
7.	Keeping journals or logs	17.3	59.1	22.0	1.6
8.	Devoting class time to discussing student writing	19.8	50.6	29.0	.4
9.	*Conferencing about a paper with a teacher	22.8	52.7	22.8	2.1
10.	Learning to edit or revise in class	21.9	53.2	23.7	1.2
11.	Critiquing a classmate's paper	15.6	64.1	19.8	.4
12.	*Studying models of well-written essays or reports	30.4	50.6	17.3	1.7
13.	Writing to different audiences	32.1	49.8	16.5	1.7
14.	*Analyzing a single student's paper in class	43.9	46.0	9.7	.4
15.	*Looking at teacher's writing	63.3	26.6	7.2	3.0
16.	*Working with a tutor in the Writing Lab	84.0	13.5	2.1	.4

*Represents activities that were less consistently emphasized during the 12 workshops given on the MTU campus between 1979 and 1983. Activities without asterisks were stressed at all 12 workshops.

one-third will write several short papers rather than one long one, share their writing with other students, or write collaboratively in some content classes; at least one-fourth will enroll in content classes that devote class time to discussing student writing; and approximately one-half of the students will brainstorm papers, keep journals or logs, learn to edit or revise, or critique papers written by peers in non-composition classes. When we expand our conclusions to include data that might have come exclusively from our first-year composition sequence (data from low, 1–2 courses, category) we believe that over 80% of our students will be exposed to 10 or more WAC activities during their stay at MTU, although only 11% or 12% will be exposed to at least 10 activities three or more times. Considering that some of the activities—such as multiple drafts of papers, journals or logs, and peer critiques—we advocated in the writing workshops are just beginning to take hold in many composition programs, the results seem promising. When we also consider that only about one-third of our current faculty has attended a workshop, we're generally pleased with our findings, even if they indicate that we still have a lot to do.

Making Connections

One of the reasons we initiated the Student Exposure Survey was to trace the effect of our university-wide program (across separate levels of our evaluation model) by examining both student and faculty perceptions. This survey provided us with what students remembered happening in their courses, and the Curricular Practices Survey told us what faculty described as happening in their courses. We wondered whether the students' reports matched the faculty reports.

Because the two surveys contained different types of data, we couldn't directly compare the findings contained in the two instruments. We could, however, transform some of the data to make some general connections between the two surveys, although not based on any statistical analysis.

We had already ranked student exposure to writing workshop activities (See Table 3). In addition, the Classroom Practices Survey told us how many faculty members who responded to the survey used these same activities in their courses. Thus, we counted the faculty members who checked that they used a particular activity, converted this number to a percentage of the total number responding, and ranked these percentages. This analysis allowed us to compare the top-ten ranked activities for both groups (See Table 4).

Although 9 of the 10 activities in both sets of ranks are the same, only one activity received an identical rank: "keep journals or logs," ranked 7th by both groups. Admittedly, these findings took us by surprise; we had expected, naively as it turned out, that the student rankings would match the faculty rankings if each survey was an accurate measure. When our initial alarm subsided, we set out to find the causes for the large discrepancies between some ranks.

One potential cause for the differences in ranks became immediately evident to us as we examined the nature of the two surveys. The ranks on the Student Exposure Survey were based on the number of courses students encountered an

Table 4. A Composite of WAC Activities Rank Ordered by Faculty and Students

	Rank		*Rank*
	Rank assigned by student sample, from highest exposure in courses to lowest.		Rank assigned by faculty participants in WAC workshops, from most commonly incorporated in classes to least commonly incorporated.
Doing more than one draft of papers	1		3
Writing several short papers rather than one long paper	2		5
Sharing your writing with other students	3		6
Working with other students on papers	4		10
Brainstorming ideas before writing (freewriting or listening)	5		7 (tie)
Giving oral reports	6		1
Keeping journals or logs	7		7 (tie)
Devoting class time to discussing student writing	8		8
Conferencing about a paper with a teacher	9		2
Learning to edit or revise in class	10		12

activity, and the ranks on the Curricular Practices Survey were based solely on the number of faculty members checking whether or not they used that activity. Obviously, if a faculty member checked one activity but exposed students to it in only one course and checked another activity but exposed students to it in several courses, then the faculty ranking for these two activities would be equal while the student rankings would not.

As a way of estimating how much the different ways of determining ranks affected our findings, we decided to contact 10 faculty members who indicated that they used oral reports (ranked 1st by faculty but 6th by students). Of these 10 faculty members, 8 responded that they used oral reports in only one course per year, thus confirming our suspicion that the different means of determining ranks was greatly affecting our comparison. Since a number of faculty had checked "oral reports" the item had ranked high on their list. However, because these teachers had used the technqiue in only one class each, relatively few students had been exposed to it, and the item ranked much lower when the students were surveyed.

Encouraged by our findings, we also asked these same faculty members if they required collaborative writing in their courses (ranked 4th in the student responses but 10th in the faculty responses) and, if so, in how many classes. Only 5 of the 10 faculty reported that they used collaborative writing, but 4 of these 5 stated that they used it in more than one of their courses, with one faculty member reporting that he required collaborative reports in 5 separates courses per academic year—again more evidence that the different means of ranking was contributing to the discrepancies between the two sets of rankings.

A final question, however, was generated by our detective work. Nine of the same 10 faculty members, when asked if they held individual conferences with students on assigned papers (ranked 2nd by faculty but 9th by students), said they conferenced individually with students about their papers. Six said that they used this technique in more than one course per year. These responses left the disparate faculty and student rankings on this item unexplained. We found our answer when we asked the 9 faculty if they required their students to attend these conferences. All responded that they didn't, and said they preferred instead to tell the students in their classes to drop in or make an appointment if they had any problems with their papers. The faculty members told us that usually between 15 to 30% of their students in any one class came in to discuss their writing. In other words, a high percentage of teachers, who conferenced with only five or six students about their papers per course, indicated that they used conferences. This, we believe, explains why student writing conferences were ranked 2nd by teachers but only 9th by students.

After we completed the additional faculty interviews, we then compared the rankings for the two sets of data. Except for the discrepancies we noted in collaborative writing, oral reports, and conferencing activities ignored, the rankings for the rest of the items were remarkably similar. We believe this suggests that while the two sets of data are not directly comparable, they are at least connected, providing evidence that one level of our trickle-down program model does affect another level.

To us, as an evaluation team, the connections we were able to make between studies were especially interesting. They gave us opportunities to see how the numerous bits and pieces of our evaluation project fit together, how the workshops affected faculty and the faculty affected the students at our institution, within our community. Because the studies that we did differed in size, scope, and design, the data that we used to make such connections often had to be reinterpreted or reevaluated. However, the exercise of explaining how information on faculty gathered in one study was connected to information about student experiences gathered for another study forced us to identify more accurately the intricate relationships that existed among the teachers, students, and curricular elements of our writing program.

Student Exposure Survey

Class ID # _____

Date: _____

Students:

The Humanities Department is trying to identify who have been exposed to certain writing activities (in Humanities courses and all other University courses) to assess the impact of Michigan Technological University's Writing-Across-the-Curriculum program.

Please complete the following questionnaire with care. To begin, look at the list of writing activities below, and circle the number of courses you have taken that have employed each technique.

number of courses

1.	Brainstorming ideas before writing (freewriting or listing)	0	1-2	3-6	7 or more
2.	Keeping journals or logs	0	1-2	3-6	7 or more
3.	Sharing your writing with other students	0	1-2	3-6	7 or more
4.	Looking at your teacher's writing	0	1-2	3-6	7 or more
5.	Giving oral reports	0	1-2	3-6	7 or more

number of courses

6. Writing several short papers rather than one long paper   0   1-2   3-6   7 or more

7. Learning to edit or revise in class   0   1-2   3-6   7 or more

8. Studying models of well-written essays or reports   0   1-2   3-6   7 or more

9. Writing to different audiences   0   1-2   3-6   7 or more

10. Doing more than one draft of papers   0   1-2   3-6   7 or more

11. Conferencing about a paper with your teacher   0   1-2   3-6   7 or more

12. Working with other students on papers   0   1-2   3-6   7 or more

13. Devoting class time to discussing student writing   0   1-2   3-6   7 or more

14. Analyzing a single student's paper in class   0   1-2   3-6   7 or more

15. Critiquing a classmate's paper   0   1-2   3-6   7 or more

16. Working with a tutor in the writing lab   0   1-2   3-6   7 or more

17. Other (please explain below)   0   1-2   3-6   7 or more

Please fill out the following section completely.

Student:_____

Major: _____

Class Rank: (circle one)   freshman   sophomore   junior   senior

Are you a transfer student?   yes   no
(please circle one answer)

If *yes*, how many quarters have you been at MTU?   _____

Chapter 8

Watching Our Garden Grow

Longitudinal Changes in Student Writing Apprehension

CYNTHIA L. SELFE, MICHAEL E. GORMAN
and MARGARET L. GORMAN

When we began our research effort in 1982, our writing-across-the-curriculum program was about to see its first crop of freshmen turn into seniors. As administrators of that program, we were anxious to know if students who attended MTU between 1979 and 1983 had changed their attitude toward writing in general and if this attitude change was related to students' encounters with the activities that had trickled down from our writing workshops.

This chapter describes Project Registrar, a study that we undertook to answer these two questions. In the following pages, we will detail our study's methodology, report on our data, and outline the conclusions we reached about students who had four years of exposure to our writing-across-the-curriculum program.

The Study

Our first difficulty in answering our questions involved selecting an appropriate sample from the 7,500 students who attended MTU. Because we designed Project Registrar to document students' involvement in the writing-across-the-curriculum program and their attitude change over a four-year period ending in 1983, we wanted to find students who had already provided us with some information at the beginning of the project in 1979.

Among the rather scattered data that had been collected in 1979 (at the beginning of a research project *who* knows *what* information will be needed at the end?), we found a dusty set of Writing Apprehension Tests that had been completed by 297 students in six randomly selected first-year Humanities courses. Fortunately, each test bore a student identification number.

Although we later found that 97 of these students were no longer attending MTU, this discovery made it possible to identify 200 students currently attending our university who had been exposed to four years of the writing program and who had indicated their feelings toward writing *before* the study began. These students became the focus of our research.

With the cooperation of our university registrar, we were able to mail these 200 students two different surveys to find answers to our questions. The first survey, which we called the Writing-Across-the-Curriculum Student Exposure Survey (ES), was one of the instruments we designed to evaluate our WAC program. It was to tell us how often MTU students were exposed to individual WAC activities such as composing multiple drafts, writing in journals, etc. (See Chapter 7). This survey lists twenty such activities and asks students to identify (on a scale to the right of each item) how many classes they took that employed that technique. We hoped that responses on the ES would tell us two things: which specific WAC activities had trickled down to the students and how often students encountered each activity.

The second survey we sent out was the Writing Apprehension Test (WAT), designed by John Daly and Michael Miller (1975). The WAT (See p. 107) includes 26 statements about writing anxiety that explore students' confidence in the process and product of their composing efforts ("It's easy for me to write good compositions"), their attitude toward evaluation of their writing ("I don't like my compositions to be evaluated"), and the degree to which they enjoy writing ("I enjoy writing"). Students mark their responses to each item on a Likert-type scale 1 = strongly agree to 5 = strongly disagree. We used the WAT in Project Registrar as a measure of attitude change toward writing tasks in general.

When we began Project Registrar we suspected that information from these two questionnaires would correlate closely with each other. We anticipated a lessening of apprehension among those students who had been exposed to a heavy dose of our WAC activities during their four years at MTU. The more WAC activities students were exposed to and the more often they were exposed, we thought, the less apprehensive they would be toward writing tasks in general.

In all, 88 of the original 200 students in the sample returned both the ES and the WAT. We used their responses to make two major comparisons. First, we compared the WAT scores of 88 students from their first year (1979) and their fourth year (1983). This comparison would tell us whether the students' writing apprehension had changed. Second, we compared the shift in writing apprehension with the number and frequency of the WAC activities to which students had been exposed. This comparison would tell us if there was a relationship between these students' exposure to WAC activities and their change in writing apprehension.

Results

The data we gathered with the student exposure survey and the writing apprehension test supported in part our initial expectations. Students who had exposure to the major writing activities exhibited decreased writing apprehension after the four-year period ending in 1983. In general, the more exposure subjects had to workshop related activities, the lower their writing apprehension dropped.

In the following sections, we will discuss these results in terms of the two major comparisons we made for Project Registrar.

Comparing Students' Attitudes Towards Writing Tasks in 1979 and 1983

Perhaps the most important comparison we made in Project Registrar was designed to identify whether our subjects' apprehensions toward writing had changed from their first year to their fourth. Using a Wilcoxson Signed Rank Test we compared students' scores on the Writing Apprehension Test from their first year at Tech with their scores in their fourth year.

For the purpose of simplifying and clarifying this analysis we clustered the 26 items on the WAT into three categories: (1) confidence in the process and product of composing; (2) attitude toward evaluation of writing; and (3) enjoyment of writing.

Table 1. Clusters of Statements on the WAT with Significance of Change

Confidence in the Process and Product of Composing

```
 **     1.  I avoid writing.
 **     5.  Taking a composition course is a very frightening experience.
  *     7.  My mind seems to go blank when I start to work on a composition.
***    11.  I feel confident in my ability to clearly express my ideas in writing.
       13.  I'm nervous about writing.
       14.  People seem to enjoy what I write.
***    16.  I never seem to be able to clearly write down my ideas.
 **    18.  I expect to do poorly in composition classes even before I enter them.
 **    21.  I have a terrible time organizing my ideas in a composition course.
       22.  When I hand in a composition I know I'm going to do poorly.
  *    23.  It's easy for me to write good compositions.
***    24.  I don't think I write as well as most other people.
 **    26.  I'm no good at writing.
```

Attitude Toward Evaluation

```
  *     2.  I have no fear of my writing being evaluated.
 **     4.  I am afraid of writing essays when I know they will be evaluated.
  *     9.  I would enjoy submitting my writing to magazines for evaluation and
            publication.
  *    12.  I like to have my friends read what I have written.
       20.  Discussing my writing with others is an enjoyable experience.
       25.  I don't like my compositions to be evaluated.
```

Enjoyment of Writing

```
        3.  I look forward to writing down my ideas.
        6.  Handing in a composition makes me feel good.
  *     8.  Expressing ideas through writing seems to be a waste of time.
       10.  I like to write my ideas down.
       15.  I enjoy writing.
       17.  Writing is a lot of fun.
       19.  I like seeing my thoughts on paper.
```

*Denotes a significant reduction in apprehension, $p < .01$, and each additional asterisk indicates a $10 \times$ increase in significance; thus, two asterisks indicate $p < .001$ and three asterisks indicate $p < .0001$.

We used simple *a priori* suggested by a close reading of the WAT itself, to define these clusters. Those items which referred to some form of confidence (or lack thereof) in composing (11. I feel confident in my ability to clearly express my ideas in writing.), we put in the "confidence" cluster. In a similar manner, we grouped those WAT items which mentioned the writer enjoying composing (15. I enjoy writing.) in the "enjoyment" cluster and those items which mentioned evaluation of one kind or another (2. I am afraid of writing essays when I know they will be evaluated.) in the "evaluation" cluster. This type of clustering, suggested specifically by an earlier unpublished analysis of the WAT (Selfe, 1979) and generally by Daly himself (1983) helped us to pinpoint the attitude changes that students exhibited in their four years at MTU.

What this first analysis told us was both encouraging and intriguing. First we found that our student sample had indeed exhibited strong shifts of attitude in two of the three clusters we had identified. We learned, for instance, that students had become generally more confident about composing, becoming significantly less apprehensive on 10 out of 13 items we had classified under that category as illustrated in Table 1. This finding suggested to us that some aspect of their education during their four years at MTU had encouraged these students to become less apprehensive about the processes involved in composing—"starting to work on a composition" or "organizing ideas"—and about the products of their composing efforts.

We also found that the students in our sample had become generally less anxious about having their compositions evaluated. Overall, they had indicated significantly less apprehension on 4 items out of the 6 identified in this cluster. Again, we were pleased with this finding and the fact that it seemed to suggest that our students had become increasingly confident about submitting their papers to the evaluation of teachers, peers, and publishers during the four years they attended MTU.

It was our third finding from this analysis, however, that surprised us the most. We found that although fourth-year students in our sample had become more confident about composing, and less anxious about the evaluations of their texts, they didn't seem to enjoy writing any more than they had as first-year students. Initially this information puzzled us, until we were honest enough to admit to ourselves just how difficult a task writing is for all of us, and how seldom even English teachers completely enjoy the hard work of composing. In further explaining this finding to ourselves, we also considered that the large majority of our sample, approximately 80%, were engineering students who, as we knew from our experience in MTU classrooms, seldom saw the importance of writing in their chosen course of study. Because they considered writing as unrelated to their personal interests, the students often found composing to be unpleasant "busy" work.

Relating Attitude Change to Writing Across the Curriculum: What Caused Our Garden to Grow?

After determining that the students in our sample had shown significant changes in their attitudes toward writing tasks, we wanted to explore the possibility of a relationship between this attitude shift and exposure to writing activities. We expected that those students who were exposed frequently to the major activities taught at our workshops would show a significant drop in one or more of the clusters we identified on the writing apprehension test. We realized that finding this kind of relationship would not guarantee that workshop activities *caused* the attitude-change because we didn't attempt to eliminate other factors that might be related to both attitude-change and exposure. But we felt a strong relationship would indicate the workshop techniques were probably influencing students' attitudes.

For purposes of this comparison, we selected 10 workshop activities that had been stressed at all of our four-day sessions over the last four years from those activities listed on our exposure survey. We made this selection with the history of our faculty workshops in mind. Although all seventeen items on the survey had been stressed at one or more workshops during the four years of the program, we felt we should identify those 10 items that had been emphasized consistently at every workshop.

The comparison seemed simple enough: just find a measure that expressed the amount each student had been exposed to the 10 WAC techniques and relate it to each student's change in apprehension. The overall frequencies and percentages of exposure to the 10 activities are shown in Table 2. More than half of the students fell into the low or no exposure categories on all but two items: doing several short papers rather than one long one and doing more than one draft of a paper. To create an overall "writing exposure" score for each student, we summed the number of times they claimed they were exposed to each activity and divided by ten. This was, admittedly, a crude global measure, but we felt it should be correlated with a reduction in apprehension.

So we computed a correlation[1] between each student's overall "writing exposure" score and a series of 26 difference scores created by subtracting a student's freshman WAT rating on each question from his or her senior rating. (The scale was standardized for all questions so that a *negative* difference score meant *decrease* in apprehension, freshman to senior.) The results were not impressive: only three statements showed significant correlations with exposure—numbers 3 (rho = -.18), 10 (rho = -.2) and 23 (rho = -.19). Although these correlations were all in the right direction, they indicated such marginal significance that they were of little interest to us.

We thought about this analysis for a while and realized there might be a good reason for the low correlations. If someone's freshman WAT score on a particular statement indicated they weren't apprehensive to begin with, we wouldn't expect a lot of WAC exposure to change them—the same problem faced in measuring

Table 2. Students Exposed to the 10 WAC Activities Stressed Most Consistently in Workshops

	No Exposure (0 classes)		Low Exposure (1-2 classes)		Moderate Exposure (3-6 classes)		High Exposure (7 or more classes)	
	%	Freq.	%	Freq.	%	Freq.	%	Freq.
1. Brainstorming ideas before writing (freewriting or listing)	8.0%	(7)	40.2%	(35)	43.6%	(38)	8.0%	(7)
2. Keeping journals or logs	9.2%	(8)	56.3%	(49)	33.3%	(29)	1.1%	(1)
3. Sharing your writing with other students	0%	(0)	43.7%	(38)	44.5%	(45)	4.5%	(4)
4. Writing several short papers rather than one long paper	0%	(0)	39.1%	(34)	57.4%	(50)	3.4%	(3)
5. Learning to edit or revise in class	16.1%	(14)	47.1%	(41)	35.6%	(31)	1.1%	(1)
6. Writing to different audiences	17.2%	(15)	58.6%	(51)	22.9%	(20)	1.1%	(1)
7. Doing more than one draft of papers	2.3%	(2)	35.9%	(28)	57.5%	(50)	8.0%	(7)
8. Working with other students on papers	18.4%	(16)	36.8%	(32)	41.3%	(36)	3.4%	(3)
9. Devoting class time to discussing student writing	9.2%	(8)	51.7%	(45)	35.6%	(31)	3.4%	(3)
10. Critiquing a classmate's paper	3.4%	(3)	62.1%	(54)	32.2%	(28)	2.3%	(2)

faculty attitudes in Chapter 5. Conversely, on statements where he or she was initially neutral or apprehensive, we would expect a lot of WAC exposure to increase his or her apprehension. An overall correlation wouldn't reflect these subtler changes. Consider a group of students who weren't apprehensive on a given statement as freshmen. Even if these students were exposed to a lot of writing techniques, their apprehension wouldn't change much and a low correlation would result.

We considered several solutions to this problem (including putting all the data in a pile and burning it) and finally decided to look at separate correlations on *each statement* for three groups:

1. those students who had entered MTU with moderate or low apprehension on that statement;
2. those students who were initially neutral;
3. and those students who were initially moderately or highly apprehensive.

We hoped we would see strong negative correlations between high exposure to WAC techniques and changes in apprehension in groups 2 and 3, but no correlation on group 1, where high exposure shouldn't affect students' already low apprehension. The pattern that emerged wasn't quite this clear. A low correlation for group 1 and higher negative correlation on groups 2 and 3 emerged on only two statements: numbers 19 and 25. However, the overall results were favorable: 19 out of 78 correlations were statistically significant, and all 19 of these were in the expected direction: high exposure correlated with a lowering of anxiety.

Table 3. Correlations Between Student's Exposure to 13 Writing-Across-the-Curriculum Technqiues and Changes in Apprehension Across Four Years at MTU, by Writing-Anxiety-Test Clusters.

(Only those statements with at least one significant correlation are reported, + denotes p < .05, * p < .01, ** p < .001)

Confidence Cluster

Statement #		Initial Apprehension		
		Low	Neutral	High
1	I avoid writing.	−.44**	.03	.18
11	I feel confident in my ability to clearly express my ideas in writing.	−.28+	.02	−.30
21	I have a terrible time organizing my ideas in a composition course.	−.11	−.47+	−.3
23	It's easy for me to write good compositions.	−.08	−.39+	−.33+
24	I don't think I write as well as most other people.	−.14	−.35+	.18

Evaluation Cluster

Statement #		Initial Apprehension		
		Low	Neutral	High
4	I am afraid of writing essays when I know they will be evaluated.	−.22+	−.62+	−.13
9	I would enjoy submitting my writing to magazines for evaluation and publication.	−.20	−.38+	−.13
20	Discussing my writing with others is an enjoyable experience.	−.51*	−.01	−.46*
25	I don't like my compositions to be evaluated.	−.14	−.28	−.62*

Enjoyment Cluster

Statement #		Initial Apprehension		
		Low	Neutral	High
3	I look forward to writing down my ideas.	−.56**	−.23	−.25
8	Expressing ideas through writing seems to be a waste of time.	−.14	−.12	−.21
10	I like to write my ideas down.	−.37+	−.55*	−.19
15	I enjoy writing.	−.34*	.01	−.37
19	I like seeing my thoughts on paper.	−.13	−.49*	−.90**

Note: Some of the correlations marked with a + *may* be due to chance because $p < .05$ means that a correlation that high should occur by chance only one time in *twenty*—and we computed *78* correlations. But by chance, some of these marginally significant correlations should be positive—and none are.

To understand these correlations, let's look at the statement (#19) that corresponded most closely to predictions: "I like seeing my thoughts on paper." The overall correlation between exposure to writing workshop techniques and change in apprehension was only −.1 on this statement, but fifty-five students entered MTU already agreeing that they liked to see their thoughts on paper. There was a slight negative correlation (rho = −.13) between exposure and change in apprehension for group 1; those who like seeing their thoughts on paper when they entered MTU changed very little. For group 2, the correlation was higher (rho = −.49) and significant ($p < .01$); ten out of the 25 students in this category didn't change. The 3 whose apprehension increased by one point had low exposure, and the students with the highest exposure became less apprehensive. In group 3, the correlation is very high (rho = −.9). There were only eight people in this group; the two who didn't change had almost no exposure to workshop technqiues; the four who dropped one point had intermediate exposure and the two who dropped two points had the highest exposure.

So, on this statement, the lack of a significant overall correlation between exposure and change masks the fact that those few students who were initially apprehensive really did learn to like their writing better if they took a fair number of courses that stressed WAC techniques.

A similar pattern emerged on statement 25, "I don't like my compositions to be evaluated." The overall correlation between exposure to workshop techniques and change in apprehension was not significant (rho = −.15), but for the group of students that were highly apprehensive when they entered MTU, this same correlation is highly significant (rho = −.62, p < .003).

On statements 1, 3, 5, and 20, this pattern was reversed, with the largest significant correlation between exposure and change occurring when students were initially low in apprehension. On statements 4, 9, 10, 21, 23, and 24, the best correlations occur in the group that entered neutral. Without more data, it's hard to interpret these findings. Are students who enter with high apprehensions more resistant to change on some statements and less on others? We don't know.

In terms of the clusters, it's interesting that many more highly significant correlations occur on the statements related to enjoyment. There was no *overall* change in anxiety on the statements in this cluster, but exposure to workshop technqiues does seem to help students enjoy their writing a bit more—if these correlations are not caused by some other, underlying factor.

When we brought these results to a meeting of the evaluation committee, a heated debate ensued over what other analyses should be done to see if we could get a more precise picture of the effect of exposure to workshop techniques on change in apprehension. We finally agreed to define our mission. In other words, before undertaking any additional analyses, we agreed that we would have to have a very precise idea of what they would accomplish. No one on our team was able to come up with further analyses that seemed justifiable on these grounds.

Most writers feel they could always do another draft; similarly, researchers often feel that they could do another analysis. Part of analyzing data is knowing when to stop.

Conclusions

From Project Registrar we learned that student apprehension about writing decreased significantly over four years at MTU, particularly in the area of confidence in writing, although also in terms of apprehensions about having their writing evaluated. We also learned that students didn't enjoy writing any more after four years at MTU than they had when they entered our institution.

Did the writing-across-the-curriculum program influence these changes? We really don't know for sure. Exposure to workshop techniques was correlated with reduced apprehension on 15 out of 23 Writing-Anxiety-Test statements, though most of these correlations were low and didn't fit into a clear pattern that we could discuss, especially in relation to the clusters of items we identified on the WAT. The absence of a higher correlation and a clear pattern could be explained if we believed that exposure to workshop techniques had only a small influence on students' apprehensions about writing, or our method of assessing the relationship between exposure and attitude change was too crude to pick up the true relationship.

The attitude test and the student exposure survey are both very general measures of attitude and exposure. For example, we may know that a student remembers having done multiple drafts three or four times in her or his college career, but we don't know whether this exposure occurred in freshman composition classes or advanced engineering classes. We also don't know how effective the use of drafts was in those classes. If the process of drafting was handled poorly in a class, the student might leave the class more anxious.

We could build a clearer picture if we could relate specific techniques on the exposure to specific items on the apprehension test. We were able to do this in a couple of cases. We felt that brainstorming (exposure # 7) ought to reduce students' fear that their minds would "go blank" when they were working on a composition (anxiety #7). The overall correlation between the two items was only .02, but a breakdown by the three exposure groups showed a significant correlation for students who entered *disagreeing* with this statement. In other words, those who weren't worried about their minds going blank when faced with starting a composition became even less worried if they were exposed to a lot of brainstorming. Those students who were very apprehensive, initially, didn't indicate that learning how to brainstorm lessened their apprehension as much.

We also related critiquing a classmate's paper (exposure #15) to "I like to have my friends read what I have written" (anxiety #12). Here again, the overall correlation is almost zero, but there is one group for which the correlation is significant: those who were initially neutral about sharing their writing with friends tended to like it more after four years at MTU if they were allowed to critique classmates' papers in several classes (rho = .51).

Specific statement-to-statement correlations showed no clearer pattern than the overall correlations. Where they were signficant, they were negative, but it's hard to explain why the highest correlation occurs for the low-apprehensive group on one statement and the neutral group on the other. To explain our results in more detail, we would need more data, especially qualitative comments from students. Because of time constraints, we weren't able to follow our usual multiple-measure approach in this study. If we decide to do a follow-up study in the future, we will redesign the exposure survey and the WAT so they fit our objectives more precisely. Specifically, on the exposure, we would find a way to determine where students had been exposed to each technique—in a humanities course, an engineering course, etc.—and how effective the student felt that exposure had been. We would redesign the Writing-Anxiety-Test so statements on it could be related more specifically to statements on the exposure survey. We would encourage open-ended comments on both instruments and pilot them carefully, interviewing selected students who took them.

All of these plans result from hindsight, however. Our study of change in anxieties about writing across four years at MTU did show that exposure to writing techniques taught at faculty workshops is significantly correlated with a reduction in anxiety on some of the anxiety test items. The workshop writing techniques seem to have had a slight positive effect on student attitudes as measured indirectly by this attitude test, though we remain uncertain about the magnitude of the effect and why it occurs for some types of anxious students but not others.

Notes

1. Because students were asked to rank only their *rough* exposure to workshop techniques, we used the Spearman rho, a correlation-coefficient that is ideal for imprecise scales (Ferguson, 1976).

Writing Apprehension Test

Below are a series of statements about writing. There are no right or wrong answers to these statements. Please indicate the degree to which each statement applies to you by circling whether you (1) strongly agree, (2) agree, (3) are uncertain, (4) disagree, or (5) strongly disagree with the statement. While some of these statements may seem repetitious, take your time and try to be as honest as possible. Thank you for your cooperation in this matter.

	sa	a	u	d	sd
1. I avoid writing.	1	2	3	4	5
2. I have no fear of my writing being evaluated.	1	2	3	4	5
3. I look forward to writing down my ideas.	1	2	3	4	5
4. I am afraid of writing essays when I know they will be evaluated.	1	2	3	4	5
5. Taking a composition course is a very frightening experience.	1	2	3	4	5
6. Handing in a composition makes me feel good.	1	2	3	4	5
7. My mind seems to go blank when I start to work on a composition.	1	2	3	4	5
8. Expressing ideas through writing seems to be a waste of time.	1	2	3	4	5
9. I would enjoy submitting my writing to magazines for evaluation and publication.	1	2	3	4	5

	sa	*a*	*u*	*d*	*sd*

10. I like to write my ideas down. 1 2 3 4 5

11. I feel confident in my ability to clearly express my ideas in writing. 1 2 3 4 5

12. I like to have my friends read what I have written. 1 2 3 4 5

13. I'm nervous about writing. 1 2 3 4 5

14. People seem to enjoy what I write. 1 2 3 4 5

15. I enjoy writing. 1 2 3 4 5

16. I never seem to be able to clearly write down my ideas. 1 2 3 4 5

17. Writing is a lot of fun. 1 2 3 4 5

18. I expect to do poorly in composition classes even before I enter them. 1 2 3 4 5

19. I like seeing my thoughts on paper. 1 2 3 4 5

20. Discussing my writing with others is an enjoyable experience. 1 2 3 4 5

21. I have a terrible time organizing my ideas in a composition course. 1 2 3 4 5

22. When I hand in a composition I know I'm going to do poorly. 1 2 3 4 5

23. It's easy for me to write good compositions. 1 2 3 4 5

24. I don't think I write as well as most other people. 1 2 3 4 5

25. I don't like my compositions to be evaluated. 1 2 3 4 5

26. I'm no good at writing. 1 2 3 4 5

Chapter 9

Assessing the Writing Skills of Engineering Students

1978 to 1983

GEORGE A. MC CULLEY and JON A. SOPER

Recent research tells us that most engineers spend at least 25% of their time on the job writing–sometimes jotting down notes or writing brief memos and reports; at other times, composing full-blown reports or carefully articulated public documents (Stine & Skarzensk, 1979). But what a blanket figure like 25% doesn't tell us is how important this amount of time is to an engineer's overall success on the job. One researcher investigated the importance of writing in determining career success by asking a sample of practicing, successful engineers: "How important is writing for professional development?" Over 70% of the engineers who responded stated that writing was very important in helping them achieve their career goals (Davis, 1977). We expect that as technology makes more information accessible, engineers will spend even more of their time writing and that their writing will have an increased bearing on job success–assumptions which contributed heavily to an increased interest in the writing skills of engineering students at Michigan Tech.

In 1978, wholly apart from the concerns of the composition faculty at Michigan Tech, the Dean of the College of Engineering formed a college-wide committee to study how the language abilities of engineering students could be improved. The members of this committee, representing the departments of electrical, chemical, metallurgical, and civil engineering, as well as mechanical engineering-engineering mechanics, pursued their task in a straightforward, no-nonsense fashion: first they wanted to assess the level of their students' communications skills, then to make recommendations based on the evaluation.

Early on, the committee began to ask questions: "What is an adequate level of communication skills for practicing engineers?" "Where should our students be in relation to this standard when they are about to graduate, assuming that some communications skills must be mastered on the job?" "How do we assess these skills?" Not easy questions.

109

At this point, the committee looked for help. Peter Schiff, then a member of the Humanities Department at Tech (now at Northern Kentucky University), helped the committee identify a standard and design an assessment methodology. Peter introduced them to Diederich's (1974) scale and methodology for writing assessment, which provide standards and a means for assessing student writing in relation to those standards. Using the method recommended by Schiff, the committee proceeded to assess the writing skills of senior engineering students in the fall of the 1978-79 academic year.

The First Assessment—1979

That year there were 627 seniors enrolled in the College of Engineering, so the committee decided that a sample of 200 or so students would be adequate for the assessment, with the number of students from each department in the college in proportion to the size of the department. The sample of 198 papers was obtained by selecting classes from each department, which contained the approximate number of senior students necessary, and then seeking each instructor's cooperation to use an hour of their class time.

At the beginning of each class, the students were given a handout (See Appendix A, p. 129) containing some simple instructions, a few questions about the student's background, a release statement for the student's permission, and a list of five topics on which the student could write. The topics were carefully chosen to be subjects about which the students would have an opinion so that the students' writing abilities, not their knowledge of a particular subject, would be evaluated. The selected topics were:

1. Criticize the 15-credit Humanities and Social Sciences elective requirement of the College of Engineering.
2. Tell why you sought or will seek a particular job at the BS level.
3. Tech is proposing a major expansion of research activity. Argue for or against this expansion.
4. What do you think of the preparation your Tech curriculum provided for developing your own writing skills?
5. Argue for your choice of either engineering *or* humanities professors as teachers of technical report writing. Do *not* consider the alternative of team teaching.

After the writing samples were collected from each class, they were numerically coded and randomly mixed. Professor Schiff then trained six raters (the committee plus volunteers, representing various disciplines within the College of Engineering) to evaluate the papers using the Diederich scale (See Appendix B, p. 130). Schiff discussed with the raters the scores of high, medium, or low on four of the categories in the Diederich scale (ideas, organization, wording and flavor) until a consensus on these criteria was reached. The raters discussed the categories under the general rubric of writing mechanics on the scale (word usage, spelling, punctuation, and neatness) until they believed that they were in agreement on these criteria as well. Then the actual scoring began, with each paper scored independently by two raters.

If the scores on any paper by the two raters were more than 10 points apart (maximum = 50), a third rater evaluated the paper, adjusting either one or both of the previous scores until they were 10 or less points apart. A third rating was necessary with only 9 percent of the papers, an impressive percentage of agreement. The mean scores for each major and by category on the Diederich scale are reported in Table 1.

The mean scores between the various groups of students (for example, between civil and mechanical engineering majors) were compared using the t-test designed for this purpose, with no statistical difference found between any two majors. There were, however, some statistical differences between majors within separate categories on the Diederich scale (for example, between metallurgical and electrical engineering students on the "content" category, 21.12 to 19.35, respectively—significant at the .05 level). But these differences between categories appeared random and not important.

To determine if writing instruction beyond the required first-year composition sequence significantly affected the results, the students were grouped by the number of credit hours of writing instruction beyond the required courses in the first-year composition sequence, as determined by student responses on the information sheet completed before they wrote the essay. Table 2 presents the mean scores by the number of credit hours.

Using the appropriate t-test to compare means, the committee found only one significant difference (at the .05 level)—between the group of students who indicated no additional credit hours of writing instruction beyond the first-year composition sequence and the group who indicated 7 or more hours of additional instruction. The committee believed this finding suggested that 7 or more additional credit hours of instruction (which translates as 3 or more writing courses in the Tech curriculum) did contribute to improved writing skills, even under the one-shot, no-revision conditions of the first writing assessment.

What remained unanswered, however, is why 7 or more additional credit hours? Why not 3? Or 6? Was growth in writing abilities so slow that under assessment conditions differences would appear only after 3 or more courses? Or in a writing program like Michigan Tech's where the entire writing process is emphasized, from invention through final editing, differences in the quality of essentially first drafts would appear only after 3 or more courses? Or was our assessment methodology not very sensitive, capable of reflecting only the grossest of differences? All important, yet at this point unanswered, questions.

As a way of comparing the first-year composition sequence at Michigan Tech with similar course sequences at other schools, the committee decided to compare the mean scores of students who originally matriculated at Michigan Tech and those who transferred from other schools, as evidenced by student responses on the background information sheet. Of course, not all transfer students would have completed their first-year writing requirements before entering Tech, but a check with the Registrar's office indicated that this was true in most cases. Table 3 presents the mean scores for both groups.

Table 1. 78–79 Diederich Composition Scores—Mean Scores by College of Engineering Major (Standard Deviations in Parentheses.)

Diederich Categories	Major					
	Chemical (N = 50)	Civil (N = 50)	Electrical (N = 27)	Mechanical (N = 56)	Metallurgical (N = 11)	All Participants Reporting Majors (N = 194)
Ideas	6.95 (1.32)	6.90 (1.60)	6.70 (1.35)	6.90 (1.43)	7.42 (1.21)	6.92 (1.42)
Organization	6.31 (1.29)	6.10 (1.62)	6.11 (1.50)	6.55 (1.61)	6.82 (1.86)	6.32 (1.54)
Wording	3.34 (0.53)	3.11 (0.56)	3.11 (0.59)	3.38 (0.58)	3.21 (0.58)	3.25 (0.57)
Flavor	3.72 (0.54)	3.68 (0.70)	3.43 (0.77)	3.63 (0.68)	3.67 (0.73)	3.64 (0.67)
Content	20.37 (3.02)	19.82 (3.90)	19.35 (3.75)	20.40 (3.80)	21.12 (3.82)	20.14 (3.62)
Usage	3.54 (0.54)	3.26 (0.69)	3.43 (0.62)	3.35 (0.58)	3.31 (0.41)	3.39 (0.60)
Spelling	3.81 (0.81)	3.74 (0.88)	3.74 (0.87)	3.83 (0.73)	3.64 (0.62)	3.78 (0.80)
Punctuation	3.75 (0.50)	3.61 (0.71)	3.65 (0.65)	3.71 (0.56)	3.67 (0.39)	3.69 (0.59)
Writing	3.49 (0.59)	3.40 (0.68)	3.22 (0.61)	3.73 (0.57)	3.53 (0.83)	3.50 (0.64)
Mechanics	14.60 (1.87)	13.99 (2.24)	13.96 (2.20)	14.61 (1.99)	14.11 (1.88)	14.33 (2.05)
TOTAL	34.98 (4.15)	33.71 (5.73)	33.17 (5.60)	35.01 (5.40)	34.32 (4.35)	34.37 (5.17)

Table 2. 78–79 Diederich Composition Scores—Mean Scores by Number of Credits of Writing Instruction Beyond Freshman English (Standard Deviations in Parentheses.)

Diederich Categories	Zero Credits (N = 50)	One Credit (N = 11)	Two Credits (N = 27)	Three Credits (N = 58)	Four Credits (N = 2)	Five Credits (N = 1)	Six Credits (N = 22)	Seven or More Credits (N = 14)	All Participants Reporting = Of Credits Taken (N = 185)
Ideas	6.96 (1.45)	7.24 (1.43)	6.89 (1.34)	6.72 (1.60)	7.00 (1.41)	6.67 (0.00)	6.73 (1.20)	7.43 (1.05)	6.90 (1.42)
Organization	6.33 (1.65)	6.78 (1.17)	6.35 (1.43)	6.11 (1.55)	6.00 (1.41)	6.00 (0.00)	6.31 (1.67)	6.45 (1.30)	6.29 (1.52)
Wording	3.23 (0.60)	3.44 (0.57)	3.36 (0.60)	3.19 (0.57)	3.50 (0.00)	3.33 (0.00)	3.18 (0.48)	3.25 (0.44)	3.25 (0.56)
Flavor	3.47 (0.69)	3.76 (0.62)	3.72 (0.49)	3.63 (0.71)	3.25 (0.35)	3.33 (0.00)	3.66 (0.78)	3.88 (0.48)	3.62 (0.66)
Content	19.93 (4.00)	21.23 (3.39)	20.41 (3.14)	19.72 (3.90)	19.75 (2.47)	19.33 (0.00)	19.82 (3.49)	20.95 (2.58)	20.07 (3.62)
Usage	3.38 (0.58)	3.59 (0.80)	3.55 (0.49)	3.26 (0.63)	3.75 (0.35)	3.67 (0.00)	3.25 (0.55)	3.54 (0.59)	3.38 (0.60)
Spelling	3.64 (0.82)	3.91 (0.80)	3.78 (0.84)	3.83 (0.80)	3.50 (1.41)	4.00 (0.00)	3.73 (0.77)	4.15 (0.62)	3.78 (0.80)
Punctuation	3.58 (0.64)	3.73 (0.61)	3.80 (0.46)	3.73 (0.63)	3.75 (0.35)	3.67 (0.00)	3.61 (0.69)	3.92 (0.32)	3.70 (0.58)
Writing	3.50 (0.72)	3.25 (0.60)	3.56 (0.54)	3.38 (0.60)	4.00 (0.00)	3.67 (0.00)	3.55 (0.71)	3.61 (0.34)	3.48 (0.62)
Mechanics	14.07 (2.30)	14.48 (2.41)	14.71 (1.73)	14.21 (2.00)	15.00 (2.12)	15.00 (0.00)	14.07 (1.90)	15.21 (1.47)	14.33 (4.08)
TOTAL	33.71 (5.75)	35.71 (5.31)	35.12 (3.89)	33.84 (5.53)	34.75 (4.60)	34.33 (0.00)	33.84 (5.09)	36.17 (3.47)	34.29 (5.15)

Table 3.   78–79 Diederich Composition Scores—Mean Scores By Whether
Participant Is a Transfer Student (Standard Deviations in Parentheses.)

Diederich Categories	Transfer to MTU (N = 67)	Originally Matriculated at MTU (N = 131)	All Participants Reporting Transfer Status (N = 198)
Ideas	6.97 (1.38)	6.90 (1.44)	6.92 (1.41)
Organization	6.39 (1.51)	6.31 (1.53)	6.34 (1.52)
Wording	3.29 (0.63)	3.24 (0.54)	3.26 (0.57)
Flavor	3.67 (0.61)	3.62 (0.69)	3.64 (0.66)
Content	20.37 (3.42)	20.05 (3.70)	20.16 (3.60)
Usage	3.32 (0.62)	3.41 (0.59)	3.38 (0.60)
Spelling	3.77 (0.79)	3.79 (0.81)	3.78 (0.80)
Punctuation	3.70 (0.55)	3.69 (0.61)	3.69 (0.59)
Writing	3.52 (0.62)	3.47 (0.66)	3.48 (0.65)
Mechanics	14.24 (1.95)	14.36 (2.10)	14.32 (2.04)
TOTAL	34.53 (4.95)	34.30 (5.26)	34.38 (5.15)

A quick glance at the data in Table 3 told the committee that there were no
large differences between mean scores. Nevertheless, t-tests between mean scores
for both groups were calculated and, predictably, produced no statistically significant differences, leading the committee to assume that the first-year composition
sequence at Tech was comparable to the required composition sequence that transfer students had completed.

The final variable that may have directly affected the writing scores of the
students was GPA, as defined by the 5 levels of GPA on the background information sheet—from "less than 2.0" to "3.5–4.0." Table 4 presents the mean writing
scores by GPA level.

The committee found statistically significant differences between both of
the groups of students with GPA's at or above 3.0 and all three groups of students
with GPA's below 3.0. The committee believed these results suggested that general
academic ability directly contributed to writing ability, particularly under examination conditions.

From these results, the committee drew the following conclusions:

1. In reference to the criteria on the Diederich scale, the writing abilities of
   seniors in engineering were a little better than average (30 = average, the sum
   of the "middle" scores from all of Diederich's categories).
2. The writing abilities of the students in each major were approximately equal,
   as were the abilities for transfer students and students originally matriculated
   at Michigan Tech.
3. Students with GPA's over a 3.0 wrote better than those under a 3.0.

Table 4. 78–79 Diederich Composition Scores—Mean Scores by Participant GPA (Standard Deviations in Parentheses.)

Diederich Categories	GPA = 2.0–2.4* (N = 37)	GPA = 2.5–2.9 (N = 72)	GPA = 3.0–3.4 (N = 59)	GPA = 3.5–4.0 (N = 28)	All Participants Reporting GPA (N = 196)
Ideas	6.58 (1.36)	6.78 (1.57)	7.12 (1.31)	7.29 (1.24)	6.92 (1.42)
Organization	6.06 (1.40)	6.31 (1.68)	6.45 (1.49)	6.53 (1.45)	6.34 (1.54)
Wording	3.23 (0.61)	3.12 (0.56)	3.35 (0.54)	3.46 (0.51)	3.26 (0.57)
Flavor	3.53 (0.67)	3.66 (0.74)	3.69 (0.59)	3.64 (0.59)	3.64 (0.66)
Content	19.29 (3.38)	19.94 (4.05)	20.60 (3.28)	20.95 (3.29)	20.16 (3.62)
Usage	3.11 (0.67)	3.28 (0.60)	3.62 (0.51)	3.52 (0.52)	3.38 (0.60)
Spelling	3.52 (0.86)	3.67 (0.88)	4.01 (0.66)	3.95 (0.66)	3.78 (0.80)
Punctuation	3.57 (0.62)	3.60 (0.68)	3.81 (0.53)	3.86 (0.30)	3.69 (0.59)
Writing	3.37 (0.73)	3.36 (0.66)	3.62 (0.53)	3.64 (0.66)	3.48 (0.65)
Mechanics	13.53 (2.17)	13.93 (2.15)	14.99 (1.76)	14.96 (1.61)	14.32 (2.05)
TOTAL	32.83 (4.94)	33.66 (5.66)	35.54 (4.62)	35.87 (4.54)	34.39 (5.17)

*No participants reported GPAs of less than 2.0.

The committee, however, deferred making any recommendations based on this first assessment because the members didn't believe that their data base was large enough. That is, they considered the scores from only one assessment of one sample in one year not sufficient. In addition, the committee realized that the writing-across-the-curriculum program at Tech, with one of its primary goals the improvement of communications abilities, was still fairly new, just beginning to take hold. Thus the committee decided to assess the writing skills of senior engineering students two years hence—the spring of 1981.

The Second Assessment—1981

From the fall of 1978 to the spring of 1981 several changes took place at Michigan Tech which directly affected the Communications Skills Committee and its writing assessment. Some committee members left the faculty and were replaced by other faculty members from the college. Peter Schiff, the ad hoc member from the Humanities Department, left for Northern Kentucky University, and George Mc Culley took his place. The writing-across-the-curriculum program continued and grew, with over 100 faculty members attending one of six residential workshops and the majority of the entire faculty attending an on-campus workshop before school began that fall. With these changes in place, the committee once again assessed the writing abilities of senior engineering students, following the procedures used in the first assessment.

In the spring of 1981, the committee obtained the sample of students by selecting classes in each department which contained a number of students proportional to the size of individual departments, with the sample increasing slightly to 225. Then the instructors in these classes were asked to donate one class period in which to carry out the assessment.

In each class, the students were given the same handout used in the previous assessment, asked to read the directions, fill in the background information, sign the release statement, and then write on any of the five topics at the bottom of the handout. The first two of the topics in the original assessment were dropped because not many students responded to them in the first assessment and were replaced with the following two topics, both of which the committee felt would test the students' writing abilities rather than their prior knowledge of a particular subject:

1. Discuss whether or not the new computer graphics facilities should be located in the ME-EM "fish bowl." If not, suggest alternatives.
2. A shortage of American faculty has increased the use of foreign-born teachers in engineering. Discuss the problems this poses and suggest alternatives or remedies.

With the help of Mc Culley, six raters (the committee, plus two additional faculty members from the College of Engineering) discussed the Diederich scale until they reached a consensus on the criteria, then independently rated the papers from the sample, with each paper read twice and any discrepancies of more than 10 points (max = 50) resolved by a third rater. Although the percentage of agreement of 86% (among all raters across all papers) was slightly lower than that in the first assessment, it was considered acceptable. Table 5 presents the results from the second assessment in comparison with those from the first.

Table 5. Mean Scores by Diederich Parameters (Standard Deviations in Parentheses.)

Parameters	1979 Scores N = 196	1981 Scores N = 225
Ideas	6.92 (1.42)	6.86 (1.37)
Organization	6.34 (1.54)	6.08 (1.44)
Wording	3.26 (0.57)	3.25 (0.67)
Flavor	3.64 (0.66)	3.24 (0.70)
Content	20.16 (3.62)	19.43 (3.65)
Usage	3.38 (0.60)	3.21 (0.66)
Spelling	3.78 (0.80)	3.93 (0.93)
Punctuation	3.69 (0.59)	3.73 (0.75)
Writing	3.48 (0.65)	3.32 (0.64)
Mechanics	14.32 (2.05)	14.19 (2.25)
TOTAL	34.39 (5.17)	33.62 (5.12)

T-tests calculated between mean scores for the 1979 group and the 1981 group indicated no statistically significant differences, whether between each category on the Diederich scale or between the total scores. The committee concluded that in reference to the Diederich criteria, which defined a score of 30 as average, the writing abilities of both groups were equivalent and a little better than average. The committee decided, however, to compare the results within the 1981 group and between the 1979 and 1981 groups by major, credit hours of writing instruction beyond first-year composition, original matriculation, and GPA.

Table 6 presents a comparison within the 1981 group and between the two groups by major.

Table 6. Diederich Mean Scores by Major Departments (Parentheses indicate the number of respondents in each category.)

Department	1979 Scores	1981 Scores
Chemical	34.98 (50)	34.06 (56)
Civil	33.71 (50)	32.33 (42)
Electrical	33.17 (27)	31.98 (44)
Mechanical	35.01 (56)	34.84 (83)
Metallurgical	34.32 (11)	- - - - -

T-tests between any pair of means within the 1981 group (for example, between mean scores for EE and ME-EM majors) indicated no statistically significant differences. The committee found identical results between the mean scores for the 1979 and 1981 groups within the same major (for example, EE). From this, the committee concluded that students across majors were writing equally well in the 1981 group and that students in the same major were writing as well in 1981 as they were in 1979. Thus, it appeared that the students' abilities to write were not affected by their choice of major.

Table 7 presents a comparison within the 1981 group and between the two groups by the number of credit hours beyond first-year composition courses.

Table 7.   Diederich Mean Scores by Writing Course Credit Above HU 101-102-103 (Parentheses indicate the number of respondents in each category.)

Credits	1979 Scores	1981 Scores
0	33.71 (50)	32.97 (72)
1	35.71 (11)	34.12 (8)
2	35.12 (27)	35.07 (28)
3	33.84 (58)	34.03 (63)
4	34.75 (2)	31.50 (2)
5	34.33 (1)	31.56 (6)
6	33.84 (22)	33.25 (23)
7 or more	36.17 (14)	36.61 (23)

T-tests between all possible pairs of means within the 1981 group indicated statistically significant differences (at the .05 level) between the group of students who indicated 7 or more credit hours of writing instruction beyond first-year composition and the group who indicated no additional credit hours (the same difference that appeared after the first assessment) and the groups who indicated 4 or 5 additional hours. Because of the small number of respondents in the 4 and 5 additional credit-hour groups (2 and 6, respectively), the committee decided that these findings were, at best, tentative. A comparison between the 1979 and 1981 students in each of the credit-hour groupings revealed no significant differences.

Once again, because the committee expected that writing instruction increases writing abilities, these results were puzzling. Maybe the students' growth in writing abilities occurred very slowly, particularly when the assessment conditions dictated only a first-draft evaluation of students trained in process-oriented writing classes? Or maybe the Diederich assessment methodology was not sensitive to small, but important, differences?

The students within the 1981 group were compared by whether or not they were transfer students. Then the transfer students and those originally matriculated at Tech in the 1981 group were compared with the corresponding groups of students in the 1979 assessment. Table 8 presents this comparison.

Table 8. Diederich Mean Scores by Transfer Status
(Parentheses indicate the number of respondents in each category.)

Status	1979 Scores	1981 Scores
Started at MTU	34.30 (131)	33.94 (168)
Transferred to MTU	34.53 (67)	32.68 (57)

As was also the case in the 1979 assessment, there wasn't a statistically significant difference between the mean scores of the transfer students and those who started at Tech in the 1981 group. There were also no statistically significant differences between the mean scores for the transfer students in the 1979 and 1981 groups and between the mean scores for the non-transfer students in both assessments. If the Diederich scores were accurate indications of the students' writing abilities, reflecting subtle but decisive differences, then the schools where the students transferred from were preparing students as well as the Tech writing programs.

Finally, like the students in the 1979 assessment, the students in the 1981 assessment were grouped into 4 categories of GPA, from 2.0–2.4 to 3.5–4.0 (no students reported a GPA of under 2.0). Grouped this way, the mean scores of the students within the 1981 assessment were compared. Then the mean scores for the students in each GPA category in the 1981 assessment (for example, those in the 3.0–3.4 category) were compared with the mean scores for the same category in the 1979 assessment. Table 9 presents these comparisons.

Table 9. Diederich Mean Scores by Grade Point Average
(Parentheses indicate the number of respondents in each category.)

GPA	1979 Scores	1981 Scores
2.0–2.4	32.83 (37)	30.23 (42)
2.5–2.9	33.66 (72)	33.80 (81)
3.0–3.4	35.54 (59)	34.71 (73)
3.5–4.0	35.87 (28)	35.31 (29)

T-tests between the pairs of mean scores indicated statistically significant differences (at the .05 level) only between the mean scores for students in the lowest category (2.0–2.4) and mean scores for the students in each of the three higher categories (2.5–2.9, 3.0–3.4, and 3.5–4.0). The analysis did not reveal any statistically significant differences for the mean scores of students within the same GPA category (for instance, 3.0–3.4) between the 1979 and the 1981 assessment.

The committee saw these results as evidence that academic ability did again affect writing ability in the 1981 assessment. Although exactly when academic ability began to differentiate writing ability differed in the two assessments (between the 2.5–2.9 and the 3.0–3.4 categories in the 1979 assessment and between the 2.0–2.4 and 2.5–2.9 categories in the 1981 assessment), the influence was clear in both assessments, indicating that the ability to write was an essential element in academic success even in the highly technological curricula of engineering. Moreover, the committee expected that if the Diederich methodology was indeed insensitive, the relationship between general academic ability and writing ability might even be stronger.

In sum, the committee believed that what was striking about all these results was how similar they were to those from the first assessment—almost identical! The committee thought that they were so similar, in fact, that only two conclusions seemed probable—either

1. the writing abilities of students evaluated in the spring of 1981 were nearly the same as those assessed in the 1979 sample; or
2. the Diederich scale and methodology was not sensitive enough to detect any but the grossest differences in the writing of senior engineering students.

The first conclusion could have been valid. The average SAT and ACT verbal scores of both the 1979 and the 1981 groups of students were almost identical, providing some indication that the language abilities of the two groups were similar before they matriculated at Michigan Tech. Furthermore, at the time of the second assessment, less than 10% of the engineering faculty had participated in the writing-across-the-curriculum program (although the figure was higher for faculty in other disciplines), making any significant impact of this program on writing abilities of the second group seem remote. Although there were significant changes in the first-year composition program between 1979 and 1981, particularly an increased emphasis on the writing process, these changes would not have affected seniors in 1981. In short, there were no compelling reasons to believe the writing abilities of the two groups should differ. However, the more the committee members used the Diederich scale to evaluate papers, the more they believed that the criteria in the scale were inadequate for their purposes and that the second conclusion was valid.

The following example, the three levels of proficiency (high, middle, and low) described by Diederich for his "Ideas" criterion, exemplifies the committee's concern about the Diederich scale:

Ideas

High.   The student has given some thought to the topic and has written what he [sic] really thinks. He discusses each main point long enough to show clearly what he means. He supports each main point with arguments, examples, or details; he gives the reader some reason for believing it. His points are clearly related to the topic and to the main idea or impression he is trying to get across. No necessary points are overlooked and there is no padding.

Middle.   The paper gives the impression that the student does not really believe that he [sic] is writing or does not fully realize what it means. He tries to guess what the teacher wants and writes what he thinks will get by. He does not explain his points very clearly or make them come alive to the reader. He writes what he thinks will sound good, not what he believes or knows.

Low. It is either hard to tell what points the student is trying to make or else they are so silly that he [sic] would have realized that they made no sense if he had only stopped to think. He is only trying to get something down on paper. He does not explain his points; he only writes them and then goes on to something else, or he repeats them in slightly different words. He does not bother to check his facts, and much of what he writes is obviously untrue. No one believes this sort of writing–not even the student who wrote it.

Obviously, there are large differences between the "high" and "middle" levels and between the "middle" and "low" levels. A high paper, well-thought-out and developed, is typical of professional writing–the carefully crafted product of several drafts, not usually the result of one 50-minute sitting. A middle paper, vacuous and undeveloped, isn't typical of what most college seniors (possibly even high school seniors) produce even in a first draft. If the "middle" criterion accurately reflects the abilities of any group of students, it may be those in junior high or the upper elementary grades. A "low" paper, largely nonsensical and juvenile, is typical of one group: beginning writers, not college seniors. Clearly, while these criteria might be valid for assessing the idea development of a student population with a wide range of abilities (like those who annually take the SAT or ACT exams), they aren't appropriate for a fairly homogenous group, such as senior engineering students at Michigan Tech. The high level is too high and the middle and low levels are too low, leaving a huge open space between the middle and high levels where the committee guessed (quite accurately) that most of the students actually fell.

Although the problems with the Diederich scale are now readily apparent, they were not when the committee first began its assessments. In fact, the Diederich scale was attractive because it had been used extensively in a wide variety of applications with little question of its adequacy and could provide information about specific skills of writing, like spelling and punctuation, that holistic assessment could not. Both reasons combined to make the Diederich scale seem like an appropriate choice for at least the first and second assessments.

Because the Diederich scale appeared problematical, the Communications Skills Committee did not make recommendations to the Dean of Engineering after the second assessment, although the results were presented to the engineering faculty with a caveat about their possible shortcomings. The committee did, however, make plans for a third assessment to take place in the spring of 1983, which would attempt to solve the problem with the Diederich scale present in the first two assessments.

The Third Assessment–1983

Because of the possible problems with the Diederich scale, the committee, with Mc Culley's aid, began looking for a way to improve the third assessment. Almost from the beginning of his involvement with the committee, Mc Culley extolled the virtues of primary-trait assessment (Lloyd-Jones, 1977) over other forms.

He told the committee that primary-trait assessment differed from the analytic assessment scales of Diederich and others and the general impression (holistic) methodology of testing organizations like Educational Testing Service in two important ways—first, the writing topics used in the assessment and, second, the criteria used to evaluate papers. In primary-trait assessment, unlike analytic or holistic assessment, the writing topics *always* contain a role for the writer, an audience, and a purpose for writing, all of which form a complete rhetorical context for the writer. For example, in the first two assessments some of the students wrote on the topic:

> What do you think of the preparation your Tech curriculum provided for developing your communications skills?

This topic, although not obvious, does contain a role for the writer—the writer as him- or herself. It does not, however, contain an audience for the writer or a reason for writing. An audience and a purpose for writing could be added to this topic by including the following instructions before the topic:

> Please respond to the following topic, assuming that Tech faculty will read your essay and truly want your honest input before making curriculum decisions.

If these directions were placed before the topic, they, along with the topic, would establish a complete rhetorical context for the writer—the writer's role (himself/herself, honestly), the audience (Tech faculty), and the purpose (to provide student input for curriculum decisions). Taken together, the directions for writing and the writing topic would constitute a primary-trait writing assignment—that is, responses to the assignment could be evaluated using primary-trait methodology.

In primary-trait assessment the criteria for the evaluation are not insular, atomistic features, like those contained in the Diederich scale or other analytic schemes. Rather, like those used in a holistic assessment, the criteria reflect general levels of proficiency. But unlike holistic criteria, primary-trait criteria can be explicit and descriptive due to the specification of a complete rhetorical context for the writer . For example, if the topic above and preceding directions were used in an assessment, the specified audience of Tech faculty suggests that logical arguments, in the sense of classical rhetoric, should carry more weight than ethical or pathetic ones. In other words, part of the criteria could spell out that because of the intended audience, papers identified as meeting the highest level of proficiency would be those which contained logical arguments, supported and developed by specific facts and details; naturally, part of the criteria for lower levels might specify unsupported logical arguments or appeals based on the author's creditability or highly connotative language. Of course, other factors besides the type of support would be added to form the complete criteria for each level of proficiency.

Mc Culley believed that the advantage of such explicit criteria is that it allows the evaluators to focus their judgments, making delineation of subtle differences possible. He also told the committee that such criteria were much more realistic because, as they all know, the criteria for quality in writing changes as the rhetorical context changes, just as committee members would not judge lab reports from undergraduate students by the same standards they used to judge professional journal articles.

The committee listened to Mc Culley's advice and then decided to develop a primary-trait evaluation for use in the third assessment in the spring of 1983. Mc Culley admitted that with primary-trait assessment it would only be possible to compare the results of the three assessments on one topic, not the results from all five topics that could be compared using the Diederich scale because five different sets of criteria (one set for each topic) would be required. Nevertheless, he felt that if a topic (one which a large enough number of students responded to in the first two assessments to make the comparison valid) was chosen for the third assessment, the committee could use primary-trait methodology to compare at least partially the results of all three assessments, realizing that the students from the first two assessments might be at some disadvantage because a complete rhetorical context was not spelled out for them before they wrote. Nevertheless, the committee then decided to choose a topic and proceed accordingly.

The topic chosen from the first two assessments was the "What do you think of the preparation your Tech curriculum provided for developing your communications skills?" discussed above. In the first assessment, 37 people responded to this topic; in the second, 49 people—both numbers which were judged large enough to make a valid comparison among respondents to all three assessments. To modify this topic so that primary-trait criteria could be constructed for it, the "Please respond to the following topic, assuming . . ." set of instructions were added.

In addition, the committee decided to evaluate papers from the third assessment also using the Diederich scale for two reasons: first, the Diederich assessment would provide a means of comparing all of the results of the first two assessments with the results of the third. Second, although not nearly as important to the committee, a third Diederich assessment would provide more evidence of the value of this scale in this type of assessment. Thus all the papers from the 1983 assessment would be evaluated using both the Diederich scale and the primary-trait criteria which Mc Culley had developed for the topic (See Appendix C, p. 134). In addition, the papers written on the "Tech Curriculum" topic from the 1979 and 1981 assessments would be rescored using the primary-trait criteria.

The procedures for the third assessment mirrored those of the first two assessments with only a couple of changes. The sample of senior students (234) was selected from classes in each department, with the exception of metallurgical engineering, and contained proportions of senior students equal in relation to the proportion of all engineering students enrolled in each department. Students were given the same handout of instructions, background information to complete, a release statement to sign, and the same amount of time (50 minutes) as in the first two assessments. After the essays were collected, student names were deleted and then they were numerically coded. Finally, the essays from the first two assessments were randomly mixed into those from this assessment.

The essays were first scored using the Diederich scale by the four members of the committee (two fewer raters than the six in the first and second assessments), who first reached a consensus of the criteria for scoring through discussion. Any discrepancies of more than 10 points (max = 50) were resolved by a third rater. The percentage of agreement among all four raters across all papers was 82%, which was considered acceptable. Table 10 presents the comparison of the third assessment results with the results from the first two assessments.

Table 10.   Diederich Mean Scores
(Parentheses indicate standard deviation.)

Category	1979 Scores N = 196	1981 Scores N = 225	1983 Scores N = 234
Ideas	6.92 (1.42)	6.86 (1.37)	6.30 (1.41)
Organization	6.34 (1.54)	6.08 (1.44)	5.81 (1.61)
Wording	3.26 (0.57)	3.25 (0.67)	3.62 (0.46)
Flavor	3.64 (0.66)	3.24 (0.70)	3.54 (6.17)
Content	20.16 (3.62)	19.43 (3.65)	19.56 (3.45)
Usage	3.38 (0.60)	3.21 (0.66)	3.65 (0.56)
Spelling	3.78 (0.80)	3.93 (0.93)	4.53 (0.69)
Punctuation	3.69 (0.59)	3.73 (0.75)	4.41 (0.41)
Writing	3.48 (0.65)	3.32 (0.64)	3.66 (0.60)
Mechanics	14.32 (2.05)	14.19 (2.25)	16.01 (1.50)
TOTAL	34.39 (5.17)	33.62 (5.12)	35.80 (5.30)

Clearly, the results from all three assessments were very similar. A one-way analysis of variance among the means of total scores for all assessment groups revealed no statistically significant difference (thus, isn't presented here), firmly suggesting that the writing abilities of all three groups of students were essentially equivalent or that the Diederich scale was not sensitive enough to detect important differences if they did indeed exist. Because of this result, a further breakdown and comparison—by GPA, original matriculation, and number of credit hours beyond first-year composition courses—of the data from the third assessment were not performed.

After all the papers had been scored using the Diederich scale and this data was being analyzed, the committee came together again to rescore the papers using the primary-trait criteria. The committee discussed this new set of criteria and the new four-point primary-trait scale (4, the highest; 1, the lowest). They then practiced scoring sample papers (written on the topic by senior engineering students not in the assessment) until they were in complete agreement in their scoring.

Each paper in the assessment was scored independently by two different raters with both scores summed to a total score (e.g., a 1st score of "2" plus a 2nd score of "3" equaled a total score of "5"). Any discrepancies of two or more points on the eight-point scale were resolved by a third rater. The percentage of agreement among all four raters across all papers was an impressive 96%. Table 11 presents the means from primary-trait scores for all three groups.

Table 11.   A Comparison of Primary-Trait Mean Scores by Assessment Group

Group	Mean Score	Standard Deviation
1978 Group (N = 37)	4.35	1.27
1981 Group (N = 49)	4.86	1.34
1983 Group (N = 236)	4.30	1.30

The results of the primary-trait assessment provide an important insight—when the writing task is "persuasion through development of issues, arguments, and evidence appropriate to the defense of a position," the writing abilities of senior engineering students at Michigan Tech from all three assessments were slightly above average, somewhat above four (2 + 2), even though a standard of adequacy needs further development. But what does "slightly above average" mean?

Consider the following excerpt from one of the papers in the 1983 assessment, given a "2" by each of the two raters for a total score of "4" (just below the mean of 4.3 for all the papers in the 1983 assessment):

Tech has done a fair job in the development of my curriculum skills. Included in this assessment is both verbal and nonverbal communication. This is not to say that these skills are great.

Before coming to Tech, I had little experience in the area of public speaking. In high school and the other university I attended, the extent of the verbal communication required from me consisted of an occasional short answer. This answer was almost always given from a seated position. None of the skills a person needs when verbally communicating with either a group or an unfamiliar individual were ever properly developed. These neglected skills included eye contact, correct pronunciation, proper posture, and sufficient preparation. Sadly, I find most of the aforementioned skills absent from most of my instructors at Tech. It was a common sight for me to see my instructor scribbling on the chalk board and mumbling his (or her) explanation straight ahead—to be lost forever more into the molecular structure of the board. This is just one example of the lack of communication skills I have observed in my instructors. As far as my verbal skills go, they have evolved slowly through necessity. Classes such as ME 370, ME 301, ME 447 and ME 440 have helped develop my skills in front of large groups of people. Interviewing has helped develop my skill of one-to-one communication.

In this paper, a position is taken and there is some support for the position, examples of both the positive and negative aspects of the student's experience. But the support for the position is generally minimal and vague. The student states that some mechanical engineering courses (ME 301, 370, 440, and 447) helped develop his or her speaking skills "in front of large groups of people" and that interviewing developed "one-to-one" communications skills. But the student doesn't specify how these skills were developed or what they were. On the negative side, the student mentions that specific public speaking skills, such as "eye-contact" and "proper posture" weren't developed in high school or at "the other university" and provides a rationale for why they were not—because he or she was relegated to supplying occasional answers, usually " . . . given from a seated position." But then the student jumps off into a complaint about some of the public speaking skills of professors at Michigan Tech, failing to relate how this accounts for the inadequacies of the "high school" and "other university" curricula. The student's anxiety over explanations "lost forever more into the molecular structure of the board" might be well-founded, if not endearing, but it isn't completely relevant to the issue at hand. Finally, the organization of the paper is random at times, definitely lacking some controlling structure.

This excerpt is typical of many of the papers written in the 1983 assessment, although some were obviously better and some worse. Considering that the writer of this paper had little, if any, time for reflection and revision, some may believe that the paper represents a pretty good effort, even for senior engineering students. In reference to the predetermined primary-trait criteria, the score of 4 (2 + 2) on this paper represents what should be the average. The members of the Communications Skills Committee based on their knowledge of and years of experience in the engineering profession, don't agree, however. They believe that this paper and the many others like it in all three assessments should have been better, that too many of the students failed to develop ideas, provide relevant support, and clearly organize their response. They believe there is much room for improvement and that the average should be higher. Possibly this position is too harsh. There is simply no way to tell until what it means to be an effective writer as an engineer is better defined.

A one-way analysis of variance among the mean primary-trait scores for all three groups was performed to determine if the writing abilities of the groups did differ in reference to the primary-trait criteria. Table 12 presents the results from this analysis.

Table 12. One-Way Analysis of Variance Among Primary-Trait Scores

Source	D.F.	Sum of Squares	Mean Scores	F Ratio	F. Prob.
Between Groups	2	12.4412	6.2206	3.648	.0273
Within Groups	319	470.5981	1.7051		
TOTAL	321	483.0393			

The difference among the means of the three groups was statistically significant at just below the .03 level—that is, one would expect a difference of this size to occur by chance a little less than 3 times out of a hundred if there were no true differences. To say the least, these results were surprising. The surprise was not, however, in the magnitude of the differences, but in where most of the difference occurs—in the results of the second (1981) assessment. For some reason(s), the students in the 1981 group were writing better than students in either the 1979 or the 1983 groups, suggesting that the writing abilities of senior engineering students first went up, then fell back down.

At first it was thought that the students in the second assessment might have been different from the students in the other two assessments in important ways, say average GPA or number of credit hours of writing instruction beyond first-year composition—two factors that contributed to significant differences in the first two analyses. Analysis of variance would have been the most direct way to determine if the three groups of students differed by GPA or number of writing classes. Much to our chagrin, however, we discovered that we only had the means of responses to the background information sheet for the first group (1979), not the individual responses we would need to conduct an analysis of variance. Faced with this reality, we chose to compare the mean GPA's and number of writing courses for all three groups using Bancroft's (1968) modification of the Duncan Multiple Range Test, realizing this sort of after-the-fact analysis technique was not clearly appropriate for what we were trying to do. When the results of this analysis indicated *no* statistically significant differences among the mean-GPA's and the mean-number of writing courses for all three groups, we felt fairly safe in concluding that the differences in writing scores among all three groups were not due to differences in GPA or number of writing courses beyond first-year composition for one big reason—the Duncan Multiple Range Test was more likely to indicate differences between means when they didn't exist in reality.

If there are no integral differences among the groups, it's very difficult to explain why the students in the second assessment were writing better. The only apparent change in the writing education of the students at Michigan Tech since 1978 has been the growth and development of the writing-across-the-curriculum program. But if this program were significantly affecting all students in engineering, it would be expected that the increase in writing abilities would have carried over into the 1983 assessment. Obviously, it did not. It might be that a larger proportion of the students in the 1981 assessment sample were exposed to the effects of the writing-across-the-curriculum program than in the 1983 assessment. The only way to determine if the program was directly affecting student writing abilities would be to track down students in this third assessment, interview them to determine how many participants in the writing-across-the-curriculum program they have taken classes from and how many different writing-across-the-curriculum activities they have been exposed to and how frequently, then to compare the assessment scores of the students with high exposure to those with low exposure—a long, complicated process that is now underway.

The initial surprise with the differences between groups in the primary-trait scores postponed an examination of the primary purposes for including a primary-trait evaluation in the third assessment—to develop a more precise standard for judging the writing abilities of engineering students and to determine how well the students compared to this standard.

The fact that primary-trait methodology in the third assessment did reveal differences among the assessment groups provides evidence that the primary-trait standards are more precise, allowing for detection of more than just gross differences in writing abilities. Whether the criteria contained in the primary-trait scoring guide represent valid standards is not clear. The only way this question can be answered will be to assess the writing of engineers (considered exemplary writers by their peers and supervisors) on a similar task, then to articulate the criteria of quality in this writing task—another difficult, complex task that the Communications Skills Committee hopes to conduct in the future.

Coda

Since the beginning of these assessments in 1978, all who have been part of them have learned a great deal. But the four basic goals of the assessment have not been totally met:

1. To determine an adequate standard of writing skills for senior students in engineering.
2. To discover how best to assess the writing skills of the students.
3. To decide how the skills of the students should compare to standard when they are almost ready to graduate.
4. To make recommendations for curricular changes based on the progress toward the three previous goals.

Yet the committee has made some progress. We believe that while an adequate standard is still partially elusive, it is much clearer than it was when the assessments began and methods for making it even clearer are now apparent. That is, the primary-trait methodology gives us what we believe is a much more precise indication of our students' abilities. We think, however, based on our experience and intuition, that the average primary-trait scores of our student groups (4 plus) should be higher, that the development of their ideas, support, and organization should be better. Maybe we're wrong. Maybe if our students had time to plan, revise, and edit, their writing abilities would approximate what we think they should be—a lot of good arguments could be put forth to support this contention. At present, we're just not certain.

Finally, our progress toward each of the above goals enabled us to make some recommendations for improving the writing skills of our students, such as adding additional courses and expanding the writing-across-the-curriculum program. In summary, if one idea can be gleaned from all of this, it is that much more research needs to be done into what adequate writing skills really mean, how writing skills should be assessed, and how closely senior students should approximate adequate writing skills. We're looking forward to future work in these areas.

Appendix A

A.   The College of Engineering wishes to develop a profile of its seniors' writing performance. The College asks that you complete an essay in order to provide material for that assessment. You have *fifty minutes* to complete this cover page and write a composition responding to one of the topics listed in D. Because the College of Engineering is interested in the quality of the senior class' writing in an impromptu situation, we are asking that you take this assignment seriously and write the best essay you can under the time and topic limitations.

B.   Please Complete the Following Items:

1. Name _____ _____ _____
                    Last   First   Middle Initial

2. Student number _____ 3. Major department _____

4. Approximate GPA (check one)
   less than 2.0 ___; 2.0-2.4 ___; 2.5-2.9 ___; 3.0-3.4 ___; 3.5-4.0 ___

5. Did you transfer to MTU from another college or university? (yes or no) _____

6. Number of credits of writing courses you have taken (*not* including HU 101, 102, or 103 at MTU or freshman English at another college/university) _____

C.   Please Read and Sign the Following Release Statement

      I hereby give the Communications Committee of the College of Engineering, Michigan Technological University, permission to use this composition as it sees fit for purposes of assessing student writing performance. I understand that analyses of my composition will be confidential and will not affect my grades in any way. I further understand that both my composition and my responses to the informational items above are for research purposes only and become the property of the Committee. The Committee agrees that all identifying data will be removed from my composition and replaced by a code number before any analyses are made. The Committee will designate project evaluator(s) who will be the only faculty having access to any of this information. Thank you for your cooperation in this endeavor to find out how our graduating seniors write an impromptu essay.

_____
                         signature

D.   Respond to *One* of the Following Topics in an Essay of At Least Three Hundred Words.

1. Criticize the 15 credit HU and SS approved elective requirement of the College of Engineering.
2. Tell why you sought or will seek a particular job at the BS level.
3. Tech is proposing a major expansion of research activity. Argue for or against this expansion.

4. What do you think of the preparation your Tech curriculum provided for developing your own writing skills?
5. Argue for your choice of either engineering *or* humanities professors as teachers of technical report writing. Do *not* consider the alternative of team teaching.

Appendix B

Diederich Criteria

1. *Ideas*

   High. The student has given some thought to the topic and has written what he really thinks. He discusses each main point long enough to show clearly what he means. He supports each main point with arguments, examples, or details; he gives the reader some reason for believing it. His points are clearly related to the topic and to the main idea or impression he is trying to get across. No necessary points are overlooked and there is no padding.

   Middle. The paper gives the impression that the student does not really believe what he is writing or does not fully realize what it means. He tries to guess what the teacher wants and writes what he thinks will get by. He does not explain his points very clearly or make them come alive to the reader. He writes what he thinks will sound good, not what he believes or knows.

   Low. It is either hard to tell what points the student is trying to make or else they are so silly that he would have realized that they made no sense if he had only stopped to think. He is only trying to get something down on paper. He does not explain his points; he only writes them and then goes on to something else, or he repeats them in slightly different words. He does not bother to check his facts, and much of what he writes is obviously untrue. No one believes this sort of writing—not even the student who wrote it.

2. *Organization*

   High. The paper starts at a good point, moves in a straight line, gets somewhere, and stops at a good point. The paper has a plan that the reader can follow; he is never in doubt as to where he is or where he is going. Sometimes there is a little twist near the end that makes the paper come out in a way that the reader does not expect, but it seems quite logical. Main points are treated at greatest length or with greatest emphasis; others in proportion to their importance.

   Middle. The organization of this paper is standardized and conventional. There is usually a one-paragraph introduction, three main points each treated in one paragraph, and a conclusion that often seems tacked on or forced. Some trivial points may be treated in greater detail than important points, and there is usually some dead wood that might better be cut out.

Low. This paper starts anywhere and never gets anywhere. The main points are not clearly separated from one another, and they come in a random order—as though the student had not given any thought to what he intended to say before he sat down to write. The paper seems to start in one direction, then another, then another, until the reader is lost.

3. *Wording*

High. The writer uses a sprinkling of uncommon words or of familiar words in an uncommon setting. He shows an interest in words and in putting them together in slightly unusual ways. Some of his experiments with words may not quite come off, but this is such a promising trait in a young writer that a few mistakes may be forgiven. For the most part he uses words correctly, but he also uses them with imagination.

Middle. The writer is addicted to tired old phrases and hackneyed expressions. If you left a blank in one of his sentences, almost anyone could guess what word he would use at that point. He does not stop to think how to say something; he just says it in the same way as everyone else. A writer may also get a middle rating on this quality if he overdoes his experiments with uncommon words: if he always uses a big word when a little word would serve his purpose better.

Low. The writer uses words so carelessly or inexactly that he gets far too many wrong. These are not intentional experiments with words in which failure may be forgiven; they represent groping for words and using them without regard to their fitness. A paper written entirely in a childish vocabulary may also get a low rating, even if no word is clearly wrong.

4. *Flavor*

High. The writing sounds like a person, not a committee. The writer seems quite sincere and candid, and he writes about something he knows—often from personal experience. You could never mistake this writing for the writing of anyone else. Although the writer may play different roles in different papers, he does not put on airs. He is brave enough to reveal himself just as he is.

Middle. The writer usually tries to appear better or wiser than he really is. He tends to write lofty sentiments and broad generalities. He does not put in the little homely details that show that he knows what he is talking about. His writing tries to sound impressive. Sometimes it is impersonal and correct but colorless, without personal feeling or imagination.

Low. The writer reveals himself well enough but without meaning to. His thoughts and feelings are those of an uneducated person who does not realize how bad they sound. His way of expressing himself differs from standard English, but it is not his personal style; it is the way uneducated people talk in the neighborhood in which he lives.

5. *Usage, Sentence Structure*

High. There are no vulgar or "illiterate" errors in usage by present standards of informal written English, and there are very few errors in points that have been emphasized in class. The sentence structure is usually correct, even in varied and complicated sentence patterns.

Middle. There are a few serious errors in usage and several in points that have been emphasized in class, but not enough to obscure meaning. The sentence structure is usually correct in the more familiar sentence patterns, but there are occasional errors in more complicated patterns, as in parallelism, subordination, consistency of tenses, reference of pronouns, etc.

Low. There are so many serious errors in usage and sentence structure that the paper is hard to understand.

6. *Punctuation, Capitals, Abbreviations, Numbers*

High. There are no serious violations of rules that have been taught—except slips of the pen. Note, however, that modern editors do not require commas after short introductory clauses, around nonrestrictive clauses, or between short coordinate clauses unless their omission leads to ambiguity or makes the sentence hard to read. Contractions are acceptable—often desirable.

Middle. There are several violations of rules that have been taught—as many as usually occur in the average paper.

Low. Basic punctuation is omitted or haphazard, resulting in fragments, run-on sentences, etc.

7. *Spelling*

High. Since this rating scale is most often used for test papers written in class when there is insufficient time to use the dictionary, spelling standards should be more lenient than for papers written at home. The high paper usually has not more than five misspellings, and these occur in words that are hard to spell. The spelling is consistent: words are not spelled correctly in one sentence and misspelled in another, unless the misspelling appears to be a slip of the pen. If a poor paper has no misspellings, it gets a 5 in spelling.

Middle. There are several spelling errors in hard words and a few violations of basic rules, but no more than one finds in the average paper.

Low. There are so many spelling errors that they interfere with comprehension.

8. *Typing, Handwriting, Neatness*

High. The typing or handwriting is clear, attractive, and well-spaced, and the rules of manuscript form have been observed.

Middle. The typing or handwriting is average in legibility and attractiveness. There may be a few violations of rules for manuscript form if there is evidence of some care for the appearance of the page.

Low. The paper is sloppy in appearance and difficult to read.

DIEDERICH SCORING SHEETS

SIDE A

Rater # _____   Essay # _____

Low		Medium		High	
2	4	6	8	10	Ideas _____
2	4	6	8	10	Org. _____
1	2	3	4	5	Wording _____
1	2	3	4	5	Flavor _____

IDEAS + ORG + WORDING + FLAVOR = Content _____

1	2	3	4	5	Usage _____
1	2	3	4	5	Spelling _____
1	2	3	4	5	Punc. _____
1	2	3	4	5	Writing _____

USAGE + SPELLING + PUNC + WRITING = Mechanics _____

CONTENT + MECHANICS = _____   TOTAL _____

SIDE B

Rater # _____   Essay # _____

Low		Medium		High	
2	4	6	8	10	Ideas _____
2	4	6	8	10	Org. _____
1	2	3	4	5	Wording _____
1	2	3	4	5	Flavor _____

IDEAS + ORG + WORDING + FLAVOR = Content _____

1	2	3	4	5	Usage _____
1	2	3	4	5	Spelling _____
1	2	3	4	5	Punc. _____
1	2	3	4	5	Writing _____

USAGE + SPELLING + PUNC + WRITING = Mechanics _____

CONTENT + MECHANICS = _____   TOTAL _____

AVERAGE

Ratings: 2   3

Ideas _____
Org. _____
Wording _____
Flavor _____
Content _____
Usage _____
Spelling _____
Punc. _____
Writing _____
Mechanics _____
TOTAL _____

Appendix C

Primary Trait Scoring Guide[1] For "Communications Skills Development"

Rhetorical Mode: Persuasive—Social/Organizational.

Primary Trait: Quality in persuasion through development of issues, arguments, and evidence appropriate to the defense of a proposition.

Rationale of Primary Trait: The directive "What do you think of the preparation your Tech curriculum provided for developing your own communication skills?" indicates the persuasive orientation of the exercise. Given that the students assume their responses are important and are going to be read by university personnel who may have some impact, however small, on the current curriculum, the students are being asked to use writing not as a way of simply expressing personal satisfactions or gripes, but as a means of communicating public need and supporting their estimations of public need. This type of evaluative writing is very common and very important in the professions entered into by college-trained personnel, including engineers, although it is one of the most difficult.

General Scoring Rationale: Since this exercise seeks to elicit reasoned and supported persuasive statements, responses to this exercise should be scored in terms of this criterion alone. Matters such as tone or format, for example, should not be weighed in scoring. Qualities that should be weighed as evidence of systematic persuasion are: (1) focus—evidenced by taking one position and offering support for this position and (2) appropriateness of development—evidenced by the logic of the reasoning, development of arguments, and consideration of the issues.

Scoring Guide Categories:

4 (the highest) = *Takes and systematically defends a position in a coherent manner.* Papers explicitly take (or strongly imply) a position, logically develop support for this position, and offer some refutation of the opposite position. (Note: refutation is usually considered the prime determination between an extremely well developed and conceived argument and one that is probably acceptable but not forceful.) In addition, all 4 papers demonstrate a sense of wholeness; in other words, there are no distinct sections in the papers that appear stacked on top of each other rather than logically interrelated. This sense of wholeness is usually achieved through the strength of the internal ordering of ideas, not superficial organizing strategies such as: "There are two reasons . . . . The first is . . . . The second is . . . ."

3 = *Takes and systematically defends a position.* These papers, like 4 papers, explicitly take a position (or strongly imply one) and logically develop support for this position. However, 3 papers do not usually offer any refutation of the opposite position. A sense of wholeness is also not present in these papers. Rather, the papers are *sections* of arguments piled on top of each other that could be rearranged without substantially altering the meaning of the papers. For example, the section following "The first reason is . . . ." could be switched with the section following "The second reason is . . ." and not change the meaning of the paper.

Some sections of support for the position are not as well developed as are those in a 4 paper. Finally, all support for the adopted position is relevant and not merely an expression of satisfaction or complaint.

2 = *Takes but does not systematically develop a position.* These papers are characterized by a lack of development, relevant support, and organization. A position is taken (or strongly implied) but each item of support for this position is not developed beyond one or two supporting ideas. In addition, most of the supporting items could easily be rearranged without altering the meaning of the paper, and some of the support is nothing more than a personal affirmation or complaint. The basic difference, then, between a 2 and a 3 paper is that 2 papers lack a sense of sectionness that the development of supporting ideas in 3 papers creates, and some of the support is not relevant.

1 = *Does not take nor systematically develop a position.* Some 1 papers do not take a position; they only give plus's or minus's and generally equivocate. Other 1 papers do take a position but offer little, if any, support for this position, often trailing off on tangents not directly related to the issue. Some typical score point one papers are:

- a. Attitudes and opinions about related social issues without a clear statement of position—these include free-floating, uncontrolled statements of opinion showing no concern for taking a stand and supporting it.
- b. Position statements but no related support—often these papers merely reiterate their stand in various forms.
- c. Position statements preceded or followed by elaborate introductions.
- d. Position statements followed by arguments and appeals not connected to the crucial issues.
- e. Position statements followed by one or two undeveloped reasons.
- f. Position statements but the paper goes off tangentially into another realm (clarifying terms, personal gripes, etc.).

0 = *No response, illegible, illiterate, or writes off the topic.*

Note

1. This scoring guide represents a modification of the "Recreation Center" scoring guide developed by the National Assessment of Educational Progress for use in their first three writing assessments ("Writing Achievement, 1969–79: Results from the Third National Writing Assessment, Volume 1 – 17-Year Olds, Report No. 10-W-01, Denver, Colorado: National Assessment of Educational Progress, 1980).

III.
Research on Writing and Learning

The comprehensive writing program at Michigan Tech was originally started to accomplish one thing—to improve student writing—but actually emphasized something else—improved student thinking. To be sure, the goals were related. In fact, so related that we realized we couldn't accomplish the first adequately until we had addressed the second. From the beginning, we believed that a program addressed solely to so-called "writing skills" would be limited in certain crucial ways: (1) it would ignore the most serious causes of poor writing, which we felt were conceptual and motivational; (2) it would not offer a long-term solution; and (3) it was unlikely to work across the curriculum—that is, faculty outside of English wouldn't either be very interested in, or skillful at, developing such a program. We did believe that a writing program with a "cognitive base," that is, one that viewed writing as primarily a conceptual activity, would better address these problems.

However, in terms of evaluation, the cognitively-based program presented some special problems. For one thing, we don't know to date of any studies—Moffett, Emig, Britton, and Flower notwithstanding—which prove conclusively that writing improves learning—we are "sure" that it does, but we're not sure it's been proven. Nor, then, were there designs or models readily available to evaluate the writing-learning connection in our program, so we made some up. And, even if we could prove that certain kinds of writing increased comprehension, or understanding, or assimilation, or analysis, could we also demonstrate that writing ability improved? This last question remains, after all, the major reason why most writing-across-the-curriculum programs came into being in the first place and why the movement continues to capture national attention.

The chapters written for this section attempt to demonstrate collectively that, yes, teachers who assign certain kinds of writing do, beyond doubt, help students to learn better. However, they probably don't succeed in establishing this "beyond a doubt." Nevertheless, the very process of defining the questions to ask and designing approaches to answers seems to us to be an important part of each of these studies.

137

In "Poetic Writing in Psychology," Gorman, Gorman, and Young argue that imaginative writing can increase our students' ability to assess values and thereby gain certain kinds of knowledge that otherwise might be unavailable. The researchers assigned poetic writing, evaluated it, and interviewed the student writers to help them discover the nature of its contribution to learning psychology.

In "Writing in Biology," Flynn, Mc Culley—English teachers—and Gratz—a biology teacher—report the results of their experimental work to determine which of several methods helps students learn to write laboratory reports best. This project is an example of the kind of research which becomes possible "across the curriculum," when questions are raised about the role of writing to improve both learning and writing.

In "The Laboratory Reports of Engineering Students: A Case Study," James R. Kalmbach does a retrospective study of *all* the assigned writing done by five engineering students during their four years at Michigan Tech. In particular, he focuses on the engineering laboratory reports which comprised more than fifty percent of all assigned writing tasks for these students. Kalmbach's analysis of these reports identifies a probable weakness in our writing-across-the-curriculum program, and his understanding of the program's theoretical basis leads to specific suggestions for improvement.

In "Writing to Learn: Engineering Student Journals," Selfe and Arbabi explain the results of a term-long project in which civil engineering students were required to write at least a page a week in a journal to improve their understanding of course concepts. A second section of the same course was taught by the same instructor, Arbabi, in the traditional manner and didn't use journals: the results are especially illuminating to those who question the value of personal writing in technical subjects, such as math, science, and engineering.

In "Journal Writing in Mathematics," Selfe, Petersen, and Nahrgang report the effects of writing expressively in journals to learn mathematical concepts. In this experiment the researchers raise questions about the frequency, length, and type of journal entries assigned by teachers in relation to the desired outcomes in student learning.

In the last study in this section, "Composing Responses to Literary Texts," Elizabeth Flynn explores what happens when first-year students are asked to write, expressively, their personal reactions to selected readings as a way of further understanding those readings. She argues, with evidence drawn from student journals, as well as from essays based on journals, that the writing made certain forms of understanding possible—forms of understanding unavailable to non-writers.

Chapter 10

Poetic Writing in Psychology

MICHAEL E. GORMAN, MARGARET E. GORMAN
and ART YOUNG

When we first thought to introduce creative writing exercises into non-English classes, we expected to meet with resistance from students, faculty, and perhaps normally supportive colleagues. We had struggled to convince doubters of the value of expressive writing in learning; thus now to suggest that creative writing might likewise play a role in courses across the curriculum might very well test the patience and goodwill of our educational community. Surely no area of composition, i.e. creative writing, is so clearly identified as an English department's responsibility. Scientists and engineers should know how to keep journals and logbooks and to prepare reports and proposals—but poetry and stories? However, we became intrigued with the idea not because scientists should also be poets, but because we had come to believe that students and teachers alike need additional opportunities to be creative with ideas and to experience the full range of resources language has to offer.

We knew that creative writing as a method of discourse and as a tool for learning plays a significant role in the theoretical models of Britton, Moffett, D'Angelo, and Kinneavy, and yet we also knew that creative writing was assigned infrequently in schools and colleges.[1] James Britton, in particular, has stressed the importance of poetic writing, to use his term, in encouraging students to explore their own feelings and values in conjunction with new learning experiences. He asserts that poetic writing involves a kind of learning different from the learning in transactional writing. The poetic discovers and delineates values and the transactional communicates information in which already held values are either implied or explicitly stated. If Britton is correct, we speculated, shouldn't students have opportunities across the curriculum to write poetically as well as expressively and transactionally?

We thus resolved to include some "creative writing" assignments in an introductory psychology class, and (over the course of several terms) to develop instruments and techniques which might enable us to evaluate the importance of such assignments. This project was a collaborative effort among Michael Gorman, a psychology teacher, Art Young, an English teacher, and Margaret Gorman, a research associate.

Poetic *thinking* in James Britton's sense, has always been part of Michael Gorman's Introductory Psychology course. Students read Mark Vonnegut's *The Eden Express,* an autobiographical account of a young man's journey into and out of schizophrenia. Vonnegut reproduces his thoughts and feelings while he hallucinates, tries to kill himself and struggles to figure out what's happening to him. A major course objective is to get students to see schizophrenia from the inside—to understand what it means to be schizophrenic, not just to memorize a series of facts about schizophrenia. For example, students evaluate several models of therapy in terms of whether they can be applied to schizophrenia. That evaluation rests on feelings as much as facts—if a student can sense what it feels like to be a schizophrenic, he or she will evaluate the therapies in a more personal and insightful way. Mark Vonnegut does just that—he talks about how it feels to take Thorazine, to be shut up in a padded room, etc.

In the standard psychology courses, students wrote essays in which they discussed how various therapeutic models could be applied to Mark's case.[2] The essays were good, but somewhat detached—students were mastering the facts without attempting to feel what he felt. According to Britton, poetic writing should encourage students to explore feelings as well as facts. Therefore, in the fall of 1981, students were given the following assignment:

> Write a poem about how the humanistic-existential perspective can be applied to schizophrenia. You may use Mark Vonnegut's case, if you like. Your poem may be serious or humorous, rhymed or unrhymed—anything you like.

The humanistic-existential perspective is one of the four the students had to understand and be able to apply in their final papers. Its major proponent is R. D. Laing who holds that "schizophrenia is a sane response to an insane world." To see Laing's point, students have to "step outside" ordinary distinctions between sanity and insanity, reality and unreality and see society from the standpoint of a schizophrenic who may reject all of our normal, everyday values. Laing himself uses poetry to express many of his ideas; poetry seemed an appropriate way to help students understand his ideas.

When we read the poems, we saw some evidence that students were engaging feelings and values in a way not observed in their formal essays. We also saw that at least some of the students found the assignment a refreshing change from the essays, so in the fall of 1982 we decided to conduct a more formal, in-depth study of the effects of a mixture of poetic, expressive and transactional assignments, hoping to observe the perhaps distinctive function of each kind of writing in learning. We settled on Britton's categories because his theory had shaped our writing across the curriculum program, and because of his insistence that poetic writing was an important and undervalued tool for learning.

Therefore, we developed the following written assignments for the Introductory Psychology class:

1. Students were first asked to write a poem about schizophrenia before they had read anything about it, to give them a chance to explore their feelings and impressions. They were told this poem would not be graded. Based on these poems, three students were selected for in-depth case studies that will be described in this essay.

2. The students were assigned a draft essay, worth 4 points (out of a total of 100 for the course), in which they had to discuss how the bio-medical and learning models, two of the perspectives on schizophrenia in the course, could be applied to Mark's case. They were told that this essay would help them with their final papers and that it would not be graded critically.

3. Next, students had to write a draft short story on roughly the same topic as their draft essay. The idea here was to compare transactional and poetic approaches to the same assignment. The story was also worth 4 points and again, students knew it would not be graded critically.

4. Toward the end of the course, students were asked to write a poem about how the humanistic-existential perspective could be applied to Mark's case, the same assignment as had been used in a previous class. This poem was expected to be closer to a final product than the first one and was worth two points. Again, the students knew they wouldn't be graded critically.

5. At the end of the course, the students had to hand in a formal paper in which they compared the bio-medical and humanistic-existential approaches to Mark's schizophrenia. This paper was worth ten points and students knew it would be graded more critically than their first draft.

6. Students were asked to keep journals throughout the quarter, making two entries a week. Mike wanted to give the students a chance to do some writing that wasn't part of a specific assignment. We intended to use the journal to help us gauge students' reactions to the assignments—particularly the case-study students. But the focus of our study was on the contrast between transactional and poetic writing; therefore, we did not attempt a detailed study of the impact of the journals.

In summary, students had three poetic assignments (the two poems and the short story), two transactional assignments (one draft and one formal essay), and one expressive assignment (the journal). In addition to these pieces of writing we collected from students (1) a checklist of attitudes and reactions to each assignment, and (2) an open-ended questionnaire about each assignment's effect on their thinking about schizophrenia. We hoped that a combination of different approaches—in-depth case studies of a few students, and checklists, questionnaires, and written reactions from all the students—would give us a more complete picture of how the assignments affected student learning and writing than if we used a single methodological approach.

Case Studies

From the more than seventy students enrolled in the class at the beginning we selected three students to work with us in two capacities: first as fellow researchers examining the writing of fellow students, recording observations and descriptions, meeting bi-weekly to discuss impressions, and brainstorming at points of departure or points of agreement, and second, as subjects for case study research: to humor us with a couple of taped interviews about their writing and classroom experiences in Introductory Psychology, to do additional journal entries on topics related to their writing and their participation in the research project, to save for us all writing (including rough drafts, outlines, notes) done in connection with this class, and to join us in frequent discussions about the role of writing in learning. Our object was to build a profile of these three students as writers in a psychology class who were doing the assignments and then collaboratively reflecting on their possible significance. We wanted this case study research to reveal how individual students reacted to the combination of assignments used in the course.

We selected the three students during the first week of class, when all of the students wrote the first poem about schizophrenia and filled out two surveys, the Writing Apprehension Test, developed by John Daly and Michael Miller at the University of Texas and the Writing Attitude Survey, developed by our MTU Research and Evaluation Team. We read these materials and identified students whose poems and survey responses we found interesting. From this group we selected two males and a female who stated that they enjoyed writing and who represented different majors and attitudes. While each of the three said that they enjoyed writing, two thought journal writing was valuable and one that it was a waste of time. Each of the three continued to express divergent opinions and react distinctly to each of the writing assignments in the class. Of primary importance to us, each of the three learned to value the creative writing assignments.

JOHN: Poetry leads to discovery, but essays are for regurgitation.

John is twenty-one years old, an electrical engineering major, mustached, reserved in conversation. He enters the class believing that journals are useful tools and that writing should be done in all classes. He believes in outlines, thesis statements, fixed rules for writing, and knowing precisely what is to be said before touching pen to paper. John likes to write, but feels some nervousness about writing and is a little uncertain about his skill. Although he copies his writing over neatly before turning it in, he is essentially a one-draft writer.

John wrote his final essay of more than 750 words in three hours, his assigned "draft essay" of 600 words in one and a half to two hours, and his short story of 700 words in one and a half to two hours. The only exception to this pattern was the writing of the poem. Here John took several drafts and two hours to write about 100 words in twelve lines. He did at least three major rewrites, each with a separate title: "Voices," "Demons," "Daemons." He discovered both the final title and new implications for his poem by looking up the word "Demon" in the dictionary, a strategy he didn't use for any of the other assignments. Thus, when writing in poetic form, he exhibited the behavior Britton terms *impelled* and Linda Waitkus (1982) refers to as *enticing*—an intense involvement with language and form.

John's Writing Apprehension Test and Student Attitude Sruvey showed little pre- to post-change except for two items. On December 1, John "strongly agreed" that "There are fixed rules that govern all good writing" and "Before beginning to write, I should know precisely what I want to say." On February 17, he "disagreed with qualification" to both statements. In an interview John was asked about this shift and he replied that it had occurred because of the creative writing assignments. In both the short story and the poem he had begun to write without a clear sense of direction, plot or substance. John was quick to point out, however, that the shift on the scale occurred only because of creative writing, that in formal essays he still believed in knowing precisely beforehand what needed to be said, saying it according to fixed rules, and saying it in one draft. This is why he checked "disagree *with qualification*" on the form; it was a considered decision. John felt that both methods of composing produced good writing for him—using precise planning and an outline for formal essays and using speculative, discovery writing for creative assignments. John's interpretation of his own experiences had delineated two separate but equally valuable writing processes that worked for him.

John had never been asked to write a poem in his college career, and only once or twice in high school. He never wrote poetry or stories on his own. However, the journal that he kept for the class contained several entries in poetic and story form, entries of his own devising since the teacher expected prose entries, and indeed the great majority of other students did expressive prose entries. His two papers were traditional in form and substance; they covered what was necessary in coherent beginning-middle-end form. It was clear that John is comfortable with this form and that it works well for him in fulfilling most of the writing tasks he is asked to do in college. (John received two B's and an A in his three quarters of freshman composition.) Both of John's poems are written from the schizophrenic's point of view, the first full of nervous energy, confusion, alienation, grotesqueness. The second, written ten weeks later, is calmer, intellectualized, sympathetic. Perhaps John's comment in his journal on reading as a researcher the writing of his fellow students may be illuminating here:

> In the first writing assignments some writers were somewhat unsympathetic with the disease schizophrenia. These same writers became more sympathetic in the second writing assignments, presumably after they learned more about the disease. It seems *possible* that by putting themselves in the position of being a Schizophrenic in the poems and story they shed prejudices concerning the disease . . . It is my opinion that the poems were valuable in the study of schizophrenia. I do not believe that they were extremely valuable in that they did not require much research into the specific facts of the subject. *However,* they were valuable in that they got me more interested in the

subject, they provided me with introductory facts, and most importantly, they allowed me to get into a schizophrenic's head. The only analogy I can think of is that of an actor who may be so involved in his role that he actually thinks he knows MacArthur personally even though he's never met him. This is a definitive increase in the understanding of the subject.

John provides an instance of the kind of reflection that can occur when students are asked to write in content classes like psychology in a variety of ways—expressively, transactionally, poetically. John feels he learned more about psychology and more about writing by experiencing this approach. However, as we have heard in John's own words, the learning in creative writing is different from the "learning the facts" writing he usually does. John felt the creative writing assignments were more difficult, more interesting, and more worthwhile. Clearly, however, one of the reasons that John viewed the prose essays so unfavorably in comparison was his understanding and use of the essay form. To John, formal essays were formulaic, a place to regurgitate the facts to demonstrate to the teacher that he knew them, a task to get out of the way with as little effort as possible. He had never discovered that some of the experiences he valued in creative writing—discovery, play, surprise, distinct point of view—could be put to use in the writing of an essay.

Consider the introductions to his assignments. He begins his poem "Daemon" with the line "Dreams I have when I'm awake—" and he begins his story with the following paragraph.

> I had been feeling quite strong for several days. In the old days my personal physician used to tell me that I must learn to control my anxieties more, as being so high strung, emotional, and very quick to anger would have some adverse effects on my heart. But that was a long time ago—the 30's to be sure—and I am a very very old man now, and since I had gotten this far with no health problems I tended to shun modern medical advice.

Only later does the reader learn that this schizophrenic person thinks he is Adolph Hitler, a complicating factor because he is being treated by a Jewish bio-medical therapist. Both the beginnings of the poem and story are notable for their quick entrance into a context, the use of the "I" persona, the establishing of reader expectations, and the playing with language and ideas.

Now notice how he begins the two essays he was assigned in this class. The first dealt with bio-medical/environmental issues in schizophrenia, and the second compared bio-medical and humanistic-existential approaches to schizophrenia.

> (First essay) Mark Vonnegut in his book, *The Eden Express,* describes what it is like to have the mental disorder schizophrenia. There were many factors that contributed to the cause of Mark's schizophrenia; some were bio-medical and some were environmental. It is the purpose of this paper to describe some of the factors that caused Mark's schizophrenia and to decide which factors, environmental or bio-medical, were most significant.

(Second essay) In the book, *The Eden Express,* the author, Mark Vonnegut, describes what it is like to become schizophrenic and then return to reality to describe the altered experiences, thoughts, and perceptions that he had. Although there are many different views as to the nature of schizophrenia, namely the cause and cure, this paper will deal with two different approaches to the topic. These approaches are the humanistic-existential approach and the bio-medical approach to the cause and cure of schizophrenia. This paper will attempt to conclude which of these two perspectives is better as applied to Mark Vonnegut's case.

In writing creatively John felt he had numerous alternatives to "play" and be "creative." But when writing an essay, John felt that he had only one alternative, the traditional essay form as he understood and practiced it, almost always with success (a good grade). During an interview, John was asked that if he knew what he wanted to say before he began to write these essays, why he waited to the middle of his papers to give a thesis, that is, inform his reader which factor was most significant or which perspective was better. He couldn't provide us with an answer. He insisted again that he knew exactly what he wanted to say, and that this essay structure was his way of reporting it. During the interview John spoke easily and from memory about the poem he had written three weeks before, but in talking about his final essay he had to stop and reread in order to remind himself of what he had written less than a week before. Thus when John writes about the value of his experience of writing a short story—"This assignment got me more interested in the topic than a non-creative assignment might have"—he is speaking the truth. However, John's truth is based on his belief that poetic writing encourages discovery and imagination and that transactional writing demands formulaic regurgitation of ideas already known to the teacher.

ANDREA: Poetry shows what's inside me, but essays are for the teacher.

Andrea likes to write and feels it is a natural part of her, "like breathing," she says. She wrote stories and poetry when she was a child (her first Girl Scout badge was for writing), and has kept a journal since she began writing one for classes her freshman year. She was her high school valedictorian and is now a junior majoring in mathematics. She maintains a 3.6 grade point average even with involvement in many extra-curricular activities.

Andrea is a classic "good" student. She knows the rules for getting good grades out of her teachers. She does little writing for school, and doesn't like academic writing very much. However, she is successful at it, and sarcastically describes her process for writing a term paper: "You go to the library and take out a whole bunch of books and you copy a paragraph here and a paragraph there and you don't learn anything." This strategy didn't work for the psychology class assignments, and Andrea had a hard time doing some of them. She tried to discover the "rules" for producing what the teacher wanted. When she couldn't, she expressed frustration and apprehension about her work.

Andrea enjoyed writing her first poem. She consulted a dictionary definition of schizophrenia, then produced three drafts for this assignment. With the first, Andrea tried to imagine herself insane. ("Does this hurt my grade, to make it up?" she asked in an interview.) She wrote one stanza, crossed it out and wrote another five stanzas as if she were a hospitalized schizophrenic receiving visitors. She then remembered the old advice to "write about what you know" and decided to write a highly personal piece about a child whose sister has a manic-depressive disorder. Andrea's sister had to be hospitalized when Andrea was ten, but she makes the voice of the poem a 5- or 6-year-old because she thought it would be "cuter." Writing the poem brought back a flood of memories and feelings for her—especially how sad she was that her sister couldn't see her new baby.

Andrea was very conscious of her reader and how the reader might respond to various parts of the poem. When she wrote a distillation of the events that led to her sister's hospitalization, she knew she liked it and she hoped her reader would like it too. With a poem she was "writing to the world so the world can catch a glimpse of the inside of me, and that's the only reason for writing it . . . This poem is different . . . other writing has a beginning, a middle, and an end, and a purpose to writing it." From poetry "they will not learn the facts but they will learn something else."

The second poem assignment was more difficult for Andrea. Whereas the first assignment asked simply for a poem about a schizophrenic, this one had students apply the humanistic-existential perspective to schizophrenia. This threw Andrea for a loop; she understood both the class material and the phenomenon of schizophrenia, but because she didn't have the connection between the two given to her she didn't enjoy writing the poem. She spent "days" on the assignment and produced more pages of draft for this poem than for the first (five instead of two). They are testament to her struggle with the assignment.

The first attempt at the poem was from the perspective of a schizophrenic who had been hospitalized. It didn't get very far before the text dissolved into masses of doodles. Andrea tried to continue the piece on the next page, but after some minor editing, she switched to another piece, a humorous television advertisement for "schiz-o-matic." She began this piece three times and produced, with much revision, two satirical fragments. The first:

Friends,
Are you bored with your present life style?
Are you falling into the same dull routines day after day?
Are you tired of the pressures, demands and competitiveness of the world?
Is the proverbial rat race getting to you?
If the answers to these questions is "yes," hold on to your hat,
because I have an amazing offer for you.
Get a pencil and paper ready because
what I am about to offer you can't be found in any store.
That's right. We are making available to you,

at a very low cost, complete with a limited
10 day moneyback guarantee, an answer
to your problems.

The second:

We are offering you a complete release from all your problems.
Dispense with the rigorous reality of life and lie back in the
luxury of your own imagination. Tired of the same old scenery?
Enjoy yourself with your own personalized hallucination.
Dissatisfied with your present emotions? We'll supply you with a
brand new set, guaranteed to be inappropriate to any occasion.
Life a little dull? Try one of our delusions.
Why be yourself when you can be Napoleon?

Later she told us she "didn't have enough imagination" to finish the piece,
i.e., it didn't convey what she wanted to say. She also didn't think it would satisfy
the assignment. Instead, she copied from Laing: "Schizophrenia is a sane response
to an insane society," and wrote another poem designed to fulfill the assignment.
She recopied it with little revision and handed it in. It lacks the energy and origi-
nality of "Schiz-o-matic." Consider the opening verse:

How can you say I'm crazy?
Just because I'm a little different,
and I don't see things the way
you do,
doesn't mean I'm not okay.

Her poem demonstrates to the instructor that she understood the humanistic-
existential perspective, but Andrea realizes something is lacking. In her survey responses, in her journal, and in conversation she said she didn't like this assignment.
She had to struggle to "come up with something even halfway acceptable"—though
she knew it wouldn't be graded. The assignment wasn't fair, she wrote in her
journal:

How can you write about something that you don't know about? You can't
really. If these assignments are supposed to get us to think more about schizophrenia and to learn something, forget it. All they do is show yourself how
little you really know and offer no way to help you learn it.

During an interview she spoke regretfully of the advertisement she had abandoned.
Andrea had similar difficulties preparing her other writing assignments. With both
the essay draft and the short story, she had trouble beginning, and wrote comments on her rough drafts to the effect that the assignments really weren't fair expectations of her. Her main concern was whether what she wrote was correct and
acceptable to the teacher.

The first draft of her essay is interesting and typical of Andrea—in the first
paragraph she protests that she is *not* a biomedical therapist and has no expertise

in schizophrenia, so how can she write a paper about this subject that is anything other than her "personal opinion"? This paragraph of scolding and apology is followed by her thesis: "Mark's schizophrenia may have been inherited, it may have been a dopamine imbalance, or it may have been a combination of other factors."

The rest of the paper illustrates these ideas. Andrea kept her own voice in the draft by writing things like "I believe" or "I wonder." She concludes with an "I think" section.

Andrea removed much of the personal voice in her revisions to the final draft because she took the teacher's casual suggestion that the paper should be "about two pages long" as an absolute limit. Eventually the paper reduced from six pages to two. In the six pages of draft Andrea moved from saying the assignment was impossible to presenting considerable evidence of biological causes of Mark's illness.

Andrea next had to write a short story. This assignment too produced a crisis for her. She later told us she was very aware of being watched by the researchers and felt that she should do good work. This pressure, in addition to her sense that she couldn't figure out what the teacher wanted, threw her into a "writer's block." She read two chapters on schizophrenia. She drew a Necker cube on her paper, labeled it "writer's block," and drew a box around it. Then she wrote a pep-talk/tirade against the assignment:

> "Ok—this is it. I'm going to write a paper about a biomedical psychologist's treatment of schizophrenia. That I know absolutely nothing about the subject makes no difference. I am going to write, regardless. If it turns out sounding stupid or wrong, I have no one to blame but my own ignorance. Of course, it's my fault that I don't know everything there is to know about schizophrenia even though I'm only in an introductory psychology class."

Finally she went to talk to her teacher. What did he want? She needed to know. The teacher assured her that he wouldn't grade her story critically, that she didn't have to produce brilliance, that she should relax and have fun with the assignment.

Thus assured, Andrea wrote her story. She appeared to be concerned about the craft of her writing when working on creative elements such as plot and character, and less concerned when describing the therapy the patient in the story received. In her final section on treatment, she changes only three words, a remarkable contrast to the earlier story-line writing. Andrea produced accurate, serious material and edited her final paragraph carefully. This draft ends:

> "I pray this was the last I'll see of Mr. David Rhodes: Schizophrenic at large."

The story as turned in reads:

> "I pray that this was the last time I'll see Mr. David Rhodes."

Andrea later told us that once she got started the story came along well. Did she understand the material better after writing it? we asked. "Yeah . . . sort of . . . I don't know . . . *maybe* I know what I'm talking about."

When Andrea wrote her final essay, a synthesis of material she covered in her earlier assignments, she discovered that the earlier assignments "caused me to think more about the topic" than conventional assignments and she wrote in her journal, "I didn't realize that those things were doing me any good until the end." The final paper was "easy to write. I now honestly believe that writing poems, etc., gave me a chance to really explore the subject. I know more about schizophrenia than I thought I could have in this short time." She writes further, "I didn't know it then but I realize it now—as much as I disliked the assignments, the more I was forced to *really think* about the subject . . . I learned more writing this way than if I had just copied my paper out of some encyclopedia."

The essay's conclusion is as follows:

> In my opinion, Mark's schizophrenia was a combination of the two perspectives: leaning more heavily towards bio-medical. Mark had to have had the genetic potential for schizophrenia and all he needed was that little nudge from his environment to push him over the brink.
>
> Obviously the drugs did wonders for him and I don't think he could have made it without them. It was also important for Mark to receive help and understanding from his doctor, family and friends.
>
> Actually, I'm torn between the two perspectives. I honestly don't believe you can have one without the other.

The final sentence calls immediate attention to itself. The rest of the essay followed the pattern established in her first essay. The voice in the essay spoke confidently about issues which she was sure of. The issues were analyzed, the evidence was marshalled, and the resolution was reached. Mark's schizophrenia could be seen as a combination of the humanistic-existential and bio-medical perspectives, but clearly "leaning more heavily towards bio-medical." And then the final unexpected sentence, which concludes the essay with uncertainty.

Andrea begins the discussion of this final essay in an interview by asserting that she is pleased with her paper because "the thoughts were just *really* in order" and it "covers everything Professor Gorman asked us to." When she is asked about the origin and meaning of the final sentence, she admits that this statement of uncertainty "must have just slipped out." However, she is quick to defend this final position: she now believes "there really is no right answer." It becomes apparent that Andrea has wrestled for some time with this issue, and it is an important issue as far as the psychology teacher is concerned because it represents a genuine synthesis and original understanding of important concepts. The teacher had carefully refrained from mentioning such possibilities in class in hopes that students would make some important connections for themselves. Although the final sentence was unsupported and inconsistent with the rest of the paper, it appeared to represent some fresh and important thinking for Andrea. Andrea herself understood this, and in the interview rejects the rest of her paper and stands on the final sentence. "It doesn't matter what I think . . . or the psychologist thinks. It's what Mark, the patient, thinks, and if he thinks the drugs work, then they work."

In an earlier draft of this essay Andrea had written: "more important than *my* opinion, though, is the opinion of the schizophrenic in question. If the schizophrenic believes in genetic causes. . . ." This draft abruptly ended here. Andrea couldn't recall why she didn't pursue this line of thought in her final essay, although talking about it in the interview strengthened her commitment to this perspective, for her an original one. We can only speculate why she didn't pursue this important line of reasoning, but rather let it "slip out" in what might have been an unguarded moment in her otherwise conventional essay. We feel the final sentence did indeed represent confusion and intellectual agitation on Andrea's part. New ideas were clashing with old ideas in ways she hadn't yet resolved for herself. The five days from the time she turned in her essay and the interview, and the experience of *talking* about her ideas with others who were interested in her ideas during the interview, had clarified her thinking and produced commitment and understanding in place of agitation and confusion.

Andrea left the final interview determined to figure out ways to use writing in her math classes when she graduates and becomes a teacher. Whereas she entered this psychology class thinking that the idea of using writing in such classes "was really dumb," she left saying "Now I can see where it might work." We feel that the poetic assignments prevented Andrea from simply regurgitating: she realized that writing can be a process of discovery.

BARRY: Poetry encourages taking risks—even on essays.

Barry is a transfer student from a community college. He believes he got good training in writing during his freshman year, because his freshman English instructor made him write a lot, taught him to form essays and term papers, and was responsive to him as an individual writer. He is now a junior majoring in engineering; his entering ACT verbal score was 17 and his current grade point average at Michigan Tech is 2.11.

Barry took forty-five minutes to write his first poem.

The Voices

The voices started out as fun.
They would come and go when I wanted.
We would talk all day,
and play all night.
They were my friends, my only friends.

The voices became my life.
They would tell me what they wanted to do.
For fear of losing them I would do it.

It was all innocent and fun.
They were my friends, my only friends.

The voices took control of my life.
For fear of hurting the voices I listened.
For fear of rejection I became a slave of the voices.
Those sweet and innocent voices.
They were my friends, my only friends.

The voices said they got bored of me.
I told them not to leave.
But they did.
Leaving an empty shell, that was once a Man.
They were my friends, my only friends.

The voices started out as fun.
Now I don't listen to them.
I don't listen to anything.
Except the stillness of the grave.
They were my friends, my only friends.

In the first stanza the voices are "fun" and the speaker is in control of them. In the second stanza the voices are getting control, and by the third stanza the voices have made the speaker "a slave." In the fourth stanza the voices desert him leaving an "empty shell"; in the final stanza the speaker reflects on the experience from "the grave," after having committed suicide.

Barry's poem came to him while he was listening to Pink Floyd and thinking about John Lennon's death. He had heard that Lennon's killer had been obsessed with voices. He also recalled two other experiences for the poem: the imaginary friends his sister played with as a little girl, and the fact that Mark Vonnegut's schizophrenia had started out as "fun." He read his poem to his roommate who liked it; Barry also likes it and considers it finished—he wouldn't revise it. Barry comments about the experience: "It was different. I enjoyed doing this. In order to write the poem I tried to think like a schizophrenic, to get in the proper mood. I know it wasn't true schizophrenia but this helped me see what *might* go on in their minds."

Barry's second poem, also written while listening to music, is untitled, fifty-six lines long, from the point of view of a schizophrenic who has committed suicide, demonstrates an understanding of the humanistic-existential perspective (the speaker escapes the world of war and pollution to his own little world of love), was fun to write, and was composed in ten minutes. This contrasts with the two other case study students each of whom took two hours or more to write their second poem; but as Barry explained: "I really didn't put too much time into it because the ideas came fairly fast." Both Barry and the teacher were satisfied with the final product: it fulfilled the assignment and was interesting to read. The one noticeable distinction between the first and second poems according to Barry: the first poem caused him to think differently about schizophrenia while the second poem "didn't change my ideas at all." Indeed all the writing assignments after the first poem primarily reinforced what Barry already knew; they didn't change his view of schizophrenia substantially. However, he enjoyed writing them all as different expressions of his views on schizophrenia.

He liked his short story because it gave him "total control over what I could do." This echoes his general feeling about creative writing. As he says in his journal: "In short stories and poems I can have just about anything happen and not really care what the reader thinks, because the author and reader are usually never together." He enjoyed his draft essay, a conventional presentation of the material, because "it made me read into the book more than usual." Barry especially liked the poetic writing assignments ("really made the creative juices flow") and keeping a journal ("journal writing is like talking to myself"). He thinks that he will keep a journal from now on.

Barry's final paper, the single most important writing assignment in the class (worth 10 points instead of 4), is as unconventional as his draft essay was conventional. In this final essay Barry tries an experiment of his own devising: to merge poetic form with transactional purposes. It is a considered decision, as his last journal entry testifies: "But these two different approaches can in some cases come together and form a good paper. For example, my last writing I took and used an interview form but included all the information needed." Barry was the only one in the class to write anything but a conventional essay for the final assignment. His scenario involves a television announcer interviewing two psychotherapists who represent different approaches to schizophrenic treatment. Here is a selection.

ANNOUNCER: What kind of drugs do you prescribe?

DR. HANS: There are many types, antianxiety, antidepressant, or antipsychotic. Each of these classifications are aimed at a specific area of abnormal behavior.

ANNOUNCER: Antipsychotic drugs?

DR. HANS: Yes, these types modify the severe manifestations of psychosis. Antianxiety are essentially tranquilizers. Antidepressants are to lift the mood of a depressed person, also vitamins are used. Besides drugs we also have at our disposal electroshock treatment and psychosurgery. But I deal mostly in the chemotherapy aspect.

ANNOUNCER: Vitamins, what do they do?

DR. HANS: Well they help bring a better physical condition of a schizophrenic and they also help in the chemical imbalance of the schizophrenic.

ANNOUNCER: Thank you. Now Dr. Irving what is the humanistic-existential perspective?

DR. IRVING: Basically we deal with the abnormal behavior that results from a failure to reach or strive one's full potential in life.

ANNOUNCER: Could you clarify that a little so our audience will be able to understand it better?

Barry isn't very verbal in an interview, and while he was clearly pleased with his "different approach," he wasn't able to express the origins and development of the approach. We were interested in why Barry chose to gamble (with his grade, with teacher expectations) and fulfill the assignment with a creative piece rather than the essay form which was assigned. Was he simply adventuresome? Did he believe he wrote better creatively than transactionally? Did he see the situation as a risk or did he feel he had nothing to lose? We weren't able to get any satisfactory answers to these questions. However, when we stopped asking questions for which we wanted answers, and listened to what Barry was telling us, we began to admire his perception and the way his "experiment" began to change our thinking.

We had designed this project with exercises in three categories—expressive, transactional, and poetic writing. We wanted to observe the different uses of each in learning. But Barry crystallized for us our emerging perception, one which grew as we read through the hundreds of student writings, that a crucial problem with school-sponsored writing is that expressive, poetic, and transactional are separated into different categories with the implied assumption that one has nothing to do with the others. This is a lesson that John knew well; he kept his composing processes for poetic and transactional writing distinct. But it's a lesson that Barry asked us to rethink. He suggests that many of the cognitive, imaginative, and language activities we use in writing a poem or story can serve us well when our purpose is transactional ("to get things done"). If many students use Andrea's and John's formulae for writing essays and term papers, then clearly we must look for other ways to assist students in establishing a sense of discovery and a sense of commitment to transactional forms. This is not to say that essays and reports should become plays and poems, but rather that essays and reports should be perceived by students as providing opportunities for original and creative thinking, structural ingenuity, language play, a voice committed to ideas and their expression, and for real communication to an audience (to provide something to the audience it doesn't already know). It is in this sense that regular practice in poetic writing, as well as practice in writing which combines features of expressive and/or poetic writing with transactional writing, may lead to improved transactional writing in the schools. All six of us who read numerous student writings for this class agree: the poems and stories were much more enjoyable and interesting to read than the essays. We are now asking ourselves—must this be so?

The Class as a Whole

After each assignment was handed in, students were asked to fill out a checklist and answer a few questions about the assignment. As we expected, the results demonstrated that students found the various assignments useful or interesting for different reasons. This variety is reflected in how students responded after each assignment to the items on our checklist. We designed it so that it would include items reflecting both positive and negative reactions as well as both transactional and poetic goals. Students could indicate which items pertained to a given assignment by checking as many or as few as they wished. The table below shows responses to four of the checklist statements. The first statement reflects a trans-actional goal; the other three reflect more poetic goals.

Table 1.   Responses to Checklist Items

(Numbers represent percent of the class who checked the response on each assignment.)

	Draft	Short Story	Second Poem	Final Essay
The writing enabled me to organize what I knew into words that will be useful whenever the topic comes up again—on a paper or an exam, or even in conversation with friends.	44	36	27	74
It gave me a chance to think and be semi-creative at the same time.	52	76	71	40
I wrote this assignment from Mark's point of view (or the point of view of a schizo-phrenic): it gave me the opportunity to get inside a schizophrenic's head.	24	23	57	4
It helped me explore my own feelings about sanity and insanity.	48	28	47	38

Responses to the first statement indicate that more of the fifty-five students in the class found the final essay and the draft essay useful for organizing their thoughts for future reference than the short story or the poem. (We refer to the poem as the "second poem" to distinguish it from the poem we assigned early in the course.)

Students believed the short story and the poem allowed them to think and be creative whereas they indicated this less often for the final essay or the draft essay. Note, however, that half the students did feel that they could be thoughtful *and* creative while writing an essay draft, and that this percentage drops to a little over a third of the students for the final essay.

The poem assignment was most effective at getting students to write from a schizophrenic's point of view and to move inside a schizophrenic's head. Over half the students checked this item after writing their poems, whereas less than a quarter checked it after completing the other assignments. About 70% of both the first and second poems were actually written from a schizophrenic's point of view,[3] whereas the essays were mostly dispassionate, third-person accounts.

The poem and the draft essay were more successful than the other assign-ments at getting students to explore their own feelings about sanity and insanity. The draft essay was the first opportunity students had to try to make sense of Mark's experience. The short story, which was done on the same topic as the draft, didn't inspire most students to explore their feelings in a novel way. But the poem, which was written on a different topic, did provide a vehicle for about half the students to explore their own feelings.

This analysis illustrates one of the major problems with interpreting these results. Whether an assignment was poetic or transactional is not the only variable affecting students' responses: the order of the assignments and the specific topics on which they were written are also important factors. We didn't wish to attempt a controlled, experimental study that would have drastically altered the normal course of the class. Instead, we wished to describe what happened when students were asked to write both poems and essays and then interpret this description speculatively.

In summary, students appeared to believe that the draft and final essay helped fulfill the transactional goal of organizing their thoughts in order to communicate them to another person. Supporting this assumption on another checklist item, 62% of the students felt that their draft essay helped them prepare for their final assignment whereas only 29% of the students felt their poem helped them prepare—even though the poem, like the draft essay, was on a topic they had to cover in their final essay. On the other hand, the poem encouraged creativity and helped students understand schizophrenia from the inside. If, as scholars tell us, empathy is an important aspect of moral sensibility, and if decentering is an important part of writing development, such assignments might assist teachers in teaching the values component of the liberal arts as well as writing skills development. Results from the story assigned in this class were more ambiguous because the story was written after an essay on the same topic, and the students' stories were very essay-like in their content.

We also asked the students how they felt about each of the assignments:

	Draft Essay	*Short Story*	*Second Poem*	*Final Essay*
Disliked	6%	16%	6%	8%
Liked	51%	50%	65%	59%
Indifferent	18%	8%	8%	18%
Hard but Useful	8%	19%	19%	10%

Students preferred the poem to the other assignments. More students found the poem and story "hard, but useful" than the other assignments.

A few representative comments students wrote on the open-ended questionnaire we gave them after completing the second poem assignment are quoted below, grouped into two categories.

Perspectives and Understanding

It gave me a new perspective on schizophrenia (to add to the bio-medical case).

I didn't realize until this assignment what Laing really believed.

I feel as though I explored schizophrenia from a new angle, from inside the schizophrenic's head.

I'm finally grasping what schizophrenia might be.

Feelings and Attitudes

By writing a poem, I could express my thoughts very differently than in a paper.

I liked [my poem] enough to feel comfortable reading it to some friends of mine who wanted to know what I wrote.

I enjoy writing the poems best. Not so much pressure and more opportunity to be creative. It seems I can express my true thoughts better in a poem form than in an informative essay.

Students' comments, as represented by these examples, tend to support what they indicated on the checklist. Many students enjoyed the assignment because it allowed them to explore and express their feelings about schizophrenia. The poem also increased students' understanding of the disorder and the psychological perspectives toward it. It helped them explore schizophrenia from the inside. Part of the students' increased understanding stems from the fact that this is the first time they wrote about the humanistic-existential perspective, but part, we feel, comes from the fact that we asked them to write a poem about it. They also wrote about the humanistic-existential perspective in their final essays and this didn't help them understand schizophrenia "from the inside."

We would like to emphasize again that we were not working with humanities students, and that these positive comments about being creative come from technically-oriented students. The student who liked his poem and read it to friends is majoring in biology, the student who believes she expresses her thoughts better in a poem is studying chemical engineering. This last student doesn't write prose well, and produced a fairly poor final essay despite her effort on it. However, she wrote an exciting poem and we're glad she could have an opportunity to express herself in another way, one that she cannot use often at the university. Here is her poem:

> She came in my office
> In yellow from top to bottom
>
> "I dream of macaroni & cheese"
>   she said
> This was her favorite food
> But later
> I concluded that
> What she was really doing
>   was being *that* food
>
> Reality
>   was school
> Bio tests and lab
> Steve the TA
>   gives another quiz,
> "Take me home, Kraft"

What an escape!
   Thin, white and hollow
She puts on her yellow
   sweatshirt
Then on goes the cheese
And all is well

The Students Respond

On the last day of class we gave all of the students an overview of the project, the theory behind assigning various kinds of assignments and some of the tentative results we were finding. The teacher had announced beforehand the plans
for the final day, and he suggested that only students who were interested in hear-
ing the report need attend class. Fifty-seven of the sixty-six students attended and
were good enough to provide us with a written response to our oral report. We
asked each student to comment on their experience with writing in this class, especially now that they had some knowledge about why the teacher thought the writing of poems might help the learning of psychology.

Forty-eight of the 57 students clearly stated that they thought the writing
assignments were valuable, for a variety of reasons. Representative comments are
quoted below:

I think that this theory makes sense. Both types of writing are necessary
to improve writing skills. After I wrote the two poems, I really had a better
grasp of the subject. I could understand a little more how a schizophrenic
would feel and could look at Mark's case from a different angle. The papers
served to analyze facts and bring together ideas logically to a conclusion.
The poems helped bring out the feelings that those facts and ideas represented, allowing a more detailed grasp of the subject.

Impressions of the Writing Project: transactional: this type of writing seems
to bore me and is only completed because it must get done. There is little
interest in the *objective* topic and thus writing quality takes a big dive.
Poetic: this type of writing is rather enjoyable and can lead to interesting
results. Sometimes I will play with the line of a poem I have written for
hours before I find the correct words to express *exactly* what I am feeling.

Writing poems through the eyes of people with problems is a lot of fun. It
gives you a chance to go "crazy" yourself. It provides insight into the lives
of people most shy away from. This is why whenever I must do any writing,
I first try to fit it into a real life situation. I try to make it a story rather
than an account. Not only does this make it more interesting, but it provides
feeling, both for myself and hopefully the reader.

I was not looking forward to doing the two poems but once I got started
they really helped me think about the different aspects of schizophrenia. I

don't think I would have thought of some of the things I did without the poems and the short story. I think they helped me understand the material better.

Conclusions

It seems to us that the results of this study suggest the value of poetic writing in a content course. Students found the poetic assignments particularly valuable for exactly the reasons Britton suggests—poetic writing encouraged them to explore their values and feelings about schizophrenia and permitted them to play with language. But the results also indicate that transactional writing can achieve some of the goals of poetic writing. Barry's case study showed us how a student can integrate poetic and transactional modes. Student reactions to the draft essay showed that it encouraged half of the students to be creative and to explore their feelings.

The poetic/transactional dichotomy may have more to do with the way students are trained. As one student noted,

> But as to the results of your study (poetry = personal, essay = informative, short story = combination) I feel this is because of the way students are trained to regard each of these styles. Essays are formal—you present facts, not opinions. Personal ideas, opinions, etc. *DO NOT BELONG*—no "I," "we"! This is drilled in. So don't expect anything other than the results you received. The same applies to poetry and short stories. Poetry is personal, anything goes.

John is the perfect example of this dichotomy. But Barry—the poorest student—was able to go beyond it, perhaps because he cared less about his grade. Andrea on her final paper was beginning to make a real discovery, but she backed away—you can't make a discovery at the end of a graded final paper because it might lower your grade. If teachers in courses across the curriculum encouraged more exploration (expressive function) and more creativity (poetic function) in transactional essays, students like Andrea might take more risks.

Another student's comment suggested a direction for further research:

> This type of approach to writing seems very useful in learning about certain issues, but I feel that some types of writing just aren't applicable to certain fields. It would be hard to get anything out of a poem written in an Engineering class. Yet I still see the process of doing different types of writing as very valuable. It allows us to get in touch with what it is that makes us different from a computer storage bank.

What would happen if we tried these different kinds of writing assignments in a highly technical class outside of the Humanities or Social Sciences? We suspect they would be useful in learning scientific and technical material as well—but there's only one way to find out.

Notes

1. For a discussion of each scholar's theoretical model, see James Britton, et al., *The Development of Writing Abilities 11–18* (London: Macmillan, 1975); James Moffett, *Teaching the Universe of Discourse* (Boston: Houghton Mifflin, 1968); Frank D'Angelo, *A Conceptual Theory of Rhetoric* (Cambridge, MA: Winthrop, 1975); James Kinneavy, *A Theory of Discourse* (Englewood Cliffs, NJ: Prentice Hall, 1971). For poetic writing in the schools in England see Britton above; in American schools see Arthur M. Applebee, *Writing in the Secondary School* (Urbana, IL: NCTE, 1981); in Australian schools see Christopher Jeffrey, "Teachers' and Students' Perceptions of the Writing Process," *Research in the Teaching of English* 15, (October, 1981) 215–28; in Canadian schools see Merron Chorny, "A Context for Writing," in Freedman and Pringle, eds., *Reinventing the Rhetorical Tradition* (Conway, AR: L&S Books, 1980).

2. For a fuller description of the course *prior* to the introduction of the poetic assignments, see Michael E. Gorman, "Using *The Eden Express* to Teach Introductory Psychology," *Teaching of Psychology*. In Press.

3. The authors gratefully acknowledge the assistance of Polly Ingall in providing this and other information about the poems.

Chapter 11

Writing in Biology

Effects of Peer Critiquing and Analysis of Models on the Quality of Biology Laboratory Reports

ELIZABETH A. FLYNN, GEORGE A. MC CULLEY
and RONALD K. GRATZ

Interdisciplinary collaborative projects designed to measure the effectiveness of techniques introduced at writing-across-the-curriculum workshops are usually initiated by composition specialists. We are the "experts" with an interest in helping workshop alumni transform their courses so that writing becomes an important tool in achieving pedagogical aims. The project we will describe here is perhaps an exception to this rule. It originated with two professors in the Department of Biological Sciences at Michigan Tech, Ronald Gratz and Martha Janners, both of whom came away from the workshops they attended determined to apply the techniques they had been introduced to. They were eager, in particular, to experiment by allowing students to critique drafts of their laboratory reports before submitting them for a grade. Entirely on their own, they introduced peer critiquing into their pedagogical repertoire and decided, as well, to prepare students for their evaluation sessions by having them analyze articles published in professional journals. Their impression was that the approach was very successful. Students, they felt, were producing much better lab reports than had students in previous classes.

They were motivated by a realization that the traditional approach they had been using was unsatisfactory. The lab reports they were receiving were often rambling and disorganized discussions of unassimilated information. In the fall of 1980 they therefore structured a three-quarter sequence in biology (embryology, anatomy, and physiology) to include both peer critiquing and analysis of models. Enrollment in the course was approximately 60–70; students attended a lecture together but were divided into five different lab sections. Both the peer critiquing and the modeling took place during lab sessions. The first two quarters, in both embryology and anatomy, students were introduced to the genre of scientific writing through the analysis of articles published in journals in the field. Initially, Gratz provided a detailed analysis of an article from a scientific journal. The topics of the articles he selected were designed to be of interest to students—turtle urine and frog sexuality, for example. Students were subsequently asked to prepare written critiques of articles they themselves selected and to discuss the critiques in small groups. In their physiology course third quarter, students prepared their own lab reports, received feedback on them in small groups, and revised them before submitting them for a grade.

Both Gratz and Janners had been experimenting with these approaches for a year before we decided to collaborate in order to convert their impressions into hard data. And throughout the two-year period of collaboration that ensued, the biologists were actively involved in the project. They set up the luncheon meetings that resulted in our experimental design; they invited us to their classes to observe their approach; they wrote a small grant that made the evaluation of the data possible; and they selected the graduate students in biology who did the holistic scoring of selected reports. They are now urging us to expand the project.

Gratz and Janners' interest in the experiment was somewhat different from ours. For them, data would be useful as a way of validating what they were already doing in the classroom and suggesting ways of improving their pedagogical techniques. For us, findings would be a contribution to composition research. Although the practice of peer critiquing is well-established in composition pedagogy and has been endorsed by numerous specialists such as James Moffett (1968), Peter Elbow (1973, 1981), Thom Hawkins (1976), and Ken Bruffee (1973), very little research has been done to substantiate the value of the approach. In an investigation of the usefulness of a "collaborative composing methods," which involved free writing, small group response, and revision, John Clifford (1981) found that the method has merit in the composition classroom. Virtually no research, however, has been done to measure the effectiveness of group inquiry in the content classroom. We saw the project as a preliminary investigation of a relatively unexplored field and an opportunity to test assumptions about the usefulness of both peer critiquing and modeling.

Composition specialists argue that the process of peer critiquing, including the drafting of essays before critiquing sessions and the revising of those essays following critiquing sessions, has value because it allows students to use writing as a discovery procedure but also provides them an opportunity to move a piece of writing in the direction of a final product that communicates with an audience. If students prepare drafts of their written work in order to receive feedback from peers they will no doubt write to explore ideas, to formulate tentative hypotheses. Such writing is what James Britton (1975) calls "expressive," writing close to the self, or what Linda Flower (1979) calls "writer-based," writing that makes sense to the writer but has not yet been shaped in such a way that it makes sense to a reader. The draft is a first attempt, a trial run, an opportunity to take risks and make mistakes. The critiquing process itself provides the writer with a friendly audience, one that will point out problems without punishing by assigning a grade. Group critiquing sessions make use of expressive talk; readers attempt to convey their appreciation of or frustration with a piece; writers attempt to explain their meaning. Through the process of communication, writers see ways in which they can clarify their ideas, sharpen their focus, and provide different emphases. Writing moves from solipsistic expression toward readable prose. In addition, critiquing sessions give students an idea of how others have tackled an assigned task. They can place their own attempts in perspective and correct misunderstandings of the assignment or of the material they are writing about.

Having students read and analyze model essays introduces them to the genre of the task at hand. In learning to analyze a piece of writing, students are also learning to write; they are gaining an awareness of what type of writing is expected. James Slevin (1983) argues, for instance, that "we need to promote something like a spirit of 'larceny' in our students, the notion that what they read is filled with techniques they can take for themselves, the way good writers constantly store away strategies for later use. We need to promote the idea that reading itself can enable writing, can answer their needs as writers, can teach them to write" (p. 206). Modeling encourages this spirit of "larceny." Students who are introduced to the genre of scientific writing, for instance, learn that it is modeled on the scientific method and that it necessitates explanations of their findings as well as straight-forward reporting of them.

The Approach

Our first responsibility as collaborators was to become familiar with the ways in which Gratz and Janners were using the techniques they became excited about in the workshops. We therefore visited their classes several times in order to observe: (1) the session in which Gratz introduced students to the technique of analysis of models; (2) the lab session on exercise physiology that we decided would serve as the basis for the lab report we would evaluate for the project; and (3) the critiquing sessions in which students provided each other feedback on drafts of their reports.

The session in which Gratz introduced students to the technique of analysis of models was tightly structured and formal; it lasted about forty minutes. He passed out a copy of an article from the Journal *General and Comparative Endocrinology* called "Pituitary and Testicular Influenced Sexual Behavior in Male Frogs, *Rana pipiens*" [21 (1973), 148-151]. Gratz asked students to read through the article, take notes on it, and try to determine its organizational structure. He then asked students to discuss the function of each of its various parts. Gratz then distributed another copy of the article. This one specified the various sections of the piece and was followed by a handout containing Gratz's own description of the functions of those sections (See Appendix A). His discussion of the particular article was placed within the larger context of the nature of the scientific method. He explained that scientific investigation involves a review of existing knowledge, design of an experiment, the experiment itself, analysis of data, and evaluation of hypotheses. In the analysis of the article itself he paid particular attention to the "Discussion" section, emphasizing that discussion of scientific material necessitates *interpretation* of data in light of theory. The session was very tightly organized and impressively professional.

After Gratz's introduction to the technique of analysis of models, students, over the course of two quarters, analyzed three more journal articles which they themselves selected from journals such as *Ecology, Physiological Zoology,* and *Comparative Biochemistry and Physiology.* They also critiqued their written analyses in small groups.

The Exercise Physiology Laboratory was an especially good one to observe because it involved the active participation of the students. It took place in the University's athletic complex and necessitated that students measure their own "physical working capacity," an indication of physical fitness, by engaging in activities such as running, pumping an exercise bicycle, and climbing up and down steps. The goals of the lab, as expressed in the handout students received in advance of the session itself, were:

1. To understand the physiological principles underlying physical working capacity.
2. To demonstrate the direct measurement of maximal oxygen consumption by a treadmill test.
3. To compare several submaximal tests used to predict maximal oxygen consumption and be able to discuss how and why these tests may differ in the prediction of physical working capacity.
4. To evaluate students' own physical working capacity and compare this with that of a normative group.

Students seemed to enjoy the lab immensely. They performed their activities with enthusiasm, and their desire to learn more about their own capabilities no doubt motivated them to perform their calculations carefully and accurately.

The critiquing sessions we observed surprised us a little in that they were considerably shorter than the sessions we usually hold in our composition classes. Whereas we usually devote an entire class period to evaluation of student papers, Gratz and Janners were constrained by time and could only afford to devote about fifteen minutes to the activity. Nevertheless, students seemed to be enthusiastic about having an opportunity to exchange lab reports before submitting them for a final grade. They shared reports, usually in groups of three, read each other's draft, and then returned the reports to their authors before discussing them. Students wrote down comments on their own reports on the basis of the oral feedback they received during the discussion. They were involved during the sessions, and several made a point of expressing their satisfaction with the approach. One commented that the critiques made more sense in biology than they did in freshman composition because he was receiving feedback from students who were truly his peers. Others indicated that they found the approach to be helpful. The classroom atmosphere was relaxed, informal.

Methods

Our research design was determined by the context within which we were working. It was descriptive rather than rigidly experimental since the pedagogical environment we would be describing had already been established. Our task, as we saw it, was to measure the effectiveness of a project that was well under way without tampering too much with curricula, teaching assignments, or student populations. For instance, we honored Gratz and Janners' request that they not teach reference or control sections that would necessitate their temporarily abandoning the techniques they had discovered in the writing-across-the-curriculum workshops and returning to more traditional methods since they felt that to do so would be to shortchange their students. Their primary concern was the quality of their teaching, not the felicity of our experimental design. Luckily a colleague of theirs was teaching a sequence of courses that was similar in content, although it was a two-quarter rather than a three-quarter sequence. He had never attended a writing-across-the-curriculum workshop and employed traditional methods in preparing his students for their lab reports, i.e., he provided students guidelines for writing their reports, but he provided no opportunity for additional assistance. He was quite willing to allow us to use his students' reports as a reference.

Our research was carried out in two phases. We first wanted to compare Gratz and Janners' students' reports with those written by students enrolled in their colleague's sections. But we decided, as well, to refine our approach the following year by creating two different treatment groups to try to distinguish between the effects of peer critiquing and analysis of models. Our final design, therefore, involved a comparison of scores on exercise physiology lab reports of four groups of students, all of whom were sophomore biology majors. We eliminated from the sample students who were not sophomores or students who were majoring in fields other than biology; the final sample was composed of a total of 140 lab reports. The four groups of students were as follows:

1. A reference group composed of 35 students enrolled in a two-quarter sequence in biology in 1980–81 taught by a professor who had never attended a writing-across-the-curriculum workshop and who prepared his students for their reports in a traditional way—by providing them with an outline of the expected report format but no additional guidance.
2. A treatment group composed of 34 students enrolled in a three-quarter sequence in biology in 1980–81 taught by both Gratz and Janners who prepared their students, as described above, through the use of peer critiquing and analysis of models.
3. A treatment group composed of 27 students enrolled in a three-quarter sequence in biology in 1981–82 taught by Gratz and Janners who prepared their students using only modeling.
4. A treatment group composed of 44 students enrolled in a two-quarter biology sequence in 1981–82 taught by Gratz who prepared his students using only peer critiquing. This was the same sequence of courses that had been

taught the previous year by the faculty member who had not attended a writing-across-the-curriculum workshop.

The design was not ideal in that it necessitated a comparison of different students in different course sequences taught by professors in two different years. In addition, when we compared the mean university grade point averages among the four groups, we found some statistically significant differences between pairs of means. We found differences between the reference group and the groups that were introduced only to modeling and to peer critiquing, but we found no significant differences between the reference group and the group introduced to both peer critiquing and modeling. Mean grade point averages for both the modeling and the peer critiquing group were higher than that of the reference group. This information had to be considered when we interpreted our results. (See discussion of "Results" below.)

The groups were comparable in other ways, though. Students in all four groups wrote their reports on the same laboratory, Exercise Physiology, received identical guidelines for the preparation of the report, and participated in identical lab sessions. Gratz prepared the groups that were introduced to analysis of models in the same way. In addition, we have reason to believe that the instructor of the reference sections was as conscientious as the instructor of the treatment sections since he has a reputation for being an excellent teacher and was a recipient of the University's outstanding teaching award.

Gratz and Janners were very much involved in the evaluation process. They helped in the preparation of the scoring guide used in the holistic scoring (See Appendix B), and Gratz was present during the session in which two graduate students in biology were trained to score the reports.

In the fall of 1982 we collected photocopies of all of the completed lab reports, from which identifying information, teacher comments, and grades had been removed, numerically coded them, and then randomly mixed them. Students had signed permission slips indicating their willingness to have their reports used for research purposes. We also had available to us lab reports from previous years that we used in establishing our initial guidelines for evaluation. Gratz and Janners ranked these sample reports on a four-point scale, with four the highest and one the lowest. After ranking was completed, we read through the reports, trying to identify features that indicated levels of proficiency, and then developed a scoring guide for the reports. Once that was constructed, we again asked Gratz and Janners to assess the guide by using it to evaluate additional sample reports from previous years. We incorporated their suggestions into the final guide.

The training session itself went remarkably well. Gratz introduced us to the two graduate students he had selected for the intensive session. Neither had had experience conducting the Exercise Physiology Lab upon which the reports were based, nor had they assisted the students who comprised our sample. Mc Culley then reviewed the scoring guide with them and asked them to practice by scoring independently a set of ten sample lab reports. They did quite well. They agreed on nine of the ten sample reports, and the two scores for the other report were only one point apart. They then began the actual evaluation—a marathon that lasted two full days—16 hours. Despite the intensity of the sessions, the raters agreed or came within one point of each other 96% of the time.

Results

The scores for all three treatment groups were higher than the scores for the reference group. The scores for the group that was introduced only to modeling were higher than the scores for the groups that were introduced to peer critiquing exclusively or to modeling plus peer critiquing. Table 1 illustrates these results.

Table 1. Mean Ratings for the Four Teaching Strategies

	Peer Critiquing	*Modeling*	*Peer Critiquing and Modeling*	*Reference*
Mean	4.23	4.93	4.09	3.03
Standard Deviation	.89	1.44	1.26	.82
Number of Sophomore Biology Majors	44	27	34	35

Note: Means are based on the sum of the two raters' assessments. Scores ranged from 1–4 with four the highest and one the lowest.

An Analysis-of-Variance indicated that the difference between the means of the scores for the four groups was statistically significant ($F(3,136) = 16.27$, $p < .001$); i.e., we would expect such a difference to occur by chance less than one time in a thousand. These findings suggested that all three of the treatments had a positive effect on the quality of the reports produced. We realized that we could not make this claim, however, unless we established that the groups were of comparable abilities.

Unfortunately, when we ran an Analysis-of-Variance on grade point average data we discovered that there was significant variation among the groups ($F(3,141) = 12.8$, $p < .001$).

The Duncan Multiple Range Test determined that there was a significant difference between the mean grade point average of the reference group and the peer critiquing group. It also determined that there was a significant difference between the mean grade point average of the reference group and the group exposed only to modeling. The test also determined, though, that there was no significant difference between the mean grade point average of the reference group and the group exposed to both peer critiquing and modeling. Table 2 illustrates these results.

It would seem, then, that the treatment of peer critiquing and modeling combined did have an effect on the quality of the reports produced.

Table 2 : Mean Ratings for the Grade Point Averages of the Four Groups

	Peer Critiquing	Modeling	Peer Critiquing and Modeling	Reference
Mean	2.83	2.95	2.66	2.51
Standard Deviation	.49	.62	.61	.50
Number of Sophomore Biology Majors	41	30	43	30

Note: Grade point averages are based on a grading system in which A is awarded four grade points per credit and F is awarded no grade points per credit.

Discussion

Our results suggest that techniques such as peer critiquing and analysis of models may be helpful in the preparation of lab reports and that further investigation of these approaches in courses other than composition would be worthwhile. It is certainly useful to speculate on why the scores for the group introduced to both peer critiquing and modeling may have been higher than the scores for the reference group.

We can surmise that students who were prepared for their lab reports in a traditional way were less aware of the function of the various parts of a research report than were the students introduced to peer critiquing and modeling. We can also surmise that their reports did not undergo extensive revision. The traditional approach places an enormous burden on the student since it assumes that a set of instructions and a brief explanation of an assignment are sufficient preparation for the activity of writing about a scientific procedure. The traditional approach emphasizes the product and elides the process. Students, some of whom have perhaps never seen a scientific article or written a laboratory report, are expected to perform the sophisticated cognitive activity of accounting for observed phenomena. Often their approach is to prepare hurriedly a single draft and submit it for a grade. What professors often receive, then, are essentially expressive, writer-based writings—descriptive accounts of undigested material.

Gratz and Janners undertook the study because they had the strong impression that the reports they received after introducing students to both peer critiquing and modeling were considerably better than those they received using traditional methods of preparation. Students were submitting reports that were better organized, provided better discussion of the data gathered during the lab sessions, and contained fewer presentations of unassimilated information. They were "doing" better biology. Both Gratz and Janners also felt that students in subsequent courses retained their understanding of the scientific method and of the components of a lab report and that the quality of the lab reports they produced remained high. Their impressions lent credence to the empirical data.

The lab report of a member of the group introduced to both peer critiquing and modeling—the group that received a higher mean score than the reference group but had a comparable mean grade point average—will illustrate effective interpretation of research data. We would like to think that the method of preparation she received contributed to the high quality of her report. The student was given the highest rating, 4, by both evaluators. Her report was ten pages long, well-organized, and clearly written. She demonstrated an understanding of the conventions of scientific writing, and she analyzed her findings thoroughly. It would seem that her exposure to scientific writing through modeling and peer critiquing allowed her to internalize the conventions of the genre. At the end of her introduction she provided a clear statement of the purpose of her report. After describing the step test, the bicycle test, and the "run," she explained:

> The values of each test will be compared with the average values shown on Table 3. Since heart rate is a relatively accurate measure of a person's PWC (Physical Working Capacity), and because PWC can be standardized and compared (de Vries, 1966), undertaking this experiment will show where the individual is lacking and can improve her PWC, and why it may vary with the different tests.

The student's descriptions of her methods and materials and her results were clear, and her discussion was fully developed. After stating that her performance on the three tests was average, she gave some possible explanations for her performance: she was "out of shape," her muscle endurance was low, and she was overweight. At the same time, however, her high motivation kept her from performing below average. The student then discussed ways in which she could improve her Physical Working Capacity:

> A large number of factors could definitely improve PWC, but they all can be categorized into a few subunits to take into account the enormous mass of improvements which can be considered. First, and most important, the only way improvement can occur is if the body, being maintained at a steady state, is challenged (de Vries, 1966). Any challenge, whether it be increasing the strength of endurance of muscles, increasing cardiac output or stroke volume, causes the steady state to shift to accommodate for the shift in the position of greater PWC. If this stress is maintained by enough *repetition,* a second requirement to increase PWC and related areas of fitness, the steady state will automatically change to adjust to this continuous change. Also, and just as important, the stresses or challenges imposed on the body should be incremental (deVries, 1966). They should still be a challenge to the body, but not with such tremendous magnitude at one time to cause damage to the body, for the person would be more than defeating his purpose to attain fitness with respect to PWC.

The student demonstrates an understanding of the implications of her findings and an ability to relate her results to relevant theory. The tone is objective and "scientific," though it is clear that the information the student is imparting has meaning on a personal level. After learning that her Physical Working Capacity is only normal, she is attempting to figure out what to do about it.

The preparation received, analysis of models and peer critiquing, no doubt helped to ready her to complete her laboratory assignment successfully. We can't distinguish between the effects of the two treatments, though, because she was introduced to both before writing her report. Presumably, both procedures were enabling.[1]

Collaborative projects that aim to describe what is already being done in the content classroom have the disadvantage of all descriptive research—a situation that can't easily be controlled. The involvement of the biologists—surely the greatest strength of the project—sometimes presented problems, for instance. In retrospect we realize that we probably shouldn't have asked them to help with the construction of the scoring guide since their biases may have been reflected in the guide and hence their input may have affected the scoring process in an indirect way. Our sense, though, is that this didn't seriously affect the outcomes. We now realize too that we should have cautioned our collaborators against removing the names on the laboratory reports too hastily. After the scoring had been done and we recognized that it would be useful to apply the statistical technique of Analysis-of-Covariance to the data as a way of compensating for the differences in grade point averages between groups, we discovered that we couldn't in most cases recover the names of the writers and so couldn't match scores on reports with grade point averages or scores on the American College Test. This also caused problems when we attempted to determine the mean grade point averages of the four groups, hence the discrepancy between the number of students listed in Table 1 and the number listed in Table 2. In collaborating with such enthusiastic colleagues, we lost a degree of control over the study.

In general, though, we were pleased with the results of our collaborative project. We saw it as an opportunity to continue the conversation we had begun at the workshops themselves, and we had an opportunity to see the techniques we were advocating actually being applied in a setting quite different from our composition classrooms. We were pleased, for instance, to see that peer critiquing and modeling could be used successfully in large classes, and we were delighted to discover that primary trait scoring can be used in the assessment of writing assignments as unwieldy as a ten-page laboratory report. Collaborative projects that involve composition specialists and content faculty can sometimes be productively and creatively imperfect.

Notes

1. Students who were introduced to both analysis of models and peer critiquing seemed to prefer analysis of models. When asked to rate the two approaches on a scale of 1–5 with 1 the most useful and 5 the least useful, students assigned analysis of models a mean score of 2.58 and peer critiquing a mean score of 3.07. If attitude is an indicator of effect, then it may be that analysis of models had a greater impact than peer critiquing on the writing of students introduced to both.

Appendix A

Analysis of "Pituitary and Testicular Influenced Sexual Behavior in Male Frogs, *Rana pipiens*"

Prepared by Ronald K. Gratz

A. Title:

A statement of what has been measured and the subject (species) used.

This is better than a more general title such as:
"Sex in Frogs" or
"Hormonal Effect on Frog Sexual Behavior"

Note also, the full names and professional addresses of the investigators are given.

B. Abstract:

A concise summary of
  a. what was done
  b. what was found (results)
  c. brief statement of conclusions

C. Introduction:

Note: in many journals, the word "Introduction" heads this area.

1. Introductory sentence. States a reason for doing the study.

2. Review of literature: A short synopsis of findings of other scientists working in the field.

3. Introduces the present study. Sets the stage for what was done and gives some hint as to results. *Note:* The closing paragraph can take on many forms depending on the nature of the study but should generally lead into the study that was done.

D. Materials and Methods:

4. The species used and where and when they were obtained are given first.

5. This section states how the animals were maintained for the study.

6. and 7. Two different sets of experiments were performed. Each is given separate treatment. Note that details of drug dosage, number of animals used, and the exact procedures are given. *Note:* If these details were used in an earlier study or are standard, published techniques, this detailed summary would be replaced by a brief statement and references.

E. Results:

Present the data collected in the experiments that were performed.

8. Data Table. Note the details given in the title: kinds of hormones, affect on amplexus, species used. A Table should be able to stand by itself, i.e., without the text. Note also that units are given where applicable [Daily Dose (mg)].

9. Figure. Again, the title is detailed although the species was not given (it would have been better to state the species name here too). An author must decide whether his/her data is best presented as a table or a graph.

10. and 12. A concise statement of the general results with a reference to the supporting data in the figure or table.

11. and 13. These sections point out the details of the results shown in the table and graph. Note that the table and graph are *not* restated here, rather the significant trends they show are pointed out. Also, note that there is no attempt made at discussing the data here.

F. Discussion:

Interpreting the data in light of theory.

14. A strong statement of a conclusion of the study.

15. Further conclusions—and questions—based on the results.

16. Here the authors discuss the results in comparison to other similar studies.

17. Here the authors interpret their results in light of what is known about the stimuli needed for sexual behavior in frogs. Again, published literature is cited where appropriate.

G. References:

An alphabetical list of citations used. Note that most biological journals do *not* use footnotes for citations but rather refer to a book or paper in the text via author and date (e.g., Jones, 1981) and then give the full citation at the end of the paper. Also be aware that different journals have slight variations in the format of the citation.

Appendix B

Biology Lab Report Scoring Guide

Primary Trait: Quality—that is, acceptable presentation of the experimental problem and purpose, methodology, results, discussion which relates to purpose, and conclusions based on results.

Rationale: In order to communicate well the results of biological laboratory experiments, researchers must present these experiments in a tightly organized, lucid report that follows the accepted format of such reports.

General Criteria: A completely successful report will fully develop all essential sections of a standard biological laboratory report. The report will be written in clear, concise language and will integrate graphics (figures and tables) when necessary without redundancy. The entire report, including references and citations, will follow the standard conventions of contemporary English and the appropriate style manual (e.g., CBE).

The reports will be evaluated in reference to the following four-point scale (4, the highest; 1, the lowest).

4 — A report receiving a score of four will contain all of the following sections, each of which must also contain fully developed sub-sections:

1. Abstract
   a. a statement of hypothesis or purpose
   b. a statement of results
   c. a statement of conclusions

2. Introduction
   a. an established context for the research, developed by citing background literature.
   b. statement of purpose—a reason for conducting the experiment.

(*Note:* The purpose of the experiment may have been to describe the subject's Physical Working Capacity [PWC] and/or to compare methods for estimating PWC.)

3. Methodology
   a. a complete description of the methodology used, or
   b. a reference to the source of the methodology, with any variances in procedures described. Future researchers must be able to replicate the experiment exactly after reading this section.

4. Results
   a. a description of trends present in the results that is evidenced by experimental data in either:
      1. tables and figures or
      2. in the prose.

b. data presentation is clear, neat, with no redundancy; all data is presented in correct units and figures.

5. Discussion and Conclusions
   a. a relevant theory (ies) is discussed
   b. relevant theory is related to results;
   c. based on the above relationship, a statement of conclusion is made.

6. References
   a. all necessary citations will be made in the correct style format—that is, statements or assertions that are clearly not the researcher's are properly cited in the text;
   b. a reference list, including all references cited in the text, will follow on the last page and will consistently use the chosen style format.

In addition, a "4" report will have few, if any, grammatical or spelling errors.

3 — A "3" report will differ from a "4" report in each section in the following ways:

1. Abstract
   a. The hypothesis, or purpose, is not clearly stated nor strongly implied. Results and conclusions, however, are clearly present.

2. Introduction
   a. Background literature is not completely cited to establish the context for the experiment. In other words, a context for the experiment is attempted, but only one or two citations are used, leaving the context incomplete.
   b. The experimental purpose is only strongly implied, not explicitly stated.

3. Methodology
   a. The description of the methodology is vague and hazy. It may be complete, but it is difficult to understand.
   b. If just a reference to the methodology is used, the reference is complete but the description of variances is confusing—that is, it would be difficult to replicate the experiment because the variances are not completely understood.

4. Results
   a. Trends in the data are only implied, not explicitly stated.
   b. Data presentation—whether in tables, figures, or prose—is made with correct units and figures, but it is not completely clear and requires at least a "second look" in order to understand it.

5. Discussion and Conclusions
   a. The discussion of relevant theory is brief and superficial.
   b. The relevant theory is related to the results, but the connection is not clear.

   c. A conclusion is present but only vaguely related to the results.

6. References

   a. Most necessary citations are made but not all.

   b. The reference list appears complete but the style is inconsistent.

In addition, there may be more grammatical and spelling errors than in a "4" report, but these errors still do not seriously detract from the report.

2 — A "2" report will differ from a "3" report in each section in the ways described below:

1. Abstract

   a. There is *not* a hypothesis or purpose, either strongly implied or stated.

   b. Results and conclusions are present but not clearly stated.

2. Introduction

   a. Background literature is tersely reviewed and little attempt is made to establish a context for the experiment. Few, if any, citations are used.

   b. The experimental purpose is not clear. An attempt is made to establish it, but it is not related to the context.

3. Methodology

   a. No description of the methodology is present.

   b. A reference to the methodology is made, but potential variances in procedures are not described or acknowledged. Replication is not possible.

4. Results

   a. It is not possible to tell whether trends in the data exist or not.

   b. Data presentation *is* made with correct units and figures, but the method of presentation—whether in tables, figures, or prose—is loosely organized and hard to interpret. Indeed, interpretation may not be possible even after careful scrutiny.

5. Discussion and Conclusions

   a. The discussion of relevant theory is present but brief, and it is difficult to relate the discussion to the present experiment.

   b. The theory is not related to the results.

   c. A conclusion is present but not related to the results.

(*Note:* A "hallmark" of the difference between "2" and "3" papers is that "2" papers do not relate results to theory.)

6. References

   a. Few, if any, citations are used.

   b. The reference list is brief and the style is not consistent.

In addition, there are several grammatical and spelling errors that do seriously detract from some sections of the report.

1 — A "1" paper differs from a "2" paper in the following ways:

1. Abstract
   a. There is not a hypothesis or purpose. Either the results or conclusions are not present and if both are present, they are not related to each other. In short, the abstract is nothing more than a brief description of the experiment.

2. Introduction
   a. There is definitely not a context established for the experiment, only a rambling description of the experiment.
   b. There is no experimental purpose established.

3. Methodology
   a. A reference to the source of the methodology is presented, but no reason for the reference is given—that is, even with the attempted reference, it would not be possible to locate its source and replicate the experiment.

4. Results
   a. No discussion of trends is made.
   b. Data presentation is unclear and may use incorrect figures or units. In short, interpretation of the data is *not* possible.

5. Discussion and Conclusions
   a. The discussion of relevant theory, if any, is not related to the present experiment.
   b. The theory is not related to results.
   c. The conclusion, if any, is not related to the results.

6. References
   a. No citations in the text are made.
   b. References do not follow any standardized format.

Finally, there are many grammatical and spelling errors throughout the report that give the entire report an aura of being hastily conceived and written.

In summary, the preceding score points in this guide can be summarized as such:

4 — An exemplary lab report.

3 — A good lab report with errors, but no substantial revision is needed.

2 — An inadequate lab report with the essential elements present, but requiring extensive revision in order to be considered adequate.

1 — A completely inadequate report, missing many essential components.

Chapter 12

The Laboratory Reports of Engineering Students

A Case Study

JAMES R. KALMBACH

As teachers at a technical institution, we have long suspected that the majority of the writing our engineering students did was laboratory reports. We also knew that the students didn't particularly value these reports. When we asked seniors about the writing they had done at MTU, they would mention freshman composition, humanities courses, technical writing perhaps, but would rarely include lab reports unless we prodded them. We saw over and over again a gap between the writing we thought they did and the writing they valued. This gap, if real, would represent a serious challenge to the concept of writing across the curriculum. In their introduction to *Language Connections* (1982), Toby Fulwiler and Art Young establish a lofty goal for cross-curricular writing programs:

> Given that writing has several functions, teachers in all disciplines can provide opportunities for individuals to explore through writing their relationship to knowledge, articulate it, and scrutinize its value. When students begin to understand and appreciate the full potential of written language, their respect for the conventions of writing well increases (p. x).

But if lab reports aren't particularly valued by engineering students, it would suggest that a large number of their writing assignments did not, in fact, lead them "to understand and appreciate the full potential of written language."

To find out what kind of writing engineering students were doing, John Flynn, Toby Fulwiler, Art Young and I decided to do a small descriptive case study of the writing of a group of Michigan Tech seniors, and to investigate the relationship between their college writing tasks and their attitudes towards writing.[1]

To collect our data, we contacted a group of randomly chosen graduating seniors and asked them if they had kept *all* the writing they had done in their four

176

or more years at Michigan Tech. If they had, were they willing to let us photocopy the papers, fill out a questionnaire, and receive $25 for their effort?

We soon learned that our data collecting procedures had a number of problems. Students proved difficult to contact and accidental gaps (papers they forgot about or never got back) proved unavoidable. Nevertheless, we were able to collect a large body of data quickly and fairly efficiently. In all, we collected twelve portfolios from students in engineering, forestry, liberal arts, and scientific and technical communications. As we examined the portfolios further, we found that five from engineering seemed particularly complete and reliable, so we decided to focus our analysis on them.

The five portfolios included 213 separate papers. Table 1 displays the number of papers written for each of our five engineering students in their various courses. We chose number of papers written as the most usable statistic—when no papers are written, no opportunity exists to explore knowledge through writing.

Table 1. A Summary of the Number of Papers Written by Five Engineering Students During Their Four Years at Michigan Tech.

Student	Major	Freshman Composition	Other Humanities*	Lab Reports	Others**	Total
#1	CE	2 (.08)	0	21 (.84)	2 (.08)	25
#2	EE	13 (.39)	4 (.12)	16 (.48)	0	33
#3	EE	14 (.38)	8 (.22)	12 (.33)	1 (.03)	36
#4	ME	11 (.20)	15 (.28)	21 (.40)	5 (.09)	53
#5	ME	21 (.32)	2 (.03)	43 (.65)	0	66
Average # of Papers		12.4 (.29)	5.8 (.14)	22.6 (.53)	1.6 (.04)	42.6

*Includes foreign languages, philosophy, literature, and technical writing.
**Mostly social science.

We found, as we expected, that 53% of these students' writing opportunities were reports for laboratory classes. To discover the students' perception of the relative significance of these writing opportunities, we asked them to rank-order the following activities: class discussions, examinations, lab experiments, papers and reports, and reading according to how important they felt each was to the development of their thinking and reasoning abilities and then to comment on each. We found that the students ranked lab experiments as the most valuable of the five activities and papers and reports as the least valuable.

That lab experiments were the most highly rated was not surprising. These were engineering students, and many of their labs were in courses that were central to their professional development. The students valued labs because:

> (They are) a real life application of theory and require in-depth thought and reasoning.

> (Labs) help the most because you have your hands on, and you make mistakes. Correcting the mistakes helps a lot.

> Lab experience is important. I can visualize a concept and therefore understand it more fully. I learn a lot by doing things.

Engineers work at the nexus of theory and practice—they take concepts from math, physics, biology, chemistry and develop real world applications. For engineering students, lab work provides contact between what they're learning in the classroom and how it will really work in the field.

While the fact that engineering students valued laboratory work most highly wasn't surprising, that they valued papers and reports the least was. I've always found writing to be a useful activity for taking ideas and putting them into practice. Indeed, those students who ranked writing highly seemed to be focusing on the value of writing as problem solving:

> First and foremost, doing papers and reports put thought into action—giving real experience in thinking and researching.

More typically, however, these engineering students ranked writing last or next to last, saying that it did help them organize their thoughts or making no comment or saying as one did:

> Reading and writing reports and papers have not been significant learning experiences for me, though I did much of both.

Our data appeared to support our intuitions. Over half of the writing opportunities engineering students had were laboratory reports, but lab reports (and papers) were the educational experience they thought contributed the least to the development of their thinking abilities.

To discover why doing laboratory work was highly valued but writing lab reports was not, I pulled the 113 lab reports in our corpus and read through them. Although I've never had a college engineering course, I quickly found that I could follow almost all of the labs. Procedures, results and discussions were clear and readable. These five students had mastered the art of precise technical reporting. It was a valuable skill, one that would serve them well on the job. The reports were, in essence, formalized narratives of the experience of doing the lab, and, as with any narrative, they communicated the student narrator's understanding of the experience. Although I didn't know the technical vocabulary, I found it relatively easy to follow their understanding of the lab.

The laboratory reports I read varied a good deal in form and complexity, from a couple pages of calculations in a freshman physics course to a seven-page typed report in a senior mechanical engineering class, but *all* of the reports followed a single format:

> purpose statement
> equipment
> procedures

data

analysis

discussion/conclusions

The simplest lab report would have only a purpose statement and calculations, or calculations and a brief conclusion. Only the most complex report contained all of these elements. The most common form was a purpose statement (usually lifted from the assignment sheet), a description of the procedures, the data and conclusions. In only a few classes were there any variations to this format, and all the variations consisted of unique sections added to the standard report. In a few classes, for example, students were required to summarize their findings in the beginning of the report. In another class, they were required to write a section on the engineering applications they saw for the lab:

Engineering Applications

When designing retaining walls the results from the direct shear test are important. When there is more lateral strength in the ground [a] larger retaining wall can be built.

Similarly, in a metallurgy class, the teacher apparently urged the students to use the discussion section of their report to write about what they learned in the lab, leading to this comment:

In a very short time (i.e. 20 minutes) I gained a lot of respect for technology. Standing in the lab, looking at a television screen, I watched in 'awe' as the microscope scanned the surface revealing remarkable facts about the specimen's topography and chemistry.

Such sections, however, were the exception, not the rule, and as I read over these lab reports, I began to see that the report form itself wasn't the problem. The reports were clear and readable. After reading, however, I was almost always left with a nagging question: "So what?" The significance of the lab was rarely clear to me as a reader outside of the class. How did what students learn in a lab apply to what they would do as engineers in the field? While I could understand what students did and found, I could rarely find any indication by the students that they understood *why* they would use a similar apparatus or procedure at work, and *what* they would do with their results once they had them. (It may be that this knowledge was implied and understood by the teachers and students in these engineering classes, but I suspect otherwise.) In short, for these five students, I believe report writing was primarily an exercise, isolated from any sort of meaningful problem-solving context. This isn't to say that the students didn't know why they would use a procedure, or what they would do with the results afterwards, but rather that *the report itself* didn't reflect a knowledge of these applications. The writing of the report was isolated from the contexts in which the content of the report would be used. Krowne and Covington, after surveying a group of technical students, noted a similar problem: "Students have been technically indoctrinated but they don't know much about the way they will be called on to perform on the job." They go on to suggest that engineering classes should assign reports modeled after the professional engineering report, as well as reports that follow the traditional format found in the data here.

The effects of isolating reports from a meaningful problem-solving context could be seen most dramatically in the section of the reports labeled "Conclusions." In general, students were supposed to use this section to decide whether or not observed data fit expected data and if not to speculate on possible sources of error. Students could be quite creative when searching for reasons why a lab failed. One student attempted to blame the instructor:

> I would like to say that I think the main reason for this human error is due to a severe lack of communication between the instructor and students. I think the instructor should try to explain a little better exactly how such an experiment should be conducted . . .

The instructor, however, refused to accept responsibility and instead responded:

> Your complaint is absolutely ridiculous since you have not approached the instructor with any of your so-called problems. If you do not understand something, it is your responsibility to see that you ask questions.

Comparing observed to expected data did not, however, leave most students much to conclude, given the time and energy they have invested in doing the lab, and they frequently used the conclusion section for a variety of other comments. They sometimes commented on the design of the lab:

> This lab is designed well. The set-up in the laboratory is such that experimental error can be minimized. With this in mind the student is forced to analyze his data reduction technique to explain why the values experimentally determined don't coincide with minimum error to those predicted analytically. Consequently the student realizes the 'subjectiveness' in evaluating dT/dt at some given surface temperature.

or the nature of the data:

> Analysis of the results in Table 1.0 shows the results by all methods to be very compatible. This was a surprise! These results demonstrate that certain assumptions can be made without introducing significant error into the results.

or the usefulness of a procedure:

> Possessing these graphic interpretations could be very useful to an engineer. For with them he can choose a pump and/or flow rate to meet his economical and/or physical requirements.

or on the educational value of the lab:

> This lab was valuable in the respect that the student wasn't 'overwhelmed.'

This lab contained an adequate amount of exposure for the first lab. I thought this was a good idea and not a waste of time.

While such commentary may be useful to both student and teacher, the variety of different topics addressed in "Conclusions" sections reflects a lack of understanding by these students of the purpose for lab reports. The "Conclusions" section is a good place for a student to discuss the issues raised by questions such as *So what? Why?* and *What* other applications outside of the lab might these results have? Perhaps teachers could encourage personal commentary in a lab notebook or in a covering memo attached to the report while at the same time providing students with a problematic context which would require them to arrive at a real conclusion in a formal report. Both kinds of writing are important learning tools—the informal writing that explores the individual's relationship to new knowledge and the formal writing which seeks to communicate significance as well as results.

In a civil engineering lab, for example, students were asked to compare five clean samples of water using various techniques and to decide which was the clearest water. The student in my sample was thus forced to write a conclusion:

When comparing one sample with another for environmental purposes, it is obvious that the distilled water is the cleanest, purest and best water for anything. After that I would highly rate Lou's well for drinking and residential areas. The ??? water is very mysterious because it looks and smells like water, but is definitely not water. Finally, the sewage and sludge should not be environmentally acceptable.

It isn't, to be sure, a particularly well-written conclusion, but it is a conclusion; it's the solution to a problem. The student has to compare a set of data to a set of values (about cleanliness in water) and make a decision as to which sample of water is cleanest. The writing of this conclusion was both an act of discovery and and act of commitment. I suspect that through many such small interactions of values and knowledge engineering students come to see the potential of writing as a tool to discover and communicate ideas.

The students in this case study apparently didn't value lab reports because their reports were written without any meaningful context. They reported procedures and results but didn't have to use those results in any sort of problem-solving. As a result, lab report writing, but not the labs themselves, was isolated from meaningful engineering experiences.

But while these students may not see writing as having played an important role in their education, they did see the value of writing as an activity:

As far as my engineering thinking and reasoning ability is concerned, I can truthfully say that writing played an insignificant role. The writing I did (even in Technical Report Writing) basically improved my thinking and reasoning ability of human affairs, e.g., ethics, myself, movies.

> Writing actually helps very little to my thinking and reasoning ability, solving problems helps more. However, to write something does require much thinking. But with me, I've written in a practice-makes-perfect style.

It would appear that this small sample of technical students left MTU valuing writing, but not valuing writing as a way to do better engineering. They understood the value and importance of communication skills, but they didn't appear to see the connections between writing and engineering. And to us at Michigan Tech this was the most important finding in the study.

Evidence collected by our research team indicates that the writing-across-the-curriculum program at MTU has been a success. The word from employers, recruiters, and teachers is that students are communicating better. Teachers are requiring more writing and using a wider range of writing activities. Writing is valued more highly across the campus. The writing these five students did in freshman composition and humanities courses all shows the influence of the program—journals, multiple drafts, etc. However, their lab reports show no influence. Lab reports constitute a major portion of engineering students' writing opportunities, but as long as they remain isolated from learning/problem-solving contexts, one wonders how much success writing across the curriculum can have with such students.

While the laboratory reports of these five students show little influence from the program, there has been some noteworthy change across campus. Faculty in a number of disciplines are seeking to develop better models for lab reporting. Faculty in civil engineering have recently started a lab course which requires professional-engineering-type reports and oral presentations in lieu of traditional lab reports. Chapter 11 reports on an experiment in biology using model reports, multiple drafts and peer review to improve the quality of formal written reports. Other faculty have reported good success with using journals in lieu of lab reports in other science courses. One science teacher, in commenting on how this teaching of writing has changed, said that:

> I have gone to the use of a log instead of lab reports in one class, and I think that it has improved the class performance by helping to organize the students' problem solving procedure instead of just using a 'try something and hope it works' type of problem solving.

Similarly, Chapter 13 reports on an experiment using journals in an advanced civil engineering course. Journals, of course, are not substitutes for traditional lab reports or for the professional-engineering-type report advocated by Krowne and Covington. Journals can, however, give students a chance to write the sorts of personal and expressive comments that often end up in the "Conclusions" sections of reports for lack of a better place. Journals used in conjunction with reports can *potentially* lead students to see the link between writing and problem-solving and thus result in students developing their abilities to do both better as well as valuing the connections between writing and engineering.

The results reported here are from a very small case study and should be viewed cautiously. In addition, the data are drawn only from civil, electrical, and mechanical engineering students, and lab reports are required in a variety of other disciplines. Still, the results aren't surprising. At the time of this study (1981) only about 20% of the engineering faculty had attended workshops, and we know that engineering faculty, on the whole, made the fewest changes in their courses after attending a workshop (Chapter 6). Moreover, many lab sections at MTU are run by graduate students and only a very few graduate students have attended workshops.

The results of this study suggest that in its next phase, the writing-across-the-curriculum program at Michigan Tech should (1) seek to increase the number of engineering faculty who attend workshops; (2) try to influence graduate students in science and engineering; and (3) investigate in more detail the rhetoric of lab reports, perhaps developing a wider and more detailed range of alternatives to the traditional report. Only then will all of the writing engineering students do lead them to explore their relationship to knowledge and give them an appreciation for "the full potential of written language." When lab reports lead students to write in more than a "practice-makes-perfect style," they'll help students better understand and communicate information, and thus become better engineers.

Notes

1. The research was supported by a Michigan Technological University Faculty Development Grant. Our work was inspired and informed by that of James Britton, et al., *The Development of Writing Abilities (11–18),* (London: Macmillan Education, 1975) and Ian Pringle and Aviva Freedman, "Writing in the College Years: Some Indices of Growth," *College Composition and Communication,* 31 (1980): 311–321.

Chapter 13
Writing to Learn
Engineering Student Journals

CYNTHIA L. SELFE and FREYDOON ARBABI

The ability of engineers to write effective letters, memoranda, reports and proposals is very important, according to surveys of practicing engineers (Davis, 1977; Kimel & Monsees, 1979; Selfe, 1983). A survey of 52 engineering firms indicated that writing proficiency is a major factor in deciding the promotion potential of an engineer (Selfe, 1983). A similar study of 68 companies revealed that engineers spend almost a third of their work time on writing activities of some kind (Faigley et al, 1981). Writing has been shown to be valuable in problem-solving, organizing and developing previously unarticulated thoughts and concepts (Britton et al, 1975; Fulwiler, 1982), and seeing the world from different perspectives (Merritt, 1981). Such findings make a strong case for improving and expanding writing programs within existing technical curricula.

The use of student journals (notebooks set aside for written responses of a relatively informal nature) is one way to incorporate writing in an engineering course. When we—an English professor and an engineering professor—experimented with having students write in journals for a civil engineering course, we found the approach yielded benefits far beyond our modest initial goals. Moreover, the journal-writing exercises provided the engineering teacher with a valuable source of information about his students and took no class time away from technical presentations. The journals required very little additional work on the part of the students or the instructor.

The Experiment

In the winter quarter of 1982, 35 students in one section of a lecture class, Structural Analysis and Design (CE 325), at Michigan Technological University were asked to write at least one page a week in personal journals. To have a basis for evaluating the results of this experiment, a second section of Structural Analysis and Design, taught by the same instructor, was given the same lectures and assignments but not asked to engage in journal writing.

The instructor explained to the first section that the journals were to consist of "a set of informal notes taken throughout the course." The description of the writing assignment handed out at the beginning of the term suggested that journal entries could be devoted to explaining a student's interest in the course, reacting to topics discussed in class, commenting on the course presentation, or exploring "anything that would relate directly or indirectly to the course, its content, or format." According to the assignment, the journals were not be be graded for content, grammar or spelling but on "how seriously the task was taken and how regularly entries were written." The journals were collected three times during the quarter and examined by the instructor, who often made comments on specific entries. He encouraged students to place a star next to those entries they considered particularly significant so that he could read them with "special care."

Benefits to the Students

Although the purpose behind requiring a journal was to incorporate more writing into the engineering classroom, it soon became evident that keeping a journal provided much more than that. It helped students clarify their thoughts, work out strategies for solving engineering problems, understand the important aspects of the structures course, and identify areas in which they needed more help.

The first reaction of most students to the journal assignment was negative. Faced with the demanding schedule of engineering majors, most saw the journal as busy-work. They didn't understand how they could use writing as an effective problem-solving tool in their courses. Even those who recognized that journal writing might sharpen their writing skills thought that journals belonged in the humanities rather than in engineering courses. The earliest journal entries reflected their dissatisfaction with the assignment.*

> Nov. 27, 1981: As far as this journal is concerned, I really can't figure out what good, if any, it is to the student. I can see how it might help the instructor to evaluate his class.

Nevertheless, once students were convinced that journal-keeping was a requirement, they wrote the entries and submitted them regularly to the instructor. After some hesitant early attempts, they adapted the journals to their individual needs and learned through personal experience how writing could help them think and solve problems. Consider the following excerpt. The student uses a journal entry to reexamine his performance on an examination taken earlier the same day:

> Dec. 9, 1981 . . . In writing this [journal entry] I can see that I did a couple of things wrong and forgot to do a couple of things altogether. In one of the problems I forgot to check all possible paths to find the net area of a cross-

---

* Because of space limitations, most quotations from journals are abridged.

section with holes drilled for bolts. I analyzed the path cutting straight down the cross section to the direction of the stress. I just assumed that this was the critical case and did not check the other paths as we were probably supposed to do.

The students came to understand how writing—manipulating and shapting thoughts on paper—might help them see a problem from a different perspective.

Students also came to realize that their journals could help them learn and understand technical content. Some experimented with using their journals to keep track of important aspects of the course, analyze points and problems they did not understand, and formulate questions that arose from readings and lectures. In these entries, students also pointed out when the course was too difficult, too easy or too repetitious. In the following example, a student discusses a problem he had with the material in the last lecture:

Jan. 12, 1982: The design of tension members isn't quite as easy as I thought it would be. The problem arises in knowing how to get the required effective area. I know you just look it up in the spec manual because it is just a reduction coefficient times the net area, but the problem arises in knowing if the member is indeed a splice plate or a short compression member, etc.

Students found the journals helpful in establishing personal rapport between themselves and their teacher. Because the size of the class—35 students—precluded lengthy personal conferences with the instructor, many students used their journal as a means of engaging in private conversations with him. These students wrote comments, suggestions and questions about the class and, in return, received personal responses. The following excerpt provides an example of this valuable student/teacher dialogue:

Dec. 11, 1981: I do have one problem and that was in the lecture of 12/9/81 where you started on loads and gave us two equations:

$$W = \frac{p}{45} \left(1 + \frac{L}{5\ a}\right)$$

$$P = \frac{Sal}{6}$$

I don't know what these are for and where they came from. This is the only question I would like to get cleared up.

Instructor's response: This is an empirical equation that allows you to estimate the weight of the truss. Without the equation, you will not be able to calculate the weight until the design is completed. However, you need this weight at the start of the design to include with other loads.

The students also used their journals to comment on the pace of the course, the assignments and quizzes, their lab sections and reading materials.

Although students started out with a negative attitude toward writing journals in an engineering class, many became more positive about the experience as the course progressed. Journal entries dated later in the quarter indicated an increasing awareness of the advantages of writing practice:

> Feb. 18, 1982: It seems logical to me that a main problem with engineers is a lack of the ability to communicate ideas even though they understand the problems themselves. This could arise from the fact that English courses, written communications skills, etc. are ignored by engineering students. Complete the required few quarters in college and English is no longer a concern. . . . Anyway, the journal did give me some excellent chances to give my compliments, my comments and criticism of the class material, books, etc. I also feel the journal would be more useful if the task would have been given more time.

Of course there were some students (we estimate less than 10 percent) who, by the end of the quarter, still believed that journal entries had no place in an engineering class. Even some of the more critical students, however, provided evidence that the journal assignment had accomplished its original goals:

> Feb. 22, 1982: Although the journal might have helped me explore problems and try to solve them, and helped me form opinions, I definitely think it has no place in this class or any other class with which I have been associated.

The initial negative comments from students led the investigators to conclude that it might be useful in other technically oriented classes to present the journal under a more subtle guise—perhaps as an "engineer's logbook" or "technical notebook."

Finally, although the journal assignment was designed to engage students in informal writing, the writing practice also seemed to improve their performance on the formal written project they handed in at the end of the quarter. With few exceptions, the section that had written journals submitted projects with more coherent, organized and complete explanations of the design process than those of the control section.

Benefits to the Instructor

While the main purpose of the journals was to give students more chance to practice their writing and, therefore, their reasoning skills, the assignment also directly benefited the instructor. The journals provided him important background information about the students and useful feedback about his teaching effectiveness throughout the quarter.

One of the most striking benefits of the first round of journals was the information they provided the instructor about his students. Early journal entries helped clarify where students were in terms of their civil engineering education.

The instructor was able to identify not only the transfer students whose background differed from the rest of the class:

> Dec. 7, 1981: Since I never had CE 202 at Tech, but had a supposedly equivalent course at a different school, I don't even know where the computer is!

and those students who had had trouble in previous professional courses:

> Dec. 10, 1981: It seems trivial now, but when I came into this class I had no idea about the simple facts of trusses!

but also those who were confident of their engineering background and could qualify as tutors:

> Dec. 4, 1981: I have had Statics, Dynamics, and Mechanics of Materials . . . a good background for the material covered in this class, so far.

This type of academic information provided only a partial portrait of the class. The journals also helped the instructor identify the more practical experiences his students had had in engineering. These experiences provided interesting anecdotal material for discussion, conferencing and lab work. The following excerpt indicates a rich vein of experience that could apply directly to the material covered in the structural analysis and design course:

> Dec. 8, 1981: Two summers ago I worked in a steel fabricating shop, building three to four story structures. We didn't erect the structures, but we did everything else. Last summer I worked for my dad. I had to check all of the rebar specs for a two roof slab on this job, which was mind boggling at first. . . . maybe I'll do take-off's for a job next summer.

Finally, the journals gave the instructor a strong sense of what these young people expected from the course and the profession of civil engineering. Such information gave him an opportunity to clarify the course goals and provide information about civil engineering in brief responses to journal entries:

> Jan. 5, 1982: The study of structures seems to be interesting and very practical. I suppose most design work nowadays is done by civil engineers with master's and they use computers. This would seem to make structural engineering a hard field to become educated in.

> *Instructor's response:* Not always. Many engineers with a B.S. degree and without a computer are involved in design. However, the design of some complicated structures would be difficult without a computer.

Students proved to be quite frank about their perceptions and capable of offering specific suggestions for changing teaching techniques they found less than helpful. Perhaps because the assignment challenged students to think responsibly, the journals seemed to invite much more perceptive comments than the more commonly used methods of evaluation.

Much of the feedback in the journals dealt with the instructor's lectures. Students had some positive comments:

Jan. 27, 1982: Today was the best . . . the lecture was thorough, put on the board in such a way that my notes aren't lacking the little details that make the subject harder to understand. The example problem began with the very basics and advanced upward.

and some negative ones:

Feb. 11, 1982: The room is full and it is awfully hard to see the bottom of the board from the back. Front row seats are hard to get if you have a class beforehand.

Suggestions ranged from the very specific:

Feb. 17, 1982: Don't use the same diagram to answer two questions. It is hard to follow when two diagrams are drawn together. . . . If asked a question about a diagram that requires a slight change in shape, draw a new figure. . . .

to more general comments on educational philosophy:

Jan. 26, 1982: This course is okay so far. You don't dwell on trivial parts of the topics. The class is wide open for questioning and the instructor does not hesitate to review what he has said in a different way.

Students felt free in their journals to discuss what they saw as the strengths and shortcomings of tests, textbooks, reading assignments and lab sessions. The timing, length and content of tests proved a popular subject. The instructor often received suggestions he could use to improve subsequent administrations of the same test. Note, for instance, the following comment on the first class exam:

Dec. 16, 1981: I would like to make a quick complaint about this test. My lab was this morning, and we just got the problems on welds then. How can we get prepared to do welds on the test? When you have a full day of classes, it makes it kind of hard to learn all the stuff on welds on one day. I would appreciate getting the problems earlier.

Because they were written and collected regularly over ten weeks, the journals also served as longitudinal records of individual progress through the quarter. Like many structural analysis and design courses across the country, one of the requirements of CE 325 has been a practical design project that students must complete, for the most part, outside of class. Traditionally, however, there has been no efficient way of checking on their progress. Instructors often can't schedule lengthy individual conferences with each class member, and they consider the alternative— reviewing partially completed projects in various stages—too time-consuming.

The journals produced by CE 325 students proved to be a practical solution to this longstanding dilemma. They served as condensed but highly descriptive records of student progress on the projects that the instructor could examine several times during the semester. The following excerpts from a single student's journal provide examples of this recordkeeping function.

> Feb. 5, 1982: I am finally making some progress on my truss project. I have the loads analyzed and have my members selected. The due date is starting to loom large as far as the remaining time goes.

> Feb. 12, 1982: Well; I was able to check my bar forces the other day with somebody else that used the computer to analyze the truss. . . . I am going to use a tee section for the top and bottom chord so I can weld my double angle interior members directly to the tees without using gussett plates. I also designed the welds for my interior members to support the capacity of the member. This makes the connections easier to design and allows for an extra factor of safety.

> Feb. 15, 1982: Everything is starting to pile up. Just getting the project completed will take quite a bit of time. I have all the calculations done and the connections designed for the truss, now all I have to do is re-copy it and add a discussion, reference the equations and specifications, and make detailed drawings. This will probably take a day or two (I hope).

> Feb. 19, 1982: I turned in my truss project on time. It was really a lot of fun except for the amount of time it took. At any rate I was satisfied with the end product.

Conclusions

Like any other complex skill, writing cannot be taught in one year, one course or one department. Journal writing can give students the opportunity to practice in engineering classes the communication skills the field demands.

From this experiment we drew five major conclusions:

- Students in the experimental section, who wrote in journals as part of CE 325, got more writing practice in general and more writing practice specifically connected to their chosen major than did students in the control section, who took the same course and did not use journals.
- The students in the experimental section, who wrote regularly in their journals for a quarter, produced final reports on design projects that were generally more coherent, organized and complete, than were the reports of students in the control section, who did not write in journals.
- Students in the experimental section, using journals to communicate their thoughts, provided the instructor more complete information on their unanswered questions, the methods they used to solve engineering problems; the material they learned from texts, tests and lectures; and their suggestions for increased teaching effectiveness, than did the students in the control section.

- Students in the experimental section, through their journals, also gave the instructor more complete information on their backgrounds, engineering experiences and progress on the final design project than did the students in the control section.
- Students in the experimental section, because they wrote regularly in journals that were read by the instructor, were more likely to establish an ongoing dialogue with a positive rapport with the teacher than were students in the control section.

On of the most positive aspects of the experiment was the ease with which journals were integrated into the engineering curriculum. Although collected only three times during the ten-week quarter and graded only on a pass/fail basis, the journals put little additional burden on the instructor or the students. It seems reasonable to suggest that the same model could be adapted to other engineering and technical courses in which class time and instructor time are limited.

Chapter 14

Journal Writing in Mathematics

CYNTHIA L. SELFE, BRUCE T. PETERSEN,
and CYNTHIA L. NAHRGANG

This chapter will describe an experiment designed to identify the effects of journal writing assignments on students in a college-level mathematics class at Michigan Technological University. We'll discuss the theoretical and pedagogical claims that inspired our research, identify the questions that informed our research, describe the study itself and the data it produced, and offer our conclusions about this experiment. We'll also talk about the process of conducting research on journals, explaining how and why we chose particular quantifiable and non-quantifiable measures, which of these measures were most useful and why. Finally, we'll share a few observations about studying the very subtle effects of journal writing on students.

Theoretical and Pedagogical Background

For the last decade, teachers from a number of disciplines—mathematics, psychology, geography, and engineering, among others—have come to regard the journal as an effective tool for facilitating thinking and learning in the classroom. Advocates of the relatively unstructured expressive language that forms the basis for most journal assignments have made a sound theoretical case for their claims that such writing activity promotes learning. They cite linguistic theorists such as Susanne Langer (1960) and L. S. Vygotsky (1962), who suggest that language is our primary method of transforming sensory data into conceptual thought, and educational theorists such as Janet Emig (1977) and Jerome Bruner (1966) who maintain that language is central to learning and intellectual development. In addition, those who support the use of journals in classrooms draw on the work of teachers such as Ken Macrorie (1976, p. 158), who see journals as "seed beds" from whence highly developed ideas and concepts can grow and James Moffett (1982, p. 235), who views journal writing as a way of "making sense" of complicated subjects. Finally, journals have strong advocates in those who administer writing-across-the-curriculum programs. These experts see journals as one way of introducing writing for learning into a variety of disciplines (Fulwiler, 1980).

There has been, however, little experimental evidence proffered to support claims that journal writing improves learning or improves students' attitudes toward learning and writing in specific classroom environments. And it was this type of evidence that we sought to support our use of journal writing across the curriculum at MTU. Thus, two of us who teach composition at MTU decided to design a controlled study that would identify the effects of using journals on college-level students in a particular content-area class. For the proposed study our first task was to find a teacher who was both experienced and comfortable with using journals in an academic classroom. Because we were at a technological university and were curious about the uses of journals in non-humanities courses, we also hoped to find a colleague who taught in a scientific or technical field. In the fall of 1983, a mathematics instructor who had been using journal writing in her classes since attending a writing-across-the-curriculum workshop two years earlier, agreed to help us. As a team of two composition teachers and one math teacher, we decided to study the use of journals in a section of Analytic Geometry and Calculus during the next winter quarter.

Central Research Questions

In planning this study, our team soon realized that the lack of experimental data on the value of journals in specific disciplines was a direct result of the methodological difficulties involved in conducting such research. In one sense it seemed relatively simple to study the effects of journal writing assignments. Using traditional statistical measures, for example, we could compare the test grades or the final course grades of students who were assigned journal writing tasks and the grades of students who were not assigned journal writing tasks.

Unfortunately, while such measures might help us determine whether journal writing helped students get better test scores or course grades, we quickly realized that they wouldn't help us get at some of the subtler and more important questions we had about using journals in specific content-area classes. We wanted to know, for example, if there was evidence that journal writing helped students to learn, and, if so, just how such learning happened.

We also wondered whether we could document journal writing's effects on students' attitudes. Did working in journals make students feel better or more confident about writing tasks in general, or even about the subject matter they discussed in their journals? These difficult questions, which had grown out of our own classroom experience in using journal writing exercises and our theoretical understanding of journal writing as a learning and thinking tool, became the guidelines for our proposed research effort.

The Study

By the winter quarter of 1983, we had set up an experiment for three sections of Analytic Geometry and Calculus (MAT 20) and two teachers. The journal study was designed to answer both of our central research questions:

1. Would writing a short series of journal assignments about math concepts help students learn or understand these concepts? If so, exactly how?
2. Would writing a short series of journal assignments affect students' attitudes toward writing in general or toward the math concepts they were writing about? If so, exactly how?

The study was to last for ten weeks, or one quarter (See Table 1).

Table 1.   Experiment Designed to Study the Effects of Journal Writing on Mathematics Students.

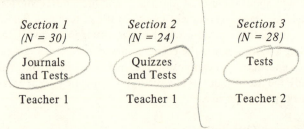

Section 1	*Section 2*	*Section 3*
(N = 30)	*(N = 24)*	*(N = 28)*
Journals and Tests	Quizzes and Tests	Tests
Teacher 1	Teacher 1	Teacher 2

We worked closely together as a team and assigned the thirty students in Section 1, which we'll herein call the experimental section, a series of twenty journal entries. These entries, written both in and out of class, asked the students to explore the various algebraic concepts traditionally covered in the MAT 20 course—quadratic equations, sines and cosines, conic sections, real and imaginary numbers, etc. For a comparison, we had the twenty-four students in Section 2, taught by the same teacher, take a series of ten quizzes in lieu of the journal entries.

Initially, we expected that those students writing journal entries in the experimental section would score at least as high on objective tests of mathematical concepts as the students in Sections 2 and 3. We also thought that the journals would encourage students in Section 1 to think about the concepts presented in the class and help them solve the problems they encountered in their texts and in lecture situations. In addition, we expected that the students in the experimental section, after writing in journals for ten weeks, would come to have a more positive attitude toward writing as a tool for problem-solving in all disciplines and toward their performance in this particular mathematics class than they had before they began using journals.

To check on the possibility that the teacher of Sections 1 and 2 might exhibit an unconscious bias in favor of the experimental section, we included a third section of the same course, taught by a different teacher outside our team, in the study. Students in Section 3 took the same tests as students in Sections 1 and 2, but took no quizzes and did no journal writing.

In an attempt to isolate and identify the effects of the journal writing treatment on the students in Section 1, and to gather data that would help us answer our central research questions, we chose five different measures to use in this study. With this multiple measure approach, we hoped to identify changes that might occur in both cognitive and affective domains and secure both objective and subjective data. We suspected that combining information from these five sources would give us a better chance of catching some of the more subtle effects of journal writing on our student sample.

1. *Content Exams:* Five hour-long exams, covering the geometry and calculus concepts in MAT 20, were given each of the three sections at two-week intervals.
2. *Student Attitude Survey:* A 25-item questionnaire, which identified students' attitudes toward various writing-across-the-curriculum practices used in MTU classrooms, was administered to each of the three sections at the beginning and the end of the quarter. (See pp. 205-7.)
3. *Writing Apprehension Test:* A 26-item test, which identified students' level of anxiety toward writing tasks in general, was administered to students in all three sections at the beginning and the end of the quarter. (See Chapter 8.)
4. *Journals:* The journals of students in the experimental section were collected and analyzed for evidence of thinking skills and problem-solving approaches.
5. *Open-ended Comments:* At the end of the quarter, both the teacher and students were asked to comment in writing on "the use of journals in this class."

Results of the Study

In this section, we'll look at the data from each measure in turn and describe which ones were most useful in identifying the effects that journal writing had on the students in the experimental section. As might be expected, not all of the measures proved equally valuable in our study. The three quantifiable analyses failed to identify any significant effects of journal writing on the students in the experimental class.

Content Exams

Our first task after having completed our study was to determine whether the journal entries (written in the experimental section) had prepared students as well as the more traditional approaches taken in the two controlled sections (Quizzes and class discussions in Section 1 and class discussions only in Section 2) for objective tests over mathematical concepts. We expected to find that students who wrote in journals "learned" the test material at least as well, if not better than, students who took quizzes over this material.

To answer our own questions on this matter, we compared the scores of the students in all three sections on each of the five, hour-long exams administered during the quarter that our study had taken place. The statistical analysis we used to complete this comparison is called a split-plot, repeated measures analysis of variance.

We found, as we had expected, that the test scores of the three sections showed no significant differences, that the journal writing exercises had prepared students equally as well for the tests as had the quizzes. Although this quantifiable finding matched our earlier expectations, it told us only that the journal writers and the quiz takers had performed equally in solving the particular math problems included on the five tests. It did not, for example, help us identify *what* specific kinds of learning journals promoted or helped us better understand *how* journals helped students learn.

Student Attitude Survey

We designed the Student Attitude Survey (SAS) to tell us how much of the information about writing across the curriculum we taught in our faculty workshops had actually trickled down to affect the attitudes of students. On the survey, students are asked to respond (1 = strongly agree to 5 = strongly disagree) to descriptive statements on the use of multiple revisions, journals, and peer editing; the value of writing as a learning tool in all classes; the benefits of non-graded writing, the need for all teachers to hold writing conferences with students and reinforce writing efforts; the advantage of writing to a number of audiences for a number of purposes, and the notion that students have trouble writing for a number of different audiences.

In our study of mathematics students, we administered the SAS at the beginning and at the end of the quarter because we hoped that the brief exposure to journal writing would encourage students in the experimental section to view writing-across-the-curriculum practices such as "summarizing lecture notes in writing," using writing "in all kinds of classes," and using journals as learning tools more positively at the end of the ten-week period than they did at the beginning. We didn't expect similar changes in the two control sections.

We used two statistical analyses to make sense of the data we obtained from our administrations of the SAS, and neither supported our expectations. First we employed a Wilcoxon Signed Rank Test (Ferguson, 1976) to measure the attitude change in each of the three sections from the beginning of the quarter until the end. Generally, these analyses yielded confusing results indicating, for example, that students in the third section (the control section with the different teacher) had made a significant attitude shift toward disagreeing with only one item on the 25-item questionnaire, "summarizing lecture notes in writing helps me learn . . ." ($p < .015$)[1] while the students in the other control section, taught by the experimental teacher, had exhibited no discernable attitude change at all as measured by the SAS. Equally as confusing was our finding that the students in the experimental section exhibited significant attitude change in the wrong direction on one item on the SAS, "Writing . . . is useful in all classes" ($p < .004$). While chagrined that the movement our experimental section had made on this instrument was in a direction we hadn't anticipated, we could perceive no larger or more consistent pattern in this data, nor could we venture a connection between the resulting change and anything we knew about the control or experimental groups.

In a second analysis, we used a one-way analysis of variance (ANOVA) to compare the attitude changes that the experimental group exhibited over a quarter's time to the attitude changes exhibited by the two control groups during the same period. This analysis of the SAS data yielded no significant differences at all among the groups.

Writing Apprehension Test

We administered Daly and Miller's (1979) Writing Apprehension Test (WAT) to each of the three sections at the beginning and at the end of the quarter to see if the experience of writing in journals for a quarter affected the students' anxiety levels when faced with composition tasks in general.

On the WAT students are asked to respond (1 = strongly agree to 5 = strongly disagree) to twenty-six judgmental statements about writing tasks in general. ("I like seeing my thoughts on paper," "Writing is a lot of fun," "I avoid writing.") Initially, we expected that those students in the experimental section would become less apprehensive, more confident, about writing as the quarter progressed and that the students in the other two sections would exhibit little or no change in their apprehension level.

We used the same two statistical analyses of the data for the WAT as we did earlier for the SAS: (1) the Wilcoxon Signed-Rank Test to identify the apprehension changes occurring within each of the three sections from the beginning of the quarter to the end of the same quarter, and (2) an ANOVA to compare the apprehension changes exhibited by the experimental group to those changes exhibited by the two control groups.

Again both of these analyses yielded confusing results. The Wilcoxon Test indicated that each of the three sections had exhibited a significant change of attitude on only one item of the 26 listed on the WAT. The experimental section, for example, made a significant attitude shift toward disagreeing with the statement, "My mind seems to go blank when I start to work on a composition" ($p < .002$). While we expected attitude shifts of this type by the experimental group, a significant change on only one item out of 26 was less than encouraging. Similarly, the movement of the two control groups was limited. Both of these groups also exhibited significant attitude shifts on only one statement each. The control group taught by the experimental teacher made a significant shift toward disagreeing with the statement "I am no good at writing" ($p < .004$). The control group taught by the second teacher made a marginally significant shift toward agreeing with the statement "My mind seems to go blank when I start to work on a composition" ($p < .05$). This confusing movement suggested to us only that something about the approach or attitude of the experimental teacher caused her students to become less apprehensive on two WAT items, whether or not these students actually participated in the journal writing assignment.

The ANOVA indicated a variance among the three sections on five items on the WAT, indicating that the changes in the apprehension level of one of the sections was significantly different than the changes in the other two sections. At first, this analysis buoyed our hope that the apprehension level of students in the experimental section had dropped dramatically while the apprehension level in the control sections had remained stable. A close examination of this phenomenon, however, showed us that changes in apprehension had occurred in both of the two sections taught by the same teacher while little change had occurred in the control group taught by the second teacher. After thinking about this movement, we identified two possible explanations. First, it again seemed possible to us that the first teacher's approach and her attitude were enough to affect the apprehension level of her students, whether or not she used journals in a particular class. Second, we speculated that other classes being taken by students in Section 3 (humanities or English classes, for instance, which often focus on writing) might have been responsible for the attitude change we observed.

Journals

At the beginning of this study, members of the Humanities Department worked with the teacher of the experimental mathematics class to design journal assignments that would get students to explore their understanding of mathematical concepts taught in the class. Typical journal assignments asked students to "Discuss all similarities of graphs of exponential functions" or tell "Why we must change a trigonometric equation to a function of one angle before solving for the unknown."

At the end of the winter quarter, we examined the journals from the experimental section for data that we could use to answer our central research questions. Initially our comprehension of these texts was hampered by their very technical nature, our recollection of exponential functions and two-dimensional arrays was fuzzy at best, and we found it difficult to generalize from journals about a subject that was so foreign to us. Eventually, however, after multiple readings, patterns began to emerge from the chaos of equations on the pages of the journals, and we found five distinct kinds of evidence that indicated how successful the writing assignments had been in getting students to think and learn about mathematical concepts. Specifically from our close readings we saw that students had rejected simplistic or rote answers to the questions on tasks posed in the assignments and instead had

1. composed useful, practical definitions of mathematical terms stated in a language and style that was entirely their own;
2. demonstrated their understanding of abstract mathematical concepts through the use of concrete analogies;
3. attempted to evaluate the usefulness of the material presented in class in terms of their own understanding or their own experience;
4. devised useful strategies or heuristics for approaching problems in analytic geometry and calculus; and
5. used the journal writing experience and the thinking that necessarily accompanied it to discover solutions to problems.

Certainly one of the more obvious pieces of evidence that the journals were encouraging students to think seriously about the context presented in analytic geometry and calculus was the language of the entries themselves, which tipped us off to the fact that students were doing much more than responding automatically to the directions given for each task. One assignment, for example, asked students to "define" three terms from the text. Rather than parroting the technical definition for the terms offered in the text itself, most students came up with infinitely more practical and understandable definitions of the complicated and relatively mathematical concepts. One student pulled no punches in explaining standard deviation as:

> a stupid way to figure out where a large percentage of values are with respect to the average of the values.

Another described median as:

> the middle number in a bunch of numbers. There are as many numbers above it as below it in a distribution.

A second obvious clue we had that students used their journals to think and to learn were the concrete analogies they created to explain abstract mathematical concepts in more familiar terms. One student, for example, when asked to explain the rules of adding and subtracting complex numbers noted:

> A rule when trying to add or subtract complex numbers is that you can only combine the like terms (the real with the real and the imaginary with the imaginary). You just can't combine real numbers with imaginary numbers. It's like trying to add apples and oranges or x's and y's. Example: 2x + 3y cannot be added together.

We found a third indication that journals made students think about mathematical concepts in the entries which incorporated elements of evaluative language. We saw that as students came to understand concepts, operations, or functions as they wrote and thought about them in a number of journal entries, they began to evaluate their usefulness. One student, for example, talked about differentiation in these terms:

> Differentiation is a weird operation. (Who thought it up?) It's really kind of handy because you can use it to find both velocity and acceleration. I think it's funny how one operation can give you both.

To us, and to the teacher of the section, such evaluative statements indicated that students had become familiar and comfortable with the concepts they were writing about and no longer saw these ideas as quite so abstract. In similar entries, students evaluated concepts in terms of their own experience:

> . . . proving the equation $\cos(-\theta) = \cos\theta$ might be a very important learning procedure for a student who is going into electrical engineering. But for civil

engineers, this type of math, proving equations, just might be a waste of time . . . I do not think that we will ever see this or use it.

We also found evidence that students used the journal assignments to record strategies for approaching the kinds of math problems they encountered in class and in their texts. The following, for example, is one student's observation on how to go about solving an exponential function:

One way I've discovered to solve an exponential function is to convert it to a logarithm problem. Then it's easy because you can solve a log problem by finding the log of both sides of the equation and work from there.

To us, such strategies, expressed in the students' own language and often dotted with cautions and notes to themselves ("You have to be careful to look at the signs of numbers here because they can throw you."), indicated that the writing assignments had required students to think about and make concrete their personal experience in solving math problems, to give previously unarticulated strategies a concrete and identifiable form.

Finally, in our readings of the journals we were fortunate enough to find direct evidence that students in the experimental section used journals to solve mathematical problems. We collected several entries that demonstrated to us the catalytic process by which writing, and the thinking that necessarily went along with it, generated or sparked the act of discovery. Students characteristically began these entries *without* a solution in mind, and *discovered* one only when the act of writing caused them to examine, to make concrete, their perceptions of the situation. The following passage, in which a student is trying to "devise a procedure" for finding a derivative that can be applied to three different problems that the teacher provided, illustrates this kind of "ah hah!" process:

I see nothing in common with the three functions except that the derivative has a power of N-1 just like all the other derivatives have. Oh—wait a sec, now I see how you did it. You took the derivative of the first term and multiplied it to the N-1 power.

Generally we found the journals to be a rich source of data. They showed us the kinds of thinking strategies students used in responding to the writing assignments and thus gave us clues about the role writing played in learning and understanding math concepts. We would, however, like to offer an important *caveat* about the interpretation of this data. Although the journals provided interesting and, we believe, useful information, we couldn't consider them as definitive statements of what went on in the students' minds as they grappled with math problems. The journals suggested that mathematical learning occurred through writing, and the volume of responses which we collected similar to those quoted above gave us evidence that these conclusions were valid, but the studies which prove that journal writing is an accurate reflection of cognitive processes remain to be done.

Open-Ended Questions

At the end of the quarter, in an attempt to get at the effects of the journal writing experience not yet addressed by the test grades, surveys, or the journal entries themselves, the teacher and the students of the experimental section commented on what they thought of "the use of journals in this class."

The teacher cited three "distinct advantages" to using journals as listed in abbreviated form below:

1. The act of writing about mathematical concepts and problems in their own language and using their own experience helped students seal such concepts and problems in their mind.
2. The journals forced students to make concrete their understanding of concepts and their strategies of approaching problems. After they had presented the material in an organized form in their journals, they exhibited increased confidence in their ability to solve problems and participate in in-class discussions about problems and concepts. Journals allowed students to build on this confidence by providing them the opportunity to work with math terms in their own language, on their own terms.
3. The journals provided a unique form of evaluation. Because students had to record their responses in prose, they could not hedge or guess at the correct answer or approach. Their level of understanding was immediately evident to the teacher. For this reason, journals were preferable to quizzes for the teacher. Journals also provided a record of individual learning styles, a written account of a student's progress as seen not only by the instructor, but by the student as well.

The students in the experimental section also saw benefits in the journal assignments. We collected 27 student responses to the open-ended question about journals at the end of the quarter and 21 of these responses indicated that journals were a positive addition to the class. Although 10 of the students made only vague positive comments about the journals—stating simply that journals were "good," "ok," or "helpful"—other students articulated five specific benefits of the journals which directly supported the teacher's perceptions.

We have listed these benefits in an abbreviated form below, including quotations to support our paraphrases. We include these items only to show the range of uses students found for their journals. They don't indicate a consensus among the group.

1. The act of writing about concepts helps students "think" about new concepts and "rethink" concepts that had been presented earlier.
2. Journals provided a place which students could "write down" what they "learned" from lectures, text and class discussions.
3. The act of writing the journal entries and the thought that accompanied this writing helped students "understand math concepts better" and "learn the material more thoroughly."

4. Journal entries helped students "remember what went on in class."
5. The strategies and explanations included in the journal entries provided "good building blocks" for further math courses.

Not all students in the experimental section, of course, were quite so enthusiastic about journals in mathematics classes. Six of the 27 students that completed open-ended responses in the experimental class wrote what we classified as negative or neutral comments about journal writing. One neutral student, for example, noted only that the "journals were better than quizzes." Another student, even less enthusiastic about the writing assignments, complained that he "didn't care for the journals" because he didn't "like to write about math functions." A third student, inspired perhaps by our penchant for journals in all classes at MTU commented in answer to the open-ended question, "Expletive deleted! I don't like journals in *any* class."

Our conclusions for this study fall into two categories: what we learned about doing research on difficult questions and what we learned about how journals affected students in our experimental mathematics class.

What We Learned About Doing Research on Difficult Questions

Perhaps the most important lesson we learned was the value of trying more than one way to find out what happened. Early in the experiment, we came to appreciate the difficulty of obtaining quantifiable data that would answer our central questions about the effects of journals. We had suspected that the benefits of journals were subtle and often hard to identify, and indeed we obtained only confusing data from our numerical analyses of students' grades and their responses to the SAS and WAT.

After a reexamination of the nature of the quantifiable measures we had used in the study, we could identify two explanations for the confusing nature of the data that these measures had generated. First, we could accept that the results of the journal treatment, themselves, were confusing and that our quantifiable measures had reflected this confusion accurately. To accept this conclusion, however, we would have had to believe that this particular series of journal writes had little effect on the students in the experimental section. For those of us who read the student journals from the experimental section and used journals ourselves or with students in other classes, this conclusion was directly counter to what we felt intuitively to be true. We had *seen* journals encourage some students to think and learn in our own classes. Our second choice, then, was to acknowledge that the three quantifiable measures we had chosen to employ in our study were inappropriate or insensitive gauges of the effects of journal writing on the students in the experimental section. These instruments were not, after all, designed specifically for this study to measure the ways in which journal writing affected students. We also suspected that the instruments might have been more appropriate and successful if used with a larger sample than our experimental section (N = 30) or with a longer series of journal writing assignments.

Fortunately, we had also collected data in other forms—in journals and from open-ended questions. This data was less quantifiable, but, in many cases, more useful to us because it was more immediate, more directly related to the journal writing experience. We learned that if we wanted to know whether journals help students learn about a subject, we needed to go directly to the journals and examine the cognitive skills and patterns demonstrated therein rather than correlating journal writing statistically with a less direct measure of content-area learning such as grades. If we wanted to find out whether journals affected students' attitudes toward writing or toward the content itself in a particular course, we learned to ask students themselves by way of open-ended questions in which they could express attitudes toward journals and toward the subject matter they had learned rather than relying on more structured and perhaps less applicable instruments that measured only writing apprehension or only student attitudes toward writing activities.

We don't mean to suggest here that, during the course of our larger effort to evaluate the effects of our writing-across-the-curriculum program, we always found material taken from journals or open-ended responses preferable to data obtained from more quantifiable measures. Indeed, in later studies we found good uses for the WAT, the SAS, and other quantifiable instruments. In these studies, in specific contexts, they gave us clear indications of gross movement and change. Our larger lesson was not to avoid quantifiable measures altogether, but to use them cautiously, with a sharp eye out for their limitations, and in combination with other sources of data—journals, interviews, homemade questionnaires—that were directly and immediately related to the central research questions we identified for each study.

What We Learned About Journals

The data we gathered from our examination of test grades, an analysis of the SAS and the WAT, the journals themselves and the responses of teachers and students led us to six conclusions about the effects of journals on the 30 students in our experimental section of Analytic Geometry and Calculus at MTU:

1. Students in the experimental section performed equally as well on content-area tests as students in the control sections.
2. The series of journal writing assignments to the experimental section did not change students' attitudes toward writing activities as identified by the SAS.
3. The series of journal writing assignments completed by the experimental section did not reduce students' writing apprehension as measured by the WAT.
4. In the experimental section, some students used their journals to think and learn about mathematical concepts and problem solving.
5. The teacher of the experimental section felt that journals were beneficial in helping most students understand math concepts and solving math problems.
6. Generally, the students in the experimental section felt that journals were a

positive addition to a mathematics class. Some students commented that journals helped them think and understand the mathematical concepts they learned in class.

These findings, while limited to one mathematics class at our own engineering university, are intriguing to us and informative, we believe, to the profession as a whole. They imply a new list of hypothetical questions for future studies on journals:

1. Do students who write in journals, because they are involved in thinking about content-area concepts, perform well on major content-area tests?
2. Do journal writing assignments, because they force students to articulate personalized strategies and analogies and to use their own language to understand material, help them to think about content-area concepts in different ways than do more traditional activities?
3. Does writing in content-area journals, because it forces students to articulate their knowledge of concepts and problem-solving approaches, increase students' confidence in their problem-solving and discussion skills in that specific area?
4. Does writing in a content-area journal, because it forces students to practice writing as a problem-solving tool, help students see the value and importance of using writing as a problem-solving tool in that particular area?
5. Does writing in a content-area journal, because it combines practice in verbal skills and content-area skills, help students transfer certain skills between classes?

Future Research

As a colleague once explained at the end of a long research project, "This experiment is less a success than a pilot." Our research, too, is a first step rather than a stopping place. The value of our findings, and, indeed our strongest findings, are those which suggest certain methodological approaches to the study of journals in future experiments. Our own study indicates, for example, that quantifiable measures on the uses of journals might be more successful if they are designed for specific experimental questions or if they are applied to larger populations or stronger treatments than our own.

Further studies should be completed to document the effects of journals in different content areas and under different conditions. We need to study, for example, how the number of journal entries per week, the length of journal entries, the duration of the course, or the type and structure of journal assignment alters the effects of journal writing on students. Moreover, we must explore the possibility that writing journals in one field may have beneficial effects in other fields.

We believe our study has been most beneficial in teaching us *how* to look at the effects of journals in content-area classrooms. We hope the lessons we learned from conducting this research will make it easier for others to undertake similar projects and provide us as teachers more useful information about employing journals in our classes.

Student Attitude Survey

Class ID #: _____

Date: _____

Student ID #: _____

Sex   M   F

Class Rank: freshman   sophomore   junior   senior

Major: _____

Transfer student: Yes   No

Directions: Please circle the appropriate number next to each item.

	strongly agree	agree with qual- ification	no opinion	disagree with qual- ification	strongly disagree
1. Journals help me think about what I learn in class.	1	2	3	4	5
2. Faculty members should grade rigorously every writing assignment done by their students.	1	2	3	4	5
3. Teachers should not grade early drafts of papers to encourage students to revise their writing.	1	2	3	4	5
4. Conscientious teachers who want to improve student writing will point out all errors on each student paper they read.	1	2	3	4	5
5. Students should read and critique each other's writing to improve their own writing.	1	2	3	4	5
6. Poor assignments from teachers often cause poor writing from students.	1	2	3	4	5
7. A major cause of poor college writing is immaturity on the part of the writer.	1	2	3	4	5
8. Writing (papers, essay tests, journals, logs, etc.) is useful in all kinds of classes.	1	2	3	4	5

	strongly agree	agree with qualification	no opinion	disagree with qualification	strongly disagree
9. History, business, engineering, math, and science teachers should evaluate the quality of student ideas not the quality of their writing.	1	2	3	4	5
10. Writing can play an important role in classes that enroll over 100 students.	1	2	3	4	5
11. Teachers in disciplines other than English should give one grade for content and a separate grade for quality of writing.	1	2	3	4	5
12. Asking students to rewrite assignments does not help most students to improve their writing.	1	2	3	4	5
13. Poor spelling and punctuation are the most serious writing problems of college students.	1	2	3	4	5
14. Summarizing lecture notes in writing helps me learn lecture material.	1	2	3	4	5
15. Many students write poorly because teachers have made them afraid to write.	1	2	3	4	5
16. Many students are afraid to write because their writing has been severely criticized in the past.	1	2	3	4	5
17. I should always make an outline before beginning to write.	1	2	3	4	5
18. Before beginning to write, I should know precisely what I want to say.	1	2	3	4	5
19. There are fixed rules which govern all good writing.	1	2	3	4	5

	strongly agree	agree with qual- ification	no opinion	disagree with qual- ification	strongly disagree
20. College students will improve their writing only when they are required to pass a writing proficiency examination in order to graduate.	1	2	3	4	5
21. I should state my thesis clearly in the first paragraph before I write anything else.	1	2	3	4	5
22. College students should always be required to write to a single audience—their teacher.	1	2	3	4	5
23. Writing should be evaluated for both grammar and content.	1	2	3	4	5
24. Students learn bad writing habits when they read and criticize each other's writing.	1	2	3	4	5
25. Visiting the Language Lab and getting help with my writing from tutors could make me a better writer.	1	2	3	4	5

Please put further comments about writing, writing in your classes at Michigan Tech, or this form, on the back of this page.

Notes

1. The probability of this attitude shift occurring by chance was less than fifteen chances in one thousand. We have abbreviated this as $p < .004$. For ease in reporting, all probability values that follow will be abbreviated in this same way.

Chapter 15

Composing Responses
to Literary Texts
A Process Approach

ELIZABETH A. FLYNN

Teachers of literature who recognize that writing is a mode of discovery as well as a mode of communication are beginning to make use of informal or exploratory writing in their classes. In his essay, "From Story to Essay: Reading and Writing," for instance, Anthony Petrosky (1982) illustrates the usefulness of response statements in a graduate seminar on reading and psychology which he taught at the University of Pittsburgh. He argues that having students write about their initial impressions allows them to make links between their reading and their own experience. Students become active participants in the creation of meaning. They "compose" their understandings of texts, and their compositions become indicators of their level of comprehension.

In their enthusiasm to introduce students to the uses of exploratory writing, however, teachers sometimes forget that response statements are means to an end rather than ends in themselves. Response is only the initial stage in a complex process. Teachers who are interested in having students revise their initial impressions of texts into finished essays need to be aware not only of the usefulness of exploratory writing, but also of ways in which exploratory writing can be transformed into writing which makes sense to an audience. They need to understand the nature of the process of responding to literary texts, a process, quite obviously, which involves reading as well as writing.

Research on the nature of the composing process is helpful in elucidating the broad outlines of the process of responding to literature. James Britton (1975) and Linda Flower (1979) describe the pattern of change which frequently occurs as writers move from "expressive" writing, to use Britton's term, or from "writer-based" writing, to use Flower's term, toward essays which communicate ideas to an audience. Writers initially write to and for themselves, and so early drafts of essays are frequently characterized by an absence of statements showing causal relations, citation of evidence, or development of ideas. Expressive or writer-based writing is close to the self, writing which reveals initial attempts to come to terms

208

with a topic. As writers begin to gain some perspective on their subject they become better able to transform their preliminary gropings into writing which makes sense to an audience. Expressive or writer-based writing is transformed into "transactional" or "reader-based" writing. This movement from writing which is close to the self to writing which communicates with an audience almost always involves significant re-conceptualization, radical revision of early drafts.[1]

The process of responding to a literary text also involves movement from expression to transaction, from writer-oriented to reader-oriented writing. In their initial responses to literature, students frequently identify with the characters they encounter and often summarize the plot of the story. They tend, in early response statements, to participate in the events depicted in the literature and have difficulty stepping back from them to make judgments or find a coherent pattern of meaning. Writing in such response statements often reflects uncertainty and is characterized by an accumulation of unfocused detail. As students attempt to transform their initial impressions into more formal essays, however, they begin to provide a sharper focus, to develop details more fully, and to rely less heavily upon plot summary. They begin to observe rather than to participate, and they move toward the discovery of a coherent pattern of meaning. In the final stages of the process of writing about literature, students evidence an ability to detach themselves from the text, to gain a critical perspective upon it, and to replace personal considerations with social ones. Writing in this last phase reflects a reenvisioning of the text, and often students discover a new focus. The result is an essay which reveals growth, expansion, metamorphosis.[2]

A set of responses to John Updike's "A&P" written by a freshman at Michigan Technological University illustrates this movement from participation to observation, from identification to critical distance.[3] Students were asked to record their initial impressions of the story in their journals. They then wrote a draft of an essay which was to focus on characterization, and that draft was reviewed and discussed by a group of three or four students during class. The student then revised the draft and submitted the revision for a grade. (*Note:* Errors have been corrected; italics are mine.)

Journal

The story "A&P" is a story that is interesting, but seems to drag on slightly. I really like the detail, and special literary effects. One such example is when the author uses the metaphor, "outside the sunshine is skating around on the asphalt." That puts a good picture in your mind of the type of day it is outside. The way the author described the girls was unique as well. The descriptions are a little strange also. For instance the author, when describing the girls, says one has a chubby berry face with lips all bunched together under her nose. I am not quite sure of exactly what a chubby berry face is but a beautiful woman does not come to mind for sure. The reference made to the woman's lips bunched under her nose has implications of being downright ugly. When the author says that the cute one's hair hadn't quite frizzed right, I am not exactly sure what that means, but the descriptions are really neat. *It is obvious that Sammy feels that the girls are sexually attractive.* He says things like, "In come the girls wearing nothing but bathing suits, as if they were obscene or something." Later on he seems to be fascinated by the fact that the Queen's suit is down below her upper shoulders. He says that it is just "her" between the suit and her head.

Draft

Sammy, in the short story, "A&P," is a person who feels the girls in the story are sexually attractive. There are many inferences in the story that reflect this feeling or opinion of Sammy's.

In the very first sentence of the story, Sammy makes mention that the girls walked in in nothing but bathing suits. This is suggestive that he finds something unique in the fact that the girls are wearing nothing but suits, as if to suggest they are indecent. Sammy later makes reference to the "sweet broad soft-looking can." The word "sweet" here seems to indicate that Sammy enjoys the scenery. Later on, Sammy says that they don't even have shoes on. The "don't even" shows that Sammy is surprised at the fact that they don't have shoes on. If he would have just said, "they don't have shoes on," that wouldn't nearly have been so suggestive of surprise.

Sammy then proceeds to describe the girls' apparel and physical appearance. He describes the not-so-tall one by calling her "Queeny." By referring to her as a queen seems to imply that he sees something sexy in her appearance. Slightly afterwards he refers to her legs as white, prima donna legs. Again he is obviously taking more than slight note of her legs. When Sammy describes her suit, he says, "What got me, the straps were down," which really goes to show he was amazed and occupied with the fact that her straps on her suit are down. This is drilled home by the words, "What got me." Sammy then describes how white her shoulders are, which shows he is taking specific notes of her physical appearance. Sammy goes on to say that there is nothing between the top of her suit and the top of her head, except just "her." His usage of the word "her" is suggestive of his thinking of her as sexy. He also says her clean, bare top is more than pretty. Quite obviously Sammy looks at her from the standpoint of a sexual object, at least to some degree.

It is obvious by the way Sammy describes the apparel of the girls that they are of some sexual appeal to him. Also, this is evident by the remarks he makes about their physical appearance.

Final paper

Sammy is a person that is anti-establishment. Throughout the entire story, Sammy continually criticizes old people, and other things established in this world. I plan to show that this attitude of Sammy's is pushing him to search for something better than he thinks can be found in life.

It is quite obvious that Sammy is quite critical of old people. An illustration of this attitude can be found in the case where Sammy describes the woman at the cash register as being a witch. He describes bitterly how she has probably been watching cash registers for fifty years and he is the first one she caught. He seems to take this incident as an attack on himself—establishment against himself. Sammy then describes the people in the store as sheep. This surely is a derogatory term, implying their ignorance and that he is better and wiser somehow. Again these people represent the established people in the world, which he is so critical of. Sammy also shows his bitterness and rejection of material objects of the establishment such as the record albums and toys that fall apart. Sammy refers to his dislike of the people in the store once again when he describes them as scared sheep in a pen, bumping into each other. Sammy shows another rejection of the establishment, this time being the church. He says Lengel is dreary, teaches Sunday school and the rest. Sammy is obviously against the established church. After Sammy quits, Lengel appears very old and gray, just like all the other sheep in the store. He sees Lengel then as part of the establishment.

The girls that walk in the store represent anti-establishment thinking to Sammy. *They are barefoot and appear seductive, although they are a distance from the beach.* They are against the establishment, an attitude he likes. *Queen's shoulder straps are even down, not something the average woman would do in a food store.* The girls walk around the store with an attitude of control and assurance, although surely anti-establishment, exactly what Sammy longs for—freedom. Further illustrating this attitude is Queeny's response to Lengel, in that she says to him that they are dressed decently. Again this response, especially with the fact that her lip juts out and that she says what she wishes, proves to be the attitude Sammy seeks after.

This attitude found in the girls is what to Sammy he has been looking for all along. By quitting the job (establishment) and chasing after the girls it is evident that he has finally found, in the girls, what he has been searching for: an escape from the establishment which he so dislikes.

In the journal entry, the student identifies with Sammy and participates in the action of the story. Like Sammy, he delights in the sexual attractiveness of the girls. Observations about the story are tentative, fragmented, and form no coherent pattern. Details come to the student's attention, but they appear to be unrelated. The student focuses on a few vivid images but is unable to place those images within a larger context.

In the draft, the student has provided a sharper focus by centering on the sexual attractiveness of the girls and eliminating material unrelated to this idea. The student is less of a participant and more of an observer. He is attentive to the language of the story in a way he was not in the journal entry, and he has gained more distance from Sammy and makes some judgments about him: Sammy looks at Queeny as a sex object. The writer still identifies with Sammy to some extent, and still delights in the sexual attractiveness of the girls, but he has gained more of a perspective and is moving toward an assessment of Sammy's character. The essay is largely descriptive, though, and organized according to the chronology of events in the story. The student has not yet related those events in the story to a broader social context.

The final essay represents a kind of breakthrough. The student has discovered an entirely new focus, one which does not appear in either the journal entry or the draft. "Sammy is a person that is anti-establishment." He has categorized Sammy and in so doing distanced himself from him. His new focus allows him to take into account a number of elements in the story which he has previously ignored— Sammy's encounter with the old woman at the cash register, and his climactic confrontation with Lengel. The sexual attractiveness of the girls now becomes a subordinate idea and is interpreted rather than simply described. The girls represent the freedom Sammy longs for and serve as a catalyst in his encounter with Lengel. In the final essay, the student has moved from participation to interpretation, from identification to detachment, from a focus on fragmented parts to a conception of the whole. The progression represents a transformation, an openness to different perspectives.

We can only speculate on the factors that brought about the student's re-envisioning of the story: learning is ultimately a mysterious process. It is likely, though, that the student was able to see beyond his initial, personal response as a result of the exploratory writing and the discussions with peers and the teacher made possible by the classroom structure. An exchange of interpretations and the process of rewriting for an audience no doubt altered his original conception of the text, provided new "schemata" or frames of reference for comprehending it, and made possible productive rereading and rewriting.

Louise Rosenblatt (1976) emphasizes that a student's initial reaction to a text is a necessary starting point in the teaching of literature. Students inevitably react to literature in terms of their own temperament and background, and this rudimentary response is an important component of the pedagogical agenda. Rosenblatt makes clear, though, that initial responses are often limited and can be enhanced by an exposure to other opinions and by a return to the text. Personal response needs to be broadened through the social exchange of ideas. She says:

> The reader must remain faithful to the text. He must be alert to the clues concerning character and motive present in the text. But he does more than that: he seeks to organize or interpret such clues. His own assumptions will provide the tentative framework for such an interpretation. He may discover that this causes him to ignore elements in the work, or he may realize that he is imputing to the author views unjustified by the text. He will then be led to revise or broaden his initial tentative assumptions (pp. 11-12).

The student came to an expanded awareness of "A&P" because the classroom situation provided him the freedom to explore the meanings of the text in personal terms but also established for him the constraint of having to compose those meanings into an essay that is convincing to an audience. In transforming personal response into negotiable interpretation he made discoveries about Updike's text and, perhaps, about the nature of adolescent rebellion. The revision, while hardly mature literary analysis, reveals development of an ability to find a consistent pattern of meaning and to communicate that pattern to others. An accumulation of such experiences should improve the student's ability to read literature and to write essays about it.

Pedagogical practices should aim toward helping students broaden their understanding of texts in order to help them broaden their awareness of themselves. Students must be encouraged to evaluate and analyze, to de-center, to transcend the limitations of their initial, private responses. The process of negotiation with others has the potential of having this effect. Sharing perceptions of texts should open students to different interpretive possibilities and enrich the re-reading and re-writing process. What is crucial is that an atmosphere of mutual trust be established and that students be encouraged to use writing to explore textual meaning. Talking should serve to complement writing. A good deal of students' time should be spent exploring, engaging in the reading and writing process. Written products which are the result of the extended process of discovery should reflect the richness of that process.

Response statements which are envisioned as links between texts and students' experiences should serve the function of expressive or writer-based writing, which can be transformed into transactional or reader-based writing. If students are encouraged to interact with texts, to respond to textual cues in their earliest encounters, they will be introduced to a literary tradition which has the potential to expand their previous sense of self and so give them ways of examining and re-creating their own past. Reading has value because it introduces students to experiences which are not their own and which challenge their conceptions of themselves and of their world. Writing has the potential of enriching the reading experience. Pedagogical structures which encourage students to read and to write in stages also encourage them to transform their perceptions of texts which, in turn, may encourage them to transform their perceptions of their worlds and of themselves.

Notes

1. Nancy Sommers, for instance, in her article, "Revision Strategies of Student Writers and Experienced Adult Writers," argues that revision is central to the writing process in mature writing. Sommers says that experienced writers "seek to discover (to create) meaning in the engagement of their writing, in revision." *College Composition and Communication,* 31 (December, 1980), 38.

2. The stages I am delineating here were suggested by Joseph Comprone's discussion of the reading/writing process in "Burke's Dramatism as a Means of Using Literature to Teach Composition," *The Rhetoric Quarterly,* 9 (Summer, 1979), 142–155.

3. I am grateful to John F. Flynn for allowing me to use material collected from students in his freshman composition course and for the very useful feedback he provided on drafts of this essay. A version of this article was presented at the Conference on College Composition and Communication in March of 1981. I wish to thank Randall Freisinger for the helpful suggestions he made for revising the paper.

IV

Writing in the Disciplines
Problems and Perspectives

As we have visited with colleagues from other campuses at conventions and at writing workshops who related tales of woe about inadequate funding, faculty mistrust, and political squabbles, we have gained a further appreciation for the support we received at our program's beginnings and for the strong continuing support.

As we look back to 1977, we have to admit that we had a relatively easy time establishing our writing-across-the-curriculum program. To be sure, there was the writing of a three-page proposal to our vice president, which we explained to faculty in every department, to university administrators, and even to the university's Board of Control; there was the writing and rewriting of the forty-page grant proposal to the General Motors Foundation; and there was the talking, the planning, and the collecting of information about programs elsewhere. But in this important formative stage we encountered little opposition or hostile reaction from faculty, students, or administrators. In 1975, everyone including *Time* and *Newsweek* seemed to agree that it was time to do something to help students become better writers, and most were pleased, or perhaps relieved, that the Humanities Department was volunteering to lead the effort. Our administration supported us, provided substantial internal university funds, and endorsed our proposal to General Motors in support of engineering education. When the grant was awarded, we were off and running—smoothly.

Yet as the program was implemented, we entered the world of campus politics, suffered the mistrust that comes with high visibility, solidified our vision of the role that writing should play in a student's education, and tried to learn from our mistakes even as we were reminded of them. The final three essays in this collection are about the setbacks and surprises we encountered as we experimented with our teaching, developed our research, conducted our workshops, administered our program, and attempted to understand what we were learning from these activities.

215

"The Politics of Research," by James R. Kalmbach, demonstrates the ideological nature inherent in research instruments such as surveys and questionnaires. Kalmbach describes the results of a senate sub-committee investigation and the colossal waste of energy which results when "scientific" data gathering is put in the service of campus politics.

"Mucking Around," by Margaret E. Gorman, is a down-to-earth introduction to collecting and interpreting the "information" that is generated by surveys, questionnaires, computer printouts, and experimental studies. The essay is written for English teachers who often have been traditionally educated in historical and literary scholarship, but who have not been exposed to research techniques in "data analysis." Such teachers' traditional education plays a vital role in writing-across-the-curriculum programs which view writing as a humanistic activity, such as the one at Michigan Tech. But we have discovered that part of the excitement in writing across the curriculum is the opportunity for classroom-based experimental studies and program evaluation, and Gorman's essay invites us to muck around and get our hands dirty.

In the concluding essay, "Reflections: How Well Does Writing Across the Curriculum Work?" Toby Fulwiler reviews some of the ideas and practices we were sure would work, but didn't and some of the ideas and practices which worked, but in ways which surprised us. This essay ends where Art Young's essay began—with the discovery that a campus-wide writing program can unexpectedly foster a deepened sense of community through collaborative research and teaching— a community of scholars in every way Paul Goodman meant.

Chapter 16

The Politics of Research

JAMES R. KALMBACH

I can still remember the shock when I looked in my mailbox and discovered a thick, mimeographed sheaf of raw numbers. They were the results of "The Freshman English Survey," a collection of data about faculty attitudes towards and perceptions of MTU's freshman composition program. The survey had been prepared by the Curricular Policy Committee of our faculty governing body—the faculty senate—as part of an investigative reivew of the program, and now the results were out.

I was shocked not by the data, but by its presentation. The entire faculty had been sent eight pages of raw numbers with no attached interpretation of those numbers. In addition, the responses had been divided into three groups of faculty: (1) Engineering (62 respondents), (2) Humanities (25 respondents) and (3) Total (189 respondents), and the number of faculty in each group varied so much that large apparent differences in raw response could reflect similar percentages of response, while similar numbers of raw response would necessarily reflect different percentages of response. If we were to make any sense of the data, raw numbers would have to be converted to percentages. I went to the office and sat a work-study student down in front of a calculator.

I was also somewhat surprised that the committee had singled out engineering and humanities faculty, but no others. They could have reported results for each college or for each department had they so chosen. I wondered if there was a hidden motive in their reporting of the data. From the very beginning of the Curricular Policy Committee's review of the freshman composition program, we had seen it as an attempt to "review" the writing-across-the-curriculum program. During the five years of the program, the Humanities Department had gradually shifted from a product to a process orientation in the teaching of writing. If the committee, none of whom ever attended a workshop, could demonstrate that we weren't doing a good job of teaching freshman composition or that the faculty wasn't satisfied with the new process approach to teaching writing, then it could, by implication, discredit the writing-across-the-curriculum program.

I had seen an early draft of the questionnaire and it had a lot of problems, including inconsistencies in question format, ambiguous phrasings, misleading statements and erroneous assumptions. I had passed along revision suggestions to our Director of Freshman Composition who, in turn, returned the document to the committee with suggestions for revision.

The original draft questionnaire had stated as its formal objective:

> The purpose of this questionnaire is to solicit the views of the academic faculty on the goals and objectives of Freshman English.

The real objective of the questionnaire, however, appeared just a few lines later:

> Some persons have expressed concern that the new focus advocated in the writing across the curriculum program on "expressive writing" (personal letters, diaries, journals, and reflections in which grammar, spelling, word usage, and overall structure are deemphasized) is consuming time and effort which might be better allocated to "transactional writing" (formal reports, themes and term papers in which grammar, spelling, word usage, and overall structure are emphasized).

The committee intended to discover whether the writing-across-the-curriculum program had distorted freshman composition at Michigan Tech. What's more, they were attacking not the program itself, but a garbled version of the theory behind the program. The committee's prose did not reflect an understanding that expressive writing was both a stage in the writing process and a particular form of writing. Our writing program was being reviewed by people who neither understood our program nor participated in our workshops.

At the root of their objection was, apparently, the process approach now widely used in freshman composition which the committee felt inhibited the teaching of "spelling, grammar, word usage, and overall structure." (They never defined "overall structure.") Five of the twelve questions (45%) in the original draft survey asked about the importance of "spelling, grammar, word usage and overall structure." Did faculty believe employers expected MTU graduates to be competent in this area? Were the students competent? Should freshman English place its priority emphasis on teaching spelling, grammar, word usage and overall structure? etc.

The single-minded focus of the original draft questionnaire on the mechanical elements of composition had brought a strong protest from our department. We all agreed that mechanical correctness was important, but we felt that our writing program encompassed other things as well. Later versions of the questionnaire were fairer, but certain questions had a habit of reappearing unchanged no matter how hard we objected. The review committee had encouraged us to submit new questions in addition to our comments on the first draft. We had suggested that the committee ask whether faculty required writing in their courses, and what sort of things they commented on when they graded their students' written work. We also offered the following as a possible area of concern:

MTU's freshman English program should establish pedagogical practices based on recent sound research in linguistics, the composing process, and the development of writing ability.

We felt it would be worthwhile to know if the University community valued a professional writing staff who kept up in the literature and who integrated research with common sense and experience when developing pedagogical practices. In the next version of the questionnaire, however, there had been a considerable transformation:

Should MTU's freshman English program establish pedagogical practices based on recent sound research in linguistics, the composing process, and the development of writing ability which indicates that spelling, grammar, and correct word usage cannot be taught?

I was astonished. I had recently completed a Ph.D. in theoretical and applied linguistics and I knew that no such research existed in linguistics. Other members of the department with backgrounds in writing research assured me that no research existed in that field either. We strenuously objected to this question on the grounds that no such research existed. The response of the committee, in the final draft mailed to all faculty, was to delete the references to the types of research: "linguistics, the composing process, and the development of writing ability," so that the question read:

Should MTU's freshman English program establish pedagogical practices based on research which indicates that spelling, grammar, and correct word usage cannot be taught?

This new version was, if anything, even worse. Although we protested again, the damage had been done. Such a poorly formulated question implied that the freshman English program was based on such misinformation. As one faculty member in the Humanities Department commented:

I am concerned that [the question] will indeed mislead MTU faculty into believing that recent research *does* indicate that "spelling, grammar, and usage cannot be taught," and that the freshman English faculty agrees with this. (In fact, in talking casually with several faculty members from other departments, I have found that that is exactly what they think we believe, primarily as a result of this question.) Since it doesn't take much intelligence to see that spelling, grammar, and usage can be, and have been taught, the question may therefore seriously undermine University confidence in the HU-101-102-103 faculty through the spread of false information.

When interpreting the entire questionnaire, these poorly formulated questions would be easy to deal with. The responses to them could not be responsibly interpreted and would have to be disregarded. Yet the possible effects on the faculty perception of the freshman composition faculty that resulted from simply asking the question would be much harder to deal with.

I began to suspect that there was a subtler design in the Curricular Policy Committee's mimeographed publication of raw numbers. They didn't include an analysis or interpretation of the survey because no reasonable inferences could be drawn from many of the questions. What they could do was simply publish the data and then let faculty draw their own inferences.

But I wondered what, exactly, the data said. I got the sheets back from the work-study student with percentages next to raw numbers and took a look. To avoid comparing the engineering and humanities faculties against themselves, I subtracted their numbers from the totals and got a fourth category of "other faculty." I soon found that if someone was trying to show how different the views of the Humanities Department were from the rest of the faculty, they had failed. As you can see in Table 1, in many of the questions, and especially the questions having to do with the goals and objectives of writing instruction, there was very little difference between the three groups of faculty, and what differences there were were not statistically significant.

Table 1.   Responses from the Faculty Senate Survey Where There Are No Statistically Significant Differences Across Disciplines:

	All Faculty $n = 189$	Engrg. Faculty $n = 62$	Other Faculty $n = 102$	Hums. Faculty $n = 25$
Are you satisfied with the quality of writing of your students?	29%	26%	29%	33%
Do you believe that most of your students are competent at formulating ideas and expressing them in writing?	40%	33%	47%	30%
Do you believe that most of your students are competent in spelling, grammar, and correct word usage?	40%	41%	38%	28%
Should the Freshman English program place some emphasis on public speaking?	81%	74%	84%	91%
Is the instilling of good communication skills, including writing, one responsibility of all members of the academic community?	91%	90%	91%	100%
Do you believe most employers of MTU graduates expect them to be competent in spelling, grammar, and correct word usage?	95%	97%	92%	100%

Note: Percentage given is the percentage of faculty who answered yes to the question.

Only about a third of the faculty were happy with the student writing they saw, though a somewhat higher percentage believed that their students were competent at expressing ideas and in spelling, grammar, and correct word usage. Similarly, faculty overwhelmingly supported the inclusion of public speaking in freshman composition; they agreed on the responsibility of all faculty to teach good communication skills; and they agreed that employers expect students to have good communication skills. And in all the categories, the viewpoints of the Humanities faculty were no different from those of the rest of the campus community.

Although the faculty as a whole agreed on the goals and objectives of writing instruction, the faculty in the humanities who completed the survey were, if anything, much tougher on student writing problems than the rest of the faculty. They were, on the whole, about 20–30% more likely to see student writing difficulties in developing a clear readable style and producing coherent papers, including such specific problems as ability to write clear sentences or coherent paragraphs, to get started, to organize, to revise, to proofread, or to use the library. Similarly, Humanities faculty were more likely than the faculty as a whole to reduce the grades of poorly written papers (92% vs. 69%) and more likely to reduce grades because of incompetence in spelling, grammar, and word usage (96% vs. 47%). They were also more likely to comment on these problems. But since the teaching of writing is one of the Humanities Department's primary responsibilities, you might expect this. We see more writing problems, and we are more likely to comment on those problems because it is our job.

The survey had so far shown that the Humanities Department shared a common set of values about writing with the rest of the faculty, that they were generally tougher in spotting writing problems, commenting on those problems and reducing grades because of them. I shared my preliminary findings with our department head, and he asked me to write up the results in a report. This report helped my humanities colleagues to see that an initially fearsome collection of raw numbers in fact showed little that they wouldn't expect.

Several months later, in the fall of 1981, the review committee produced a draft recommendation about the freshman English program. The draft recommendation began with a brief history of their investigation. There then followed a paragraph expressing concern about the use of expressive writing in freshman composition:

> *Expressive Writing and Keeping Journals.* Some persons have expressed concern that the new focus advocated in freshman English and in the writing-across-the-curriculum program on "expressive writing" (diaries, personal journals, and reflections in which grammar, spelling, word usage, and overall structure are deemphasized) is consuming time and effort in the freshman English program which might be better allocated to "transactional writing" (formal reports, themes, and term papers in which grammar, spelling, word usage, and overall structure are emphasized).

This paragraph sounded oddly familiar. It was, in fact, word-for-word the paragraph quoted earlier that had appeared in the very first draft of the survey, a paragraph which the committee had deleted after our protests. The committee also attached the summary of their findings which they had earlier sent faculty, but they included no data from the survey in their document and made no effort to interpret the survey results for faculty. It appeared, to us at least, that the committee had a preconceived notion of what it thought was wrong with freshman composition at MTU. When their survey had failed to produce data which supported that notion, they had ignored the survey.

As you can imagine, the draft recommendation brought another round of protest from my colleagues, and the committee withdrew it.

That winter the Curricular Policy Committee produced another rewording of their recommendation and placed it on the senate agenda where it was published and sent to every faculty member on campus. The paragraph about expressive writing which had crept back into the earlier draft was again deleted, as were other references to the writing-across-the-curriculum program. We began to see a pattern in their revision process. Each time we objected to a question or statement, they revised or deleted the question or statement without changing their intent. It appeared that our input had helped them design a politically more astute attack on the competence of the Humanities Department. For, after all our protests, the substance of the recommendation had not changed: the Freshman English program should emphasize the six writing abilities which the College Entrance Examination Board feels students need to do college work. These writing abilities include:

1. The ability to conceive ideas about a topic for the purpose of writing.
2. The ability to organize, select, and relate ideas and to outline and develop them in coherent paragraphs.
3. The ability to write Standard English sentences with correct sentence structure; verb forms; punctuation; capitalization, possessives, plural forms, and other matters of mechanics; word choice and spelling.
4. The ability to vary writing style, including vocabulary and sentence structure, for different readers and purposes.
5. The ability to improve writing by restructuring, correcting errors, and rewriting.
6. The ability to gather information from primary and secondary sources; to write a report using this research; to quote, paraphrase, and summarize accurately; and to cite sources properly.

These "abilities" seemed innocent enough; we were already emphasizing something like them in our classes. They were, in fact, already part of our Freshman English guidelines. Why was the committee recommending things we already did?

In the draft recommendation, the review committee also referred to their survey: "through the survey of faculty, the committee found that members of the faculty are less than saitsfied with the quality of writing displayed by their students." Their observation was clearly correct; only 29% of all responding faculty were satisfied with the writing they received in their classes, a less than impressive number. The committee, after withdrawing their first document, had also asked for and received a group of freshman composition course syllabi. They concluded, on the basis of the course syllabi but with no other research, that there was insufficient control over the different sections of freshman composition. They did not attempt to interview teachers or students, nor did they visit any classrooms. Their final recommendation is quoted below in its entirety:

> The Senate of Michigan Technological University recommends that the Faculty of the Department of Humanities re-examine the implementation of the goals and objectives of the freshman English program (HU 101-103) in the light of the Curricular Policy Committee findings. As a minimum, the six writing abilities identified by the College Board should be emphasized. Closer control should be exercised over the various sections of the course to insure achievement of these abilities. This proposal is not to be interpreted as a recommendation to eliminate the study of literature or oral communication from these courses.

This recommendation evoked anger, frustration, and general depression in my department. Faculty perceived the committee's recommendation as an attempt to tell them how to teach their classes. The committee was implying that despite the national reputation of the department, the academic training of the faculty, and our countless years of experience, we didn't know how to teach freshman to write or how to supervise freshman composition instructors. Personally, however, I was struck more by a sentence that appeared earlier in the document:

> In addition, the committee understands that the faculty in the Department of Humanities is *not* of a single mind as to what constitutes the best pedagogical approach to improving student writing.

This sentence struck me because the committee didn't say where they got their understanding (I assume from informal discussion with members of the department) and because it appeared to be one of the few statements in the recommendation which could be verified from the committee's survey.

Although the statement appeared innocent enough, it was an important point. On the one hand, the committee could be saying that different people teach writing in different ways. So what? I always assumed that diversity was healthy in a writing program. Not only did it keep everyone honest, but because people are different, it enabled them to tailor their teaching to their strengths and weaknesses as teachers. Indeed, the committee appeared to be endorsing precisely this view when they went on to say:

> The committee makes no attempt to discern whether the variety of teaching methods and course requirements, in themselves, adversely affects the quality of student writing. In fact, we recognize that such variety is often necessary due to the diversity of writing skills among students.

But then, the committee suddenly and subtly shifted gears:

> Many committee members feel that there is a need for more consistent set of classroom teaching expectations and requirements than those which are currently employed.

Instead of differences in teaching methods, the committee was suggesting that there were differences in teacher expectations—in the goals and objectives of different sections of freshman composition. The two were quite different. It is one thing to have teachers who delay comments on mechanics until later drafts and teachers who comment on mechanics in every draft. These faculty disagree in their teaching methods but share common goals—correct, well-written papers. Such diversity is healthy. It's quite another to have a group of faculty who announce that mechanics aren't important and who refuse to correct or teach them and another group of faculty who believe that mechanics are important and teach accordingly. This is a disagreement in "expectations and requirements." The committee, in the report, began by suggesting that the first situation was the case in the Humanities Department at Michigan Tech, and ended by implying that the second situation was the case, implying, therefore, that the program was in disarray and that it was up to the committee to recommend "expectations and requirements" for freshman English.

Since the committee offered no evidence to back up their contention, I wondered if I could find anything in their survey which supported the claim that freshman composition teachers were not of one mind. Three groups of questions concerning issues of what affected grading, what comments faculty made in papers, and when faculty required papers to be revised seemed to address the question of what expectations faculty had. These questions are presented in Table 2.

Table 2. Questions Concerned with Teacher Expectations and Requirements from the Faculty Senate Freshman English Survey:

	All Faculty $n = 189$	*Engrg. Faculty* $n = 62$	*Other Faculty* $n = 102$	*Hums. Faculty* $n = 25$
5. Will students' grades suffer in *your* courses which require writing if they are not competent in formulating ideas and expressing the ideas clearly in writing?				
Yes	.69	.67	.56	.92
No	.03	.02	.04	0
Only if they are grossly incompetent	.29	.31	.33	.08
6. Will students' grades suffer in *your* courses which require writing if they are not competent in spelling, grammar, and correct word usage?				
Yes	.47	.37	.45	.76
No	.08	.08	.09	.04
Only if they are grossly incompetent	.43	.51	.46	.20

	All Faculty n = 189	Engrg. Faculty n = 62	Other Faculty n = 102	Hums. Faculty n = 25
7. When you return written assignments, term papers, exams, and reports, do you comment on any of the following if there is a problem?				
Clarity of writing				
Often	.62	.59	.55	.92
Sometimes	.36	.39	.42	.08
Never	.02	0	.03	0
Style of writing				
Often	.28	.24	.19	.68
Sometimes	.51	.57	.58	.20
Never	.19	.16	.23	.12
Spelling				
Often	.73	.67	.73	.88
Sometimes	.24	.31	.24	.12
Never	.02	.02	.02	0
Grammar				
Often	.61	.53	.59	.88
Sometimes	.33	.43	.35	.08
Never	.06	.06	.06	.04
Word Usage				
Often	.51	.51	.41	.84
Sometimes	.41	.41	.49	.16
Never	.07	.06	.10	0
Organization				
Often	.59	.55	.55	.88
Sometimes	.34	.45	.35	.08
Never	.06	0	.10	.04
8. Do you require students to revise their assignments, papers, or reports if they have not formulated and expressed ideas clearly?				
Usually	.18	.12	.12	.52
Sometimes	.39	.43	.36	.40
Rarely or never	.43	.45	.52	.08

Issues such as what will affect student grades, what faculty will comment on in papers, and the frequency with which faculty required revision, define the expectations and goals of a class as much as specific writing assignments do. As you can see in Table 2, the Humanities faculty's expectations about these matters were remarkably consistent: 92% of the humanities faculty said that grades would suffer in their courses which require writing if the writing is not competent in formulating ideas and expressing them clearly; 72% of the humanities faculty said grades would suffer if students were not competent in spelling, and another 20% said only if they were grossly incompetent.

Similarly in question 7, the Humanities faculty were consistent about the problem areas they would comment on, and in question 8 they were consistent in whether or not they would require revision—88% to 100% of the Humanities faculty responded 'often' or 'sometimes' to these questions.

It was beginning to look like all of our hard work suggesting revisions to the original questionnaire was actually going to pay off. The committee had made an assertion which was contradicted by their own survey data.

The senate met on a weekday night to discuss the recommendations of the Curricular Policy Committee. I wasn't able to attend, and heard the details second-hand. Our defense was in three parts. First, we argued that the Department of Humanities had a national reputation in the teaching of composition and didn't need to look to the College Board for leadership. Second, our current Freshman English guidelines already encompassed those of the College Board, but were tailored to the needs of our institution. And finally, on many points, the committee simply hadn't done adequate research, that the controls we already had were strong, and that the committee's survey in fact demonstrated that "we were of one mind" in the teaching of composition. A handout based on the data in Table 2 was distributed, but my data played at best a minor role in the proceedings. For the issue was not ultimately the quality of the survey or the merit of the recommendation but rather, would the senate reject a report prepared by a committee of their peers? It would be a major political step to have the committee's proposal reversed by the senate as a whole.

Aware that we had prepared a strong and academically sound critique of their report, the committee first moved that their recommendations be tabled for further study. Our department head, assistant head and director of Freshman English opposed this move on the grounds that the committee had had three years to prepare its recommendations and that to table it would imply tacit approval of its points. The move to table was defeated. The committee then recommended adoption of their proposal. The proposal was defeated by a vote of 11 for to 12 against.

*   *   *

Writing-across-the-curriculum research is political. Efforts to get teachers to use more writing in their classes take place within curricular and institutional contexts, and research to assess the effectiveness of those efforts takes place within that same context. The act of choosing certain features of a program to study carries political costs and implies political outcomes. Such political considerations are part of doing research. They are dangerous only when they keep you from asking interesting and significant questions or from using the best methods possible to answer those questions.

In their investigative review of the freshman composition program at Michigan Tech, the Curricular Policy Committee chose to survey faculty perceptions and to focus on the teaching of "grammar, spelling, word usage, and overall structure" for largely political reasons. They sought to find evidence that the writing program, with its "process" orientation, was poorly run and that it didn't meet the needs and expectations of the faculty rather than try to assess what actually went on in our classes. As a result, they produced a weak survey. And, quite frankly, our contributions to that survey didn't necessarily improve it as a research instrument; rather our revisions were as politically motivated as theirs: we hoped the survey would reflect favorably on the quality of writing instruction we offered at MTU.

Our experience with the Freshman English Survey was, however, an extreme example of the ways politics can limit research. It's possible to do a variety of interesting and significant experimental, curricular, and collaborative research within the complex institutional contexts of writing-across-the-curriculum programs, as I hope the work reported in this book demonstrates. Still, political battles, such as our fight to protect our freshman composition program, are inevitable. You cannot avoid these battles; you can only prepare for them.

Chapter 17

Mucking Around

MARGARET E. GORMAN

There are a lot of statistical dazzlers in the social sciences—psychology in particular. That's part of our reputation—to carry loads of computer output around the campus, to talk about computer time and to share secretively with our fellow researchers techniques to "rotate our data" and "account for covariates." A while back when psychologists got hold of sophisticated calculators and computers, we seemed to use the most complex multivariate tests that imagination could create; our literature from this time is filled with blinding dazzle. Similarly, the composition journals reflect a broad range of complexity in reporting research results, from simple accounts of students' experiences to dissertations that leave us lost in a sea of p's, r's, r's and f's. Do researchers really understand the statistical tests that they use, or do they simply want to impress us with the complexity of their work?

Recently, psychologists such as John Tukey (1977) are moving away from mere complexity to looking at their data in a careful but simple way. You don't have to be an expert statistician to collect and make sense of data. Even English teachers—or especially English teachers—should be able to ask good questions, collect information (data) and learn to "read" it. The trick is to be willing to muck around in the stuff you collect, without getting stuck in it.

Data

Data can be almost any kind of information that is collected and examined in some systematic way. Why collect data? Because you can't always trust your own intuitions about the effects of a teaching technique, or a program, or a research variable. You want to collect some specific information that has the potential to support, or disprove, or even just illuminate your intuitions. For example, in our poetry study (see Chapter 10) we could have simply noted that many of the poems were interesting and concluded that therefore the assignments were valuable. Instead, we decided to check our intuitions, so we included

228

several kinds of data—survey responses, written comments from students and the student writing itself. Different data require different analysis, sometimes with numbers and statistical tests, but they all provide a similar product: they help the investigator answer questions about some topic.

Data collection can be as simple as giving students a sheet of paper with questions like "How long did you spend on the assignment?" and "How do you feel about what you produced?" after they hand in poems they wrote for class. But you should know which questions are interesting and need to be asked. It may take a while to identify these precise questions; we developed the checklist for the poetic study out of responses to more general questions that we gave an earlier psychology class that wrote poems. We based our original list of general questions on some hunches we had about how students might react to writing poems for the class.

Hypotheses and Hunches

Sometimes we can state our questions clearly. In our poetry study we wanted to know, "Will students enjoy writing their poetic assignments more than their transactional ones?" However, other times we have no idea what will happen when we do something and therefore our questions are more general: "What will the poems these students write be like?" Data can help us approach both kinds of questions. In the first instance, with our specific question, we had a tool to assess students' feelings because we asked them to tell us how they felt about each assignment; we could count the number of positive and negative comments they made. But in the second instance, with the general question, we had the poems themselves to look at and draw conclusions from; here we were exploring rather than conducting hard-nosed analyses.

Doing research is often following a hunch about something. Although we didn't know what to expect from the student poems, on reading them we were struck by the number that rhymed—by how many seemed to struggle to find those words to rhyme with "schizophrenia." However, when we actually sorted the poems into stacks of rhymed or unrhymed pieces, we found we were wrong. Fewer than half rhymed. We must have been so amazed by the tortured patterns and weak limericks that we didn't notice that these represented a minority of the class writing. The moral is to be skeptical about those hunches and to look for data to document them . . . or to correct them.

The Value of Mistakes

Knowledge progresses *because* we make mistakes. A way to state this in research language is "Pilot your instruments!" Test your tools with a few samples before you mail out a thousand surveys. Try to answer the questions on your survey yourself, or give it to someone you know. We once designed a Curricular Practices Survey (see Chapter 6) that looked great to us because it would be easy to analyze on the computer. However, when we asked members of our evaluation team to fill it out, they were unable to *begin* to answer the questions on it and so we had to revise. Another time, we tested the instrument used to gauge student exposure to writing across the curriculum (see Chapter 7) on just one student. He was to indicate on a scale of one to seven how often he had classes that used journals, group work, and so on. This single student pointed out that since he had never experienced some of the activities on the list, he needed a zero on the scale. We changed the scale and Cindy Selfe tested it again with several students. Fortunately, that omission proved to be its only real problem.

Counting

You've collected some data to explore one of your hunches. Now what? A mass of data can be distressing. How can one person ever read it all and make any sense of it? As a researcher, I've felt this way many times; I know the frustration of being unable to make a connection between the statistical tests I've read about and the piles of raw numbers and responses that I wanted to analyze somehow. I learned through experience and now I have an idea of what to do first and a process to follow in examining a stack of survey responses or questionnaires.

Just start counting. I usually use a computer for my work because it's fast, but it's not essential. Many surveys ask "How many" questions: How many students kept journals for their classes? For how many classes did they keep journals? How many faculty members felt their courses improved after attending a workshop? When did students last write poems on their own? Answering this last question for the poetry study is a matter of counting how many students responded "grammar school," how many "junior high," and so on. We asked this question of the psychology students. Their responses are summarized in a frequency table as follows:

When Students Last Wrote a Poem on Their Own

	number of responses
never	18
grammar school	2
junior high	3
high school	10
early in college	16
Total	55

Notice the labels on the table. This table has a title, a clumsy one, but it describes what the table shows. It also labels what the numbers stand for (actual *number* of students), the total number of students (which you could add up each time you wanted to know, but why not write it down once and not re-add it each time you need the total?) and a description of each item on the scale ("never" to "early in college"). I've learned to be compulsive about carefully labeling my tables. When I have only one or two tables to cope with, I can remember that the third number down refers to the number of students who last wrote a poem for fun in junior high. However, as I draw more tables, or if I go on a vacation and return to my work a month later, or if I show the table to another person, it's good to have all that information clearly displayed on paper.

Sorting

What's next after counting some numbers? It depends on the questions that the data is attempting to study. Should we want to know if one group of people answers a question differently from another, we divide the mass of data up into groups and start counting again. In the Curricular Practices Survey, we wanted to know if the workshop had a different impact on participants from the various academic disciplines. To answer this, we divided the data according to discipline (Business, Engineering, Biology, etc.) and made a frequency table of how each group felt the workshop affected its teaching. A summary table, where we combined several disciplines into Engineering, Humanities/Social Sciences, and Other, appears as Table 2 of Chapter 6. Since we wanted to know if the workshop affected courses differently depending on enrollment we also sorted data according to enrollment and counted frequencies of responses. Table 3 of Chapter 6 shows these frequencies and also results for two other ways we used to sort data: number of times taught per year and academic rank.

Dazzle

You have drawn several tables of results and maybe calculated a mean score for each measure. What happens now depends on the research questions. If the issue is one like "When did students last write a poem?" the analysis is essentially complete in a summary table of their responses. We did nothing more sophisticated in the Curricular Practices Survey than calculate frequencies and percentages. This kind of report is impressive; you can really "see" what people think without having to do fancy contortions with the data.

Up to now, we have been talking about descriptive statistics. As Richard J. Harris says in his book, *A Primer of Multivariate Statistics,* "In their descriptive applications, statistical procedures provide a set of tools for summarizing efficiently the researcher's empirical findings in a form which is more readily assimilated by his audience than would be a simple listing of the raw data" (1975, p. 1). In other words, descriptive statistics organize and summarize data so that the researcher—and not just others, as Harris suggests—can see patterns in the numbers. Statistics, like writing, can be used for expressive as well as transactional purposes. Percentages, means, standard deviations and correlation coefficients are examples of descriptive statistics that can be arranged in tables or plotted on graphs to show trends in the data.

When you hear researchers drop terms like *analysis-of-variance* and *multiple regression,* they're talking about inferential statistics. Harris, again: "The inferential application of statistics provides protection against the universal tendency to confuse aspects of the data which are unique to the particular sample of subjects, stimuli, and conditions involved in a study with general properties of the populations from which these subjects, stimuli, and conditions were sampled. For instance, it often proves difficult to convince a subject who has just been through a binary prediction experiment involving, say, predicting which of two lights will be turned on in each of several trials that the experimenter had used a random number table in selecting the sequence of events" (p. 688).

Many researchers, like our subject trying to predict which light will flash, have a tendency to read enormous significance into subtle differences in their data. Inferential statistics were created to check the possibility that apperant patterns in data were simply random—due to chance. For example, the attitude changes we found on our Faculty Attitude Surveys (Chapter 5) might simply be the result of chance variations in participants' responses, e.g., because a few mistakenly marked the wrong number on the post version of the survey and almost all of these mistakes happened by chance to be in the predicted direction. However, our statistics assure us that the differences we reported could not have arisen by chance alone. Of course, anyone looking at these differences would have known they didn't arise by chance.

And that's the point. When the patterns in your data are *very* obvious, inferential statistics serve only to confirm what you already know. In cases where differences are smaller, they can give you a probability that the pattern you see arose by chance. One of the dangers of mucking around is that you can discover *some* kind of pattern even in a set of random numbers. Inferential statistics can help you distinguish results that arose simply by chance from results that are highly improbable. What statistics cannot tell you is what caused the results you observe. It's up to you, as the researcher, to explain why your data fell into a particular pattern. Information from essay questions, interviews and case-studies can be particularly useful in interpreting your numerical results. An example of this occurred when Art Young decided to ask participants to comment on how the workshops had changed their attitudes after they had filled out a series of rating scales covering specific attitudes. Their responses helped us understand what the numbers meant.

It isn't necessary to be a statistical whiz to do statistical tests such as the t-test or analysis of variance, but you do need to know what you're doing. There are a couple of ways to go about gaining this knowledge. One is to take a statistics course. Don't, however, rush over to a math department for a course in "Probability and Statistics" because it will probably be highly theoretical. Take a look instead at the more practical courses such as "research methods and statistics" offered in the social science departments, school of education or agriculture school.

Another way to learn about statistical tests is to read about them. Ask around for a good undergraduate statistics book. We recommend books used in one of the social sciences departments; they limit the discussions of theory to what is believed absolutely necessary for a conceptual understanding, and they emphasize real-world applications. In psychology, we have many good books, for example Vicki Sharp's *Statistics for the Social Sciences,* and Paul Herzberg's *Principles of Statistics.* Look at the delightful *How to Lie with Statistics* by Darrell Huff too.

The Consultant

Actually, the best way to get help with analyzing data is to find a consultant. Some colleges have statistical consultants on staff, but a competent graduate student—whose training in psychology, biology, sociology, mathematics or education includes several statistics courses—can help you design a study and analyze the data.

The first thing a consultant will ask you is, "What are you looking for? What is the goal of this study?" Be ready for this—be able to tell the consultant why you want to collect data and what you hope to do with it. If you are exploring a hunch, the consultant will help you figure out appropriate descriptive statistics. If you are testing a precisely formulated hypothesis, the consultant may agree to run some inferential analyses for you. But remember: try to see the consultant *before* you collect your data. The consultant may be able to save you from gathering data that can't be analyzed. Every consultant has horror stories about the time someone came in, dumped a wheelbarrow full of data on the desk and said, "Help me analyze this." After five minutes of discussion, it became apparent that no amount of statistical dazzle could sort out that mess. Like computers, statistics follow the golden rule: "garbage in, garbage out."

The Computer

If you want to do your own statistical tests, don't sign up immediately for a course in Fortran or Pascal either. Instead, ask about the statistical packages available on the computer at the institution, and find out who to talk to for instruction in using the packages. A statistical package contains instructions that can be fairly simple to learn and assume little knowledge of statistics, as in the case of a package called Mini-Tab, which is designed to teach statistics to beginners (Ryan, Joiner and Ryan, 1976). We do much of our work at Michigan Tech with a package called SPSS (Statistical Package for the Social Sciences). It's difficult for a beginner to use; get a consultant to help you with it. In either Mini-Tab or SPSS we type into the computer a set of instructions that tells the computer to do a certain procedure, such as a t-test or a frequency table. We then get a pile of computer output showing what we asked for, or listing errors that we made in our instructions. This is much easier than writing a Fortran or BASIC program to do all the arithmetic involved in statistics. Two other sophisticated statistical packages are SAS (Statistical Analysis System) and BMDP Statistical Software. SAS produces especially nice tables and charts. If you're not an experienced data-analyst, try learning Mini-Tab. It will teach you statistics while you learn to use it. For any of the other packages listed above, work with a consultant. Used properly, a statistical package will save you hours of hand calculations. But the danger of these packages is that they will seduce you into doing analyses that are much more complicated than you really need. Never do an analysis that you can't explain in general terms to a colleague—because someday someone will ask you to justify your analysis when you don't have your consultant with you to start babbling about "arc sine transformations" and "canonical covariates."

Conclusion

So, you want to do more than report your impressions, and the impressions of your friends, that your writing-across-the-curriculum program is working wonderfully. You don't need to have two years of graduate training in statistics to collect and analyze data that will tell you the real effects of your program—if you keep a few simple principles in mind.

1. Think about how you're going to analyze your data *before* you collect it. Check with a consultant, if one is available, first. But come to the consultant with some ideas of your own. Even if you don't have a consultant, don't despair. Design simple, descriptive analyses that will summarize the data in tables or charts.

2. Gather different kinds of data—both quantitative and qualitative. Interviews and open-ended questions can help you make sense of numbers and add an important human element to your research. Conversely, numbers can keep you from reading your biases into the open-ended responses. We know how participants felt about the writing-across-the-curriculum workshops and we also know what techniques they added to their courses as a consequence of the workshops; the two kinds of data complement each other.

3. Don't be afraid to play with your data—to look for surprises. Donald Murray (1984) talks about the value of surprise in writing and teaching. The same holds true for research. When you begin a research project, you should have a plan, but you should always hope the data will surprise you. Sometimes, the surprises may be unpleasant; your program didn't produce the effects you expected it to. But that's when the exciting part begins—you can figure out what your program actually did, and how to make it better.

Chapter 18

Reflections

How Well Does Writing Across the Curriculum Work?

TOBY FULWILER

This essay is my attempt to set down, as frankly as possible, some of the lessons I've learned from overseeing a writing-across-the-curriculum program and conducting faculty workshops for the past six years. The goals and objectives, the theories and the successes of writing-across-the-curriculum programs have been fully described elsewhere in books, periodicals, and conferences; this essay will try not to repeat those assertions and descriptions. Suffice it to say that I believe the programs do work and that the interdisciplinary writing workshops are the very best way to introduce those programs to college and university faculties.

Teaching writing in English classes or outside of English classes remains more art than science; we still know very little about what happens at the moment of insight, inspiration, or ideation. Nor do we know predictable routes of faithful translation from thought to language, from pen to paper. So in every attempt to "teach" others to teach writing more often and more thoughtfully in their classes, problems arise with translation, motivation, situation, assumptions, pedagogy, terminology, personality, and turf. At the same time we who started such programs hoping to amplify the lessons of freshman composition soon found that we had stumbled into fertile territory for pedagogical research, faculty development, institutional cohesion, and personal growth.

The following personal reflections address two central issues which may never yield answers solely in numbers: what didn't work that we thought would—and why it didn't; and what happened that we didn't expect, but liked when it happened.

Problems

In the course of conducting some forty workshops, both at Michigan Tech and elsewhere, I encountered numerous questions for which I didn't have good answers. Sometimes I used language that conjured up inappropriate images; other times I hazarded solutions to problems with which I had no direct experience. But I learned and I think my answers have become more accurate, qualitied, and careful. While some of these problems are institutional, others are specific to the disciplines or personalities of workshop participants. All nonetheless need to be dealt with, one way or another, by people who plan and conduct writing-across-the-curriculum programs

Terminology

From the start we designed our program around a particular unified set of ideas and hoped to stick to those ideas consistently from workshop to workshop. We did so hoping the entire academic community would soon share common assumptions about writing and terminology to describe those assumptions and perhaps assign and evaluate student writing with a good measure of consistency. In particular we introduced our colleagues to James Britton's scheme for explaining the functions of writing: "expressive" (personal, informal writing to yourself to find out what is on your mind); "transactional" (writing to inform, instruct, or persuade someone about something); and "poetic" (writing used as art, where form, structure, and style may be more important than content). We felt this schema made sense, was easy to explain, and pointed toward certain overlooked solutions to the underuse and misuse of writing throughout the curriculum; namely, that more expressive writing in all subject areas would help students both to learn better and to learn to write better.

Often, however, we had trouble explaining exactly what the term "expressive" writing meant: to many teachers "expressive" connoted a dangerous freedom of language that suggested all sorts of educational license. We could usually dispel these anxieties over the duration of a several-day workshop, but the problem kept surfacing when people who had attended workshops tried to explain the ideas to colleagues back at campus or when we made brief presentations using that term without having the time to explore it fully. As a colleague in the School of Business recounted later: "Toby and Art Young came over trying to sell the department on workshops and then we got involved in the expressive-transactional argument again. And I think that the whole department has gotten a negative attitude." No matter how hard and lucidly (we thought) we explained the crucial distinction and relationship between the two functions of language, a number of faculty would never accept the idea that informal writing to oneself had anything to do with formal communication to somebody else—teachers, for instance. My School of Business friend tried to explain his colleagues' misconceptions: "I think the attitude of the School of Business for the most part is that . . . transactional writing has been replaced by expressive writing, poor sentence structure and no concern for spelling.

This fundamental misunderstanding lasted for over three years until we finally arranged a special exam-week, two-day workshop for his whole department and cleared up the problem once and for all. Some of my co-directors substituted terms like "exploratory" or "speculative" writing to avoid some of this terminology problem; however, the concept of informal, personal, or journal writing is of questionable value to faculty outside the humanities and no matter what language you describe it in, you must be prepared for some unsettling questions. Ironically, I had fewer problems with this on campuses where I came in as an "outside consultant": my pedestal was higher and so my terminology was less debatable.

Resistance

We learned right away that writing workshops can't inspire or transform unmotivated, inflexible, or highly suspicious faculty members. Participants must volunteer with an open mind and be willing to share ideas, rather than compete with them in order for the workshops to work. Some people seem to be constitutionally uncomfortable with workshop-style activities which require a lot of participant risks, such as reading aloud one's own writing to colleagues or generating consensus ideas or writing in a personal journal. These same teachers may never feel comfortable generating classroom dialogue, assigning journals, or trusting students to evaluate each other's writing. Such people often attend with good intentions, but can't adapt the informal workshop style to their own learning and teaching styles. One person, for example, from mathematics couldn't identify with any activity that encouraged multiple drafts as the route to good writing: he *always* wrote well in one draft and couldn't understand why others couldn't also. I believed that he spoke truly about his own writing process, but his vocal resistance was such that many in the workshop found him difficult to work with and I had a hard time being patient with his intolerance. The mode of writing and learning we presented in our model didn't match his model at all.

Other participants who have been ordered by their department heads to attend the workshops and who do so out of resentment rather than personal interest often pose more serious problems. These professors most often block things by negation, by what they won't do: they won't keep journals, they won't try freewrites, they won't share writing with colleagues or revise or participate in peer group exercises that would affirm the value of the workshop. While such participants have been few, I can vividly remember each one of them. Their participation—or lack thereof—puts such a strong damper on workshops that we think leaders should go to great lengths to insist that participants attend voluntarily. Yet we realize that if only the already committed attend, we're not reaching out as widely as we would like.

Turf

People sometimes ask me, with a twinkle in their eyes, what disciplinary group is most difficult to work with at workshops, from which disciplines do I expect trouble. I could generalize (dangerously) and say that philosophers and English teachers, on whose language turf the workshops most obviously intrude, raise the most skeptical questions. "How do you know Britton's theories are correct?"

"What empirical evidence proves that journal writing facilitates learning?" "The ideas of Quine and Chomsky contradict what you are saying." Philosophers especially question every assumption and argue fine points of terminology and language use. In the process they have taught me to stay closer to ideas verifiable by personal experience and to stay away from too much theory, which is always debatable from one point of view or another anyway. English teachers, especially those who view their proper domain as literature, often don't believe that their colleagues in other disciplines can teach anything about writing: consequently they often want to instruct them on how to do it—which gets dangerously close to telling them how to teach—and that raises severe problems in all sorts of directions.

To be fair, I could also say that some of the most helpful people in workshops have been astute philosophers and savvy English teachers. Critical colleagues with open minds who raise questions of concern to all are the very best people in a writing workshop; however, people out to celebrate their own wit and wisdom cause problems and often incur the wrath of the other participants who are confused by too much disagreement among experts. All this is, of course, predictable; the remarkable fact is how well most of the mixed discipline people get on most of the time.

Translation

A good workshop offers a smorgasbord of strategies, practices, and techniques to improve both writing and learning, and participants are free to adopt those that suit their personality, pedagogy, or situation. But it doesn't always happen the way we expect, predict, or prefer. As a group, mathematics teachers seem to have the hardest time figuring out how workshop ideas apply to their teaching. One mathematics teacher, for example, who seemed to understand theoretically most of what went on at the workshop, stated later that the only thing he could think to do, practically, was send all his 150 calculus students to tour the writing lab—under penalty of failing the course. He did, and they all went, but we believe such translations are as likely to make students resentful of the lab as to seek help in it. Another mathematics teacher who enthusiastically used writing in a small upper-division project-oriented course found it virtually impossible to include it in her several first-year calculus courses: "The course material itself is not very conducive to writing. You can have students read a story problem or maybe make up some of their own, but . . . they don't have the mathematical sophistication, because they're just starting out, to create story problems." So, while I may think writing workshop ideas translate to all disciplines, my colleagues often tell me differently, and I have learned to accept that.

Numbers

Professors who teach courses with enrollments larger than fifty or sixty, often several hundred, report major difficulties in including more writing in their classes, even though, in theory, there are ways to do this. I have stopped arguing with them. Large classes are lousy places in which to ask for writing, unless well-trained graduate assistants or "readers" are available to help out. A colleague who teaches electrical engineering technology, when interviewed a year after attending a workshop, described his situation this way: "Labs are part of our teaching load each term and generate approximately 80 labs [reports] a week. Correcting these labs makes it very difficult to be motivated to ask for additional writing assignments." A mathematics professor who teaches in a fixed three-term calculus course, one of many such sections offered by her department, explained that "not only is the class large, but our courses are so full of material that must be covered and because the students have to take these courses in sequence, the engineering departments tell us we have to cover a certain amount of material in a certain amount of time." In other words, general ideas only translate into specific practices when an instructor perceives the conditions are right and appropriate. Although there are a variety of non-graded writing assignments that do work for some instructors, large numbers of students in a class remain a problem.

Trust

Perhaps the most difficult practice for teachers across the curriculum to use is peer review, where students read (aloud or silently) and critique each other's papers in a draft stage and then revise them for the instructor's review. An otherwise successful forestry professor, after trying peer review in his class, called it "a lead balloon," explaining that some good students "suffered because his peers didn't do a good review." Another colleague in civil engineering noted: "Some students take it kind of lightly and they don't do a very good job. And then the other student that's being reviewed, of course, resents that." He went on to say that even when students take it seriously, they don't like to hurt their classmates' feelings: "Most of the time they're afraid to be critical."

I fully understand that problem. Peer review only works for me when I trust both the process and the students enough to work them hard; that is, when I return to the process more than two or three times during the term in the same groups of four or five. Used less than that, students simply don't have the time to develop trust in each other or to develop that critical skeptical eye so important to good revision. The teacher in content-area courses who tries this once or twice, with or without specific guidelines, will have a real problem making it work. The teacher who makes peer review work—and several of my cross-curricular colleagues do have good success stories here—modifies his or her course substantially to make enough time and room for it to happen.

Dabbling

I've come to believe that you can only teach a writing process approach to process-oriented people. This implies first, that some colleagues, already on our wavelengths, are already doing some of the things we suggest and use the workshops primarily for reinforcement. That's good. But it also implies that many others who attend have a rather product-oriented approach to the whole teaching business: students must learn that what counts in the real world is the final report, the finished letter, the completed project—not the evidence of effort as one struggles to get there. (My own bias shows strongly here.) For these teachers, no matter how much we stress techniques and strategies to *generate* good final products (journal writes, freewrites, multiple drafts, etc.), the workshop produces only superficial change in their attitudes or practices. (Six months after she attended a workshop and told us how much it meant to her, a professor who teaches in forestry said that the main things she looks for on papers are "spelling, style, and neatness." While we don't dismiss these items, her answer dismays us.)

On the one hand, we're not surprised when product-oriented teachers leave the workshop with one or two ideas, but no real commitment to process-oriented education. On the other hand, we are surprised when the process-oriented teacher can't get a good process idea to work. And this problem haunts a lot of really good committed teachers. If we only try peer reviews a few times they'll fail; if we don't keep a journal ourselves the journals will seem like busywork; if we don't carefully plan papers to come in at different draft stages, they'll all come in at once at the end of the term. The point is that lots of good ideas fail because we don't fully commit ourselves to make them work; we don't or can't spend the requisite time to make them work. Large classes, or too many classes, or research and publication pressure—whatever the reason, teachers need to be awfully dedicated to make a new idea a regular part of their pedagogical repertoire. We don't mean to, but we often do dabble rather than commit ourselves.

Location

On a related note, it's instructive to examine the colleges where writing across the curriculum seems to work best. It doesn't get too far at large, research-oriented universities where teaching is not a high priority. Or if it does, the program is shaped like that at the University of Michigan, where one upper-level writing course and one committed teacher per discipline is the solution; no attempt is made to make most teachers pay attention to writing. Nor is writing across the curriculum needed at certain places—at well-endowed small liberal arts colleges with high SAT students and low teacher-student ratios—because writing has been an integral part of instruction all along: teaching was always valued and writing remained a natural way to teach well. The places where such writing-across-the-curriculum programs seem most likely to be needed and have a chance of success are the public schools where faculty have fairly high teaching loads and medium to low research and publication pressure. But these same institutions, like my own, work their teachers hard, and good ideas therefore need to be awfully practical and good teachers awfully dedicated to get writing back into the curriculum.

Overselling

I learned that when I strongly endorse one idea which works well for me, I can set up other teachers for failure: no idea will work for absolutely everyone every time. This has happened several times with journals, for example, an idea which I probably oversold at earlier workshops. A business teacher who tried to use journals found herself feeling silly asking classes of 100 students to "take out your journals"; it's a phrase you actually need to practice to feel comfortable saying out loud. Another colleague in metallurgy collected student journals from all of his three sections at the same time and was overheard cursing me out loud in his office, 180 journals piled high on his desk: he overdid what I oversold and the result was not good. To teach journals well, teachers need to keep one themselves and learn how it works firsthand. The same is true for multiple-draft assignments: teachers need to watch their own writing process to know how to assign and evaluate best. And while a workshop of several days allows some opportunity for teachers to learn what it takes to write and read certain kinds of assignments, it's never really enough unless a teacher is sympathetic to begin with. This last point is crucial: the teachers who take the most away from a workshop are always those who were already doing some of the things we talked about. Perhaps the greatest value of the workshops is reinforcing one's current predispositions and practices. But even those sympathetic to a good idea know better than I when an idea *won't* work in their classes. One teacher explained that journals had no place in her course because "In mathematics, at least at the stage we're talking about, something's either right or wrong—there's seldom an in-between. You don't offer opinions about it in the same way you would discussing D. H. Lawrence, Hemingway, or Shakespeare."

Follow up

Short-term attitude changes don't guarantee long-term pedagogical changes. We already know that ideas which seemed bright and shiny in the workshop light have dimmed considerably after a year or two in our long, dark Michigan winter, due to increased teaching loads, large classes, administrative responsibilities, lack of collegial support, pressures to research, publish, write grants, and the like. We would be naive to believe we could maintain workshop-level intensity throughout the academic year. As my co-director Cynthia Selfe put it: "Of course they write and think about writing in the pine-scented wilderness that surrounds Alberta [where we do our summer workshops]. What else is there to do?" So while some teachers change their syllabi to reflect a new awareness of the role of process in assignment making, others do not. While some teachers immediately try out journals, others don't—and some who optimistically assigned journals one term find them too much trouble to assign the next.

But just as many follow-up problems can be traced to those of us who lead the workshops. Some years we have had alumni reunions, winter workshops, guest speakers, discipline-specific seminars with individual departments and informational mailings—one year we even published a monthly newsletter. Other years we, who were supposed to keep the writing spirit alive on campus, initiated nothing at all, for whatever reasons, because we were careless, overworked, lazy, or forgetful. In fact, it is hard to assess "blame" here; universities are busy places with lots going on, pulling all of us in multiple and different directions. We don't believe a writing-across-the-disciplines program can maintain white heat (or even red) throughout its term of operation. At the same time we remain convinced that these programs only work when they are long-term; that is, follow-up activities must continue no matter how difficult it becomes to find something new to do or how discouraging when no one shows up. As Art Young, the co-founder of our Tech program, puts it: "Ours is a model that will need continual care and thought—even after the five-year period [of external funding]—because it is primarily a faculty program rather than curricular." In other words, the teacher-centered model depends on teacher energy and informed pedagogy to keep working.

Carrots

At the very time we initiated our writing-across-the-curriculum program with the strong encouragement of our deans and academic vice president, these very same administrators were encouraging higher standards for tenure and promotion, asking for more research, more publications, and the generation of more external money. Over the past six years these competing movements have actually pushed faculty at our university in opposing directions, suggesting that they spend more time assigning and evaluating student writing, on the one hand, while asking them to research and publish more of their own work on the other. Mixed messages. One colleague in mechanical engineering wearily described himself in a double bind: the better his teaching, which included using lots of workshop ideas, the further behind he fell with his own research, and the less recognition he received from his department or profession. This, again, may be a faultless position, one of the many double binds that serious teacher-researchers face all the time. I have no doubt that the pressure to be a publishing professional modifies, to some extent, the energy available to be an innovative teacher—which doesn't mean that the two roles can't be kept in some sort of positive balance. But it isn't easy. A colleague in anthropology confided: "I have been, as you know, an enthusiastic supporter of student writing assignments, but to be honest, I'm souring. It's taken a lot of time and I feel it's not rewarded. Hence I have decided that next year I won't spend so much time 'teaching'; I am going to spend those 30 hours of student conference time doing my own writing. I agree it was valuable for them . . . it's just not so for me."

Unexpected Benefits

When we initiated our writing-across-the-curriculum program, we articulated our central concern as "improving students' writing ability." We soon learned—as we should have expected—that "writing ability" was related to all sorts of social, intellectual, and emotional domains which involved the entire campus community. As soon as the business of teaching writing, as well as the act of writing itself, was placed in this larger context, and as soon as we decided to offer our workshops as "explorations" rather than "conclusions" about the teaching of writing, we opened a much larger door than we ever anticipated. This part of the essay describes some lessons we didn't expect to learn and testifies to the power of an open-ended model to continue to stimulate and inform all involved.

Community of Scholars

We all learned, after the very first workshop, how wonderful it was to join with one's colleagues to discuss substantive issues of mutual concern without the everyday distractions of phone calls, mail, meetings, and memos. Prior to the writing workshops no such mechanism for promoting collegial interactions existed in a regular way on campus: neither department, senate, and committee meetings nor special-topic seminars provided the focused time for social and intellectual stimulation across disciplinary lines. As one colleague put it: "The support of colleagues has been magnificent. I appreciated the opportunity to become better acquainted with my colleagues, the opportunity to form friendships." Another said: "Many faculty members who did not know each other or did not understand each other's discipline now feel a common bond. I think this will be useful and valuable to the college in a number of ways . . . committee assignments, interdepartmental projects, advice, etc." The chance for such interaction, even more than the reason for the interaction in the first place, has proved the most powerful reason for the program's success. The workshops actually remind some people why they became college teachers in the first place—before they retreated to separate buildings, isolated offices, and competitive research.

Environment

There has been a noticeable, but difficult to measure, shift in the general campus atmosphere about writing. It crops up in lunchroom talks, when colleagues joke that they'd better get out their journals for a quick entry now that I've arrived. But the jokes suggest to me an increased and not unpleasant consciousness about writing that didn't exist before. In a conversation I had with the president of our university, Dale Stein, who had helped initiate the program in 1977, he said that recruiters had been telling him recently that MTU graduates were better at both writing and speaking than in former years. I mentally raised my eyebrows in disbelief, not willing to accept that such a generalization, nice though it was to hear, could possibly be true. But President Stein added that he firmly believed that an attitude shift had occurred which elevated writing to serious business in the campus community and that this was reflected in the communication skills of graduating seniors. I want, of course, to believe in such an improvement—but it remains difficult to prove. Informal clues like this tell us that something is at work here that may never show up in one or two concrete assessments of teacher attitudes or student writing abilities.

Teacher Writing

By being asked to write themselves, many participants gained confidence in their own writing ability, or at least an awareness of why they were nervous about it. As one participant wrote: "I was quite apprehensive about attending this workshop when I found out that we would be writing a lot. . . . Writing has not always been my strength. . . . But I found that the apprehension was unwarranted; I found I could write OK, even my colleagues in the English Department said so. This was a pleasant surprise and morale/ego booster." Another wrote: "I now see that much of my hesitancy and anxiety about writing comes from a fear of censure from . . . my professional peers. I've assumed that all my writing must be witty, intelligent, elegant, etc., so that composing takes on crisis dimensions. This is something I will have to grapple with." What this teacher sees is how unwitty and inelegant his colleagues can be too. Such insights are, I believe, crucial for progress in one's own composing skills as well as for increased empathy for student writers.

Sometimes those of us who teach English, who enjoy using language and don't fear writing, forget how many of our colleagues have had unpleasant experiences themselves at the hands of English teachers in high school or freshman composition classes. Sadly enough, our profession has become better known for its concern with conventionality and correctness than for its celebration of joy and risk-taking in writing. Not only do current students fear our "red pencils," so do all our past generations of students who are now PhD's and who now teach biology, history, geography, and business in many university departments. Some of them too, along with carpenters and shopkeepers, exclaim when they meet us: "Better watch my grammar." It's not enough to come back with a flip, "It ain't so." The John Simons and Edwin Newmans have terrified us all.

One of the really nice things that happens at these workshops, sometimes, is that our colleagues gain confidence in their writing which extends to their professional work. A participant from political science who attended our first workshop later credited that session with giving him the confidence to write a book—which was published two years later. And my colleague, Art Young, received a letter from a workshop participant who wrote: "You probably don't need at this point further proof that your workshop processes work, but I thought I'd write and tell you that my essay that I wrote during the 1st Augusta College workshop . . . 'The Poor Man's Word Processor' was just accepted by [a professional business journal]. And I did it with almost no further revision other than that suggested by you and the other readers in my group. . . .'"

Teaching Methods

Some teachers learned that they could still learn something about teaching. We suspect that, at the college level in particular, teachers often assume they are talking to adults and that all they need to do is impart knowledge in some matter-of-fact way and it will be learned. And of course no college teacher worth his or her salt will ever admit to having taken an "education course" during college—whatever the merit of such courses. As a consequence, the model of the faculty workshop, which is inquiry based, and in which problems are posed for group solution and answers generated by participant interaction, offers a process view of teaching quite different from the traditional lecture and discussion format to which many teachers are accustomed. One geography professor told me a year later that ideas from the workshop ("WAC ideas") changed the learning atmosphere in his class: "When I have used WAC ideas, I have found my courses, especially the larger enrollment courses, are less stiff, formal, and dependent on lectures. Especially the use of freewrites has been a great help in stimulating discussion and class participation. I have been more likely to *plan* a class so that discussion will occur." Such translations occur when sensitive teachers watch how they themselves enjoy learning and in turn pass those "lessons" on to their students.

We interviewed a forestry professor six months after he attended an August workshop and found that he had already tried out a lot of specific workshop ideas in his fall classes: some worked well, like the "field-trip journals" he required in place of field notebooks, and "audience-specific assignments" in which his students wrote reports for multiple audiences in the forest management industries. But more than applying any specific practice, the instructor reported modifying his basic pedagogical approach because of the overall learning model introduced at the workshops. In his own words he began moving "away from the evaluation approach and more toward the process. I feel more attuned to teaching thought processes." Along with Dewey, Piaget, Bruner, and Britton, we believe strongly in the power and authenticity of discovery learning and are pleased when this larger translation occurs, but we don't expect it.

Tenure and Promotion.

One administrator told us that the workshops should improve overall faculty performance: "I am frankly most impressed by the potential for *faculty development* that stems from this program. Granted the students will benefit, but I will be much surprised if the individuals who have completed the experience do not perform better as researchers and in their service activities, as well as in the classroom." We know this is true in cases where the workshops give teachers more confidence about their writing ability, but I would also propose that the workshops have been stimuli for new pedagogical research questions in a variety of disciplines. In our own department there has been a documentable rise in faculty publications since the project began, most of which stem from the project work itself. In particular, a number of collaborative research-in-writing projects have developed involving an English instructor and someone from a different discipline. (These projects are reported on elsewhere in this volume.)

Cohesion

Neither Art Young nor I entered the project with the idea of writing a book, nor could we have predicted that the department, as it was formulated in 1977 when we began the project, could author a book. But that is what happened. As we recruited new faculty for our department, who had varying specialities from "technical writing" and "reading" to "problem-solving" and "conferencing," we realized that we did, in fact, have the material for writing a book aimed at workshop participants from all disciplines. Consequently, the process of planning, writing, and editing the book, *Language Connections: Writing and Reading across the Curriculum* (Urbana, Ill.: National Council of Teachers of English, 1982), helped unite a dozen teachers on our staff in a collaborative effort providing both intellectual and social cohesion among the participating writers. Constructing this book gave us a common concern, apart from teaching and conducting workshops; in some cases, it actually provided colleagues with their first substantial professional publication. And it gave us a goal to shoot for: finishing the manuscript.

The collaborative book became a symbol of the collaborative activity and research which this project inspired from the beginning. The workshops are always conducted by teams from our department, which rotate from year to year. Other department members make guest appearances to present special workshops on "reading" or "speaking" or "the language laboratory" within the larger workshop. New teams were created to visit different departments and publicize and recruit for the workshops. Through it all we met off and on, as a group, planning what to do next to make things work. The net professional effects of this cooperative effort were numerous joint teaching experiments, collaborative grant proposals, and co-authored articles: for example, I have co-authored articles with eight different colleagues in the department over the past five years.

I think that, in general, the scientific and technical fields do more cooperative research and scholarship than those in the humanities, though there are notable and admirable exceptions, usually promoted by NEH. This project taught us well about the fruits of working together on funding, teaching, researching, and writing to effect positive changes in both our university and the profession at large.

*   *   *

So we did not know when we started our program in 1977 that what began as an effort to improve student writing skills would grow into a comprehensive long-term program to develop more fully all the interrelated learning and communication skills of the whole campus community. Nor did we realize in how many different directions research and evaluation questions would take us, nor the degree of local cooperation and national publicity we would receive. Nor did I know, personally, that this project would become the substance of my professional life for the better part of a decade.

The Humanities Department will continue to monitor and nurture the program which now possesses a life of its own. Remember, there are more than two hundred Michigan Tech teachers out there doing all sorts of stuff in the name of "writing across the curriculum." Research, both qualitative and quantitative, has taught us a great deal about the program we created. Yet it's hard to "prove" absolutely that something works. As I said at the outset, the program we have conducted is amorphous, hard to pin down, and impossible to keep total track of. As my dissertation advisor, Merton Sealts, used to say when I wanted to try something off-beat or experimental: "What works, works." To which I add, "But not all the time, nor for everyone, and sometimes better than we guessed."

References

Applebee, A. (1983). *A study of writing in the secondary school.* Urbana, IL: National Council of Teachers of English.

Applebee, F. L., & Auten, A. (1981) Learning to write in the secondary school: How and where. *English Journal, 70.* 78-82.

Bancroft, T. A. (1968). *Topics in intermediate statistical methods.* Ames, IA: Iowa State University Press.

Berthoff, A. (1978). *Forming/thinking/writing: The composing imagination.* Rochelle Park, NJ: Hayden.

_____. (1983). *The making of meaning.* Montclair, NJ: Boynton/Cook.

Bleich, D. (1975). *Readings and feelings: An introduction to subjective criticism.* Urbana, IL: National Council of Teachers of English.

_____. (1978) *Subjective criticism.* Baltimore: Johns Hopkins University Press.

Britton, J. (1970). *Language and learning.* Harmondsworth, U.K.: Penguin.

Britton, J. Burgess, T., Martin, N., McLeod, A., & Rosen, H. (1975). *The development of writing abilities 11-18.* London: Macmillan Education Press.

Bruffee, K. (1973). Collaborative learning: Some practical models. *College English,* ✓ *34,* 634-643.

Bruner, J. S. (1966). *Toward a theory of instruction.* Cambridge, MA: Harvard University Press.

Chorny, M. (1980). A context for writing. In A. Freedman & I. Pringle (Eds.), *Reinventing the rhetorical tradition* (pp. 1-8). Conway, AR: L & S Books.

Clifford, J. (1981). Composing in stages: The effects of a collaborative pedagogy. ✓ *Research in the Teaching of English, 15,* 37-53.

Comprone, J. (1979). Burke's dramatism as a means of using literature to teach composition. *The Rhetoric Society Quarterly, 9,* 142-155.

Cronbach, L. J. (1982). *Designing evaluations of educational and social programs.* San Francisco: Jossey-Bass.

Daly, J. (1983). *Writers' dispositional attitudes and beliefs: Conceptualization, measurement, and interrelationships.* Paper presented at the AERA Conference, Montreal.

Daly, J. & Miller, M. D. (1975). The empirical development of an instrument to measure writing apprehension. *Research in the Teaching of English, 9,* 242–249.

D'Angelo, F. (1975). *A conceptual theory of rhetoric.* Cambridge, MA: Winthrop.

Davis, R. M. (1977). How important is technical writing? A survey of the opinions of successful engineers. *The Technical Writing Teacher, 4,* 83–88.

Davis, B. G., Scriven, M., & Thomas, S. (1981). *The evalauation of composition instruction.* Inverness, CA: Edgepress.

Diederich, P. (1974). *Measuring growth in English.* Urbana, IL: National Council of Teachers of English.

Dyson, F. (1979). *Discovering the universe.* New York: Harper.

Elbow, P. (1973). *Writing without teachers.* New York: Oxford University Press.

_____. (1981). *Writing with power.* New York: Oxford University Press.

Emig, J. (1971). *The composing processes of twelfth graders.* Urbana, IL: National Council of Teachers of English.

_____. (1977). Writing as a mode of learning. *College Composition and Communication, 28,* 122–128.

_____. (1978). Eye, hand, and brain. In C. R. Cooper & L. Odell (Eds.), *Research on composing: Points of departure,* (pp. 59–72). Urbana, IL: National Council of Teachers of English.

_____. (1981). *The web of meaning.* Montclair, NJ: Boynton/Cook.

_____. (1982). Inquiry paradigms and writing. *College Composition and Communication, 33,* 64–75.

Faigley, L. & Witte, S. (1981). Analyzing revision. *College Composition and Communication, 32,* 406–411.

Faigley, et al. (1981). *Writing after college: A stratified survey of the writing of college-trained people* (Writing Program Assessment, Technical Report No. 1, Fund for the Improvement of Post-Secondary Education Grant No. G008005896). Austin: University of Texas.

Ferguson, G. A. (1976). *Statistical analysis in psychology and education.* New York: McGraw-Hill.

Field, J. & Weiss, R. (1979). *Cases for composition.* Boston: Little, Brown.

Flower, L. (1981). *Problem-solving strategies for writing.* New York: Harcourt Brace Jovanovich.

Flower, L. & Hayes, J. (1979). Writer-based prose: A Cognitive basis for problems in writing. *College English, 41,* 19–37.

_____. (1980). The cognition of discovery: Defining a rhetorical problem. *College Composition and Communication, 31,* 21–32.

_____. (1981). A cognitive process theory of writing. *College Composition and Communication, 32,* 365–387.

_____. (1981). Identifying the organization of writing processes. In L. W. Gregg & E. R. Steinberg (Eds.) *Cognitive processes in writing* (pp. 3-33). Hillsdale, NJ: Lawrence Erlbaum Associates.

_____. (1981). The pregnant pause: An inquiry into the nature of planning. *Research in the Teaching of English, 15,* 229-243.

Forum for Liberal Education, Vol. 3 (6). (1981, April).

Freire, P. (1970). *Pedagogy of the oppressed.* New York: Herder and Herder.

Freisinger, R. (1980). Cross-disciplinary writing programs: Theory and practice. *College English, 42* (7), 154-166.

_____. (1982). Respecting the image: A transactional view of language and cognition. *Iowa English Bulletin, 31,* 5-9.

Fulwiler, T. (1981). Journals across the disciplines. *English Journal, 69,* 14-19.

_____. Interdisciplinary writing workshops. *CEA Critic, 43* (2), 27-32.

_____. (1981) Showing, not telling, at a writing workshop. *College English, 43* (1), 55-63.

_____. (1981). Writing across the curriculum at Michigan Tech: Theory and practice. *WPA: Writing Program Administration, 4* (3), 15-21.

_____. (1982). The personal connection: Journal writing across the curriculum. In T. Fulwiler & A. Young (Eds.) *Language connections: Writing and reading across the curriculum* (pp. 15-31). Urbana, IL: National Council of Teachers of English.

Fulwiler, T. & Young, A. (Eds.). (1982). *Language connections: Writing and reading across the curriculum.* Urbana, IL: National Council of Teachers of English.

Goodman, K. (1976). What we know about reading. In D. Allen & D. J. Watson (Eds.) *Findings of research in miscue analysis: Classroom implications* (pp. 57-70). Urbana, Il: National Council of Teachers of English.

Goodman, P. (1962). *Compulsory mis-education and the community of scholars.* New York: Random House.

Gorman, M. E. (In press). Using *The Eden Express* to teach introductory psychology. *Teaching Psychology.*

Goswami, D. et al. (1981). *Writing in the professions: A course guide and instructional materials for an advanced composition course.* Unpublished manuscript produced by the Document Design Project, National Institute of Education.

Graves, D. (1975). An examination of the writing processes of seven year old children. *Research in the Teaching of English, 9,* 227-241.

_____. (1979). Research doesn't have to be boring. *Language Arts, 56,* 76-80.

_____. (1983). Teacher intervention in children's writing: A response to Myra Barrs. *Language Arts, 60,* 841-846.

_____. (1979). What children show us about revision. *Language Arts, 56,* 312-319.

_____. (1982, winter). Break the welfare cycle. *Forum,* 75-77.

Harris, R. J. (1975). *A primer of multivariate statistics.* New York: Academic Press.

Hawkins, T. (1976). *Group inquiry techniques for teaching writing.* Urbana, IL: ERIC/National Council of Teachers of English.

Herzberg, P. (1983). *Principles of statistics.* New York: John Wiley & Sons.

Hollingsworth, A. (1979). Review of L. Rosenblatt, *The reader, the text, the poem: The transactional theory of the literary work. College English, 41,* 223-227.

Houp, K. & Pearsall, T. (1984). *Reporting technical information* (5th ed.) New York: Macmillan.

Huff, D. (1954). *How to lie with statistics.* New York: W. W. Norton & Co.

Janis, I. L. (1972). *Victims of groupthink.* Boston: Houghton-Mifflin.

Jeffrey, C. (1981). Teachers' and students' perceptions of the writing process. *Research in the Teaching of English, 15,* 215-228.

Kalmbach, J. & Powers, W. (1982). Shaping experience: Narration and understanding. In T. Fulwiler & A. Young (Eds.) *Language connections: Writing and reading across the curriculum* (pp.99-106). Urbana, IL: National Council of Teachers of English.

Kimel, W. R. & Monsees, M. E. (1979). Engineering graduates: How good are they? *Engineering Education, 70* (2), 210-212.

Kinneavy, J. (1980). *A Theory of discourse.* New York: W. W. Norton & Co.

Langer, S. (1960). *Philosophy in a new key* (3rd ed.). Cambridge, MA: Harvard University Press.

Lanham, R. A. (1981). *Revising business prose.* New York: Scribners.

Lloyd-Jones, R. (1977). Primary-trait scoring. In C. Cooper & L. Odell (Eds.), *Evaluating writing* (pp. 33-66). Urbana, IL: National Council of Teachers of English.

Macrorie, K. (1970). *Telling writing.* Rochelle Park, NJ: Hayden.

_____ . (1976). *Writing to be read* (2nd ed.). Rochelle Park, NJ: Hayden.

Martin, N., D'Arcy, P., Newton, B. & Parker, R. (1976). *Writing and learning across the curriculum.* London: Ward Lock Educational.

McCrimmon, J. (1970). Writing as a way of knowing. *The promise of English: NCTE distinguished lectures.* Urbana, IL: National Council of Teachers of English. Reprinted in *Rhetoric and composition: A sourcebook for teachers* (pp. 3-11). R. L. Graves (Ed.). Montclair, NJ: Boynton/Cook.

Merritt, R. H. (1981). Liberal studies in civil engineering: A modest proposal. *Civil Engineering, 51* (11), 71-73.

Moffett, J. (1968). *Teaching the universe of discourse.* Boston: Houghton Mifflin.

_____ . (1981). *Active voice: A writing program across the curriculum.* Montclair, NJ: Boynton/Cook.

_____ . (1982). *Coming on center: English education in evolution.* Montclair, NJ: Boynton/Cook.

_____ . (1982). Writing, inner speech, and meditation. *College English, 44,* 231-246.

Murray, D. (1978). Internal revision: A process of discovery. In C. Cooper & L. Odell (Eds.), *Research on composing: Points of departure* (pp. 85-103). Urbana, IL: National Council of Teachers of English.

_____. (1982). Teaching the other self: The writer's first reader. *College Composition and Communication, 33,* 140-147.

_____. (1984). Writing and teaching for surprise. *College English, 46,* 1-7.

Odell, L. & Goswami, D. (1982). Writing in a non-academic setting. *Research in the Teaching of English, 16,* 201-204.

Odell, L., Goswami, D. & Quick, D. (1983). Writing outside the English composition class: Implications for teaching and for learning. In R. W. Bailey & R. M. Fosheim (Eds.), *Literacy for life: The demand for reading and writing* (pp. 175-194). New York: Modern Language Association.

Ohmann, R. (1976). *English in America.* New York: Oxford University Press.

Petersen, B. (1982). Writing about responses: A unified model of reading, interpretation, and composition. *College English, 44,* 459-468.

Petrosky, A. (1982). From story to essay: Reading and writing. *College Composition and Communication, 33,* 19-36.

Polanyi, M. (1958). *Personal knowledge: Toward a post-critical philosophy.* Chicago: University of Chicago Press.

Pringle, I. & Freeman, A. (1980). Writing in the college years: Some indices of growth. *College Composition and Communication, 31,* 311-321.

Raimes, A. (1980). Writing and learning across the curriculm: The experience of a faculty seminar. *College English, 41,* 797-801.

Reddish, J. C. (1983). The language of the bureaucracy. In R. W. Bailey and R. M. Fosheim (Eds.), *Literacy for life: The demand for reading and writing* (pp. 151-174). New York: Modern Language Association.

Rose, M. (1979). When faculty talk about writing. *College English, 41,* 272-279.

Rosenblatt, L. (1976). *Literature as exploration* (3rd ed.). New York: Noble and Noble.

Ryan, T. A., Joiner, B. L. & Ryan, B. F. (1976). *MINITAB student handbook.* North Scituate, MA: Duxbury Press.

Sapir, E. (1961). *Culture, language and personality.* Berkeley: University of California Press.

Selfe, C. L. (1979). *Evidence of a multifactor structure in the writing apprehension test.* Unpublished paper. The University of Texas.

_____. (1983). Decoding and encoding: A balanced approach to communicating skills. *Engineering Education, 74* (3), 163-164.

Selzer, J. (1983). The composing processes of an engineer. *College Composition and Communication, 34,* 174-187.

Sharp, V. F. (1977). *Statistics for the social sciences.* Boston: Little Brown.

Shaughnessy, M. P. (1977). *Errors and expectations: A guide for the teachers of basic writing.* New York: Oxford University Press.

Slevin, J. (1983). Interpreting and composing: the many sources of kind. In J. N. Hayes, P. A. Roth, J. R. Ramsey & R. D. Foulke (Eds.), *The writer's mind: Writing as a mode of thinking.* (pp. 197-210). Urbana, IL: National Council of Teachers of English.

Smith, F. (1978). *Understanding reading: A psycholinguistic analysis of reading and learning to read* (2nd ed.). New York: Holt, Rinehart, and Winston.

Sommers, N. (1978, December). *Revision strategies of student writers and experienced adult writers.* Paper delivered at the meeting of the Modern Language Association. Slightly revised version was published in *College Composition and Communication, 31* (1980), 378-388.

Stine, D. & Skarzensk, D. (1979). Priorities for the business communication classroom: A survey of business and academe. *Journal of Business Communication, 16,* 15-30.

Tukey, J. W. (1977). *Exploratory data analysis.* Reading, MA: Addison-Wesley.

Vygotsky, L. S. (1962). *Thought and language.* Cambridge, MA: MIT Press.

Waitkus, L. (1982). *The effect of poetic writing on transactional writing: A case-study investigation of the writing of three high school seniors.* Unpublished dissertation, Rutgers University, Rutgers, NJ.

Watson, J. (1968). *The double helix.* New York: Atheneum.

Williams, J. (1981). *Style: Ten lessons in clarity and grace.* Glenview, IL: Scott Foresman.

Young, A. (1982). Considering values: The poetic function of language. In T. Fulwiler & A. Young (Eds.), *Language connections: Writing and reading across the curriculum* (pp. 144-156). Urbana, IL: National Council of Teachers of English.

Contributors

FREYDOON ARBABI is Associate Professor of Civil Engineering at Michigan Technological University. His area of specialty is structural engineering. He has just completed the construction of a structural behavior laboratory where students build and test small scale models of structures and compare the measured values with computer results in a lab report.

ELIZABETH A. FLYNN is Associate Professor of Reading and Composition and director of Michigan Tech's Communications Institute. She has published articles in *College English, College Composition and Communication, The New Orleans Review,* and elsewhere. She is co-editing an anthology on relationships between gender and reading and edits *Reader: Essays in Reader-Oriented Theory, Criticism, and Pedagogy.*

TOBY FULWILER directs the writing program at the University of Vermont. From 1977 to 1983 he held a similar position at Michigan Tech. He is co-editor, with Art Young, of *Language Connections: Writing and Reading Across the Curriculum* (NCTE, 1982), and has published a variety of articles in professional journals about both writing-across-the-curriculum programs and student journals. Currently, he is at work on a book about writing workshops.

MARGARET E. GORMAN is a research assistant at Michigan Technological University where she collaborates on research in composition and cognitive psychology. She formerly performed research at the National Institutes of Mental Health, and has published in composition, cognitive psychology, and psychiatry.

MICHAEL E. GORMAN is an Assistant Professor of Psychology who holds a joint appointment in Humanities, Social Sciences, and Education at MTU. His publications include experimental studies of scientific problem-solving, articles on the teaching of psychology, and reviews of computer hardware.

RONALD K. GRATZ is Associate Professor of Biological Sciences at Michigan Technological University. He is the instructor for the two-term course: Principles of Anatomy and Physiology and for two advanced physiology courses. He has authored numerous papers in comparative physiology and is a member of The American Physiological Society, The American Society of Zoologists, and The American Society of Ichthyologists and Herpetologists.

JAMES R. KALMBACH is Assistant Professor and Director of Tutoring Services in the Language Skills Laboratory at Michigan Technological University. He teaches courses in reading and publications management and supervises students tutoring in area schools. His research interests include narrative analysis, program evaluation, and the interrelationship of reading and graphic design.

GEORGE A. MC CULLEY was Assistant Professor of Rhetoric and Composition at Michigan Technological University (1981–84), where he taught first-year composition, business and technical writing, and humanities. He recently accepted a position with the Utah State Department of Education.

CYNTHIA L. NAHRGANG is Instructor of Mathematics for the School of Technology at Michigan Technological University. She recently presented a paper, "The Use of Writing in the Math Class," at the 1983 Annual Conference on School Science and Mathematics.

BRUCE T. PETERSEN was Associate Professor of Rhetoric and Composition at Michigan Technological University. He died unexpectedly in July, 1984, as this manuscript was being readied for publication. Bruce was an integral member of MTU's writing-across-the-curriculum program and a close personal friend of his colleagues represented in this book. His good sense, good humor, inquiring mind, and warm companionship are sorely missed. At the time of his death, he had nearly finished editing a collection of essays for NCTE on the connections between reading and writing. Publication is expected in 1985.

CYNTHIA L. SELFE is Assistant Professor of Rhetoric and Composition and Director of the Language Skills Laboratory in the Humanities Department at MTU. She has published articles on writing across the curriculum, writing and reading connections, and writing with computers. She is co-editor of *Computers and Composition.*

JON A. SOPER is Professor and Assistant Head of Electrical Engineering at MTU. For the past six years he has served as chairman of the College of Engineering Committee on Communication Skills where he has been active in assessing the writing skills of senior engineering students. He teaches courses in electromagnetic theory, microwave circuits and antennas and has made writing a significant part of two of these senior engineering courses.

ART YOUNG is Professor and Department Head of Humanities and Project Director of the MTU's writing-across-the-curriculum program funded by the General Motors Foundation. He is co-editor, with Toby Fulwiler, of *Language Connections: Writing and Reading Across the Curriculum* (NCTE, 1982) and has authored a number of articles in English studies.